RICHARD R. GAILLARDETZ

Witnesses to the Faith

Community, Infallibility and the Ordinary Magisterium of Bishops

D1713689

PAULIST PRESS
New York/Mahwah, N.J.

Library of Congress Cataloging-in-Publication Data

Gaillardetz, Richard R., 1958–
    Witnesses to the faith: community, infallibility, and the ordinary
magisterium of bishops/by Richard R. Gaillardetz.
        p.   cm.
    Originally presented as the author's thesis (University of Notre Dame).
    Includes bibliographical references and index.
    ISBN 0-8091-3350-4 (pbk.)
    1. Catholic Church—Teaching office.   2. Catholic Church—Bishops.
3. Church.   I. Title.
BX1746.G33   1992
262′.12—dc20   92-28043
                                                                      CIP

Published by Paulist Press
997 Macarthur Boulevard
Mahwah, NJ 07430

Printed and bound in the
United States of America

Contents

Acknowledgements

This book has its origins in a dissertation which I completed at the University of Notre Dame. There I benefited from the counsel of several distinguished theologians in that university's theology department. In particular, I would like to extend my gratitude to Professor Thomas O'Meara for the time and guidance which he so graciously provided throughout this project. I count myself fortunate to find in him both a mentor and a friend. Professors Richard McBrien, Richard McCormick and Lawrence Cunningham were also most encouraging and supportive. Research in Rome would not have been possible without the grant I received from the Zahm Foundation. My good friends and colleagues, Nancy Dallavalle and Mark Miller, deserve special thanks for graciously indulging me in my need to "talk through" portions of this book. I am grateful as well for the support of my colleagues at the University of St. Thomas School of Theology at St. Mary's Seminary in Houston, Texas. Finally, I would like to thank Donald Brophy and Paulist Press for their expert guidance in bringing this book from manuscript to publication.

Dedication

This book is dedicated to my wife, Diana—her patience, support and tender companionship have been indispensable in bringing this book to completion—and to our twin sons, David and Andrew—whose birth has marvelously eclipsed the conclusion of this more modest creation.

Introduction

Recent events of the past twenty-five years have encouraged ecclesiastical commentators to declare the teaching authority of the Roman Catholic church to be in a state of crisis. From controversies surrounding *Humanae vitae* to the schism created by the followers of Archbishop Lefebvre, both liberals and conservatives agree that the credibility of the church has suffered, in many quarters, a tremendous loss of prestige. Some blame this on liberal theologians and others on repressive church structures, but most agree that the church stands at a decisive point in its history. But how unique is our current situation?

Let us consider the following scenario. In a period of enormous change in the fields of politics, philosophy and science, the Roman Catholic church finds itself in the position of having to defend its *raison d'être*. Numerous theologians rise to the occasion and attempt to bring the Catholic faith into critical engagement with the modern world. In order to do so, it becomes necessary for these theologians to make use of modern philosophy and the burgeoning field of historical inquiry as a means of buttressing the church's credibility. These theologians find it necessary to distance themselves from the static, a-historical thought-forms of the dominant theological school, neo-scholasticism. They are convinced that the church must abandon outmoded expressions of the faith and restore the legitimate freedom of academic inquiry, even with regard to theological matters. If the credibility of the church is to be maintained, there can be no repeat of the humiliating Galileo affair. This means distinguishing between those doctrinal expressions which have been solemnly defined by the church and are essential to the faith from those which have not been taught with the charism of infallibility and are therefore subject to revision. The views of these theologians elicit profound consternation from curial officials in Rome. In the minds of these officials, the renegade theolo-

1

gians are in danger of undermining the divinely guaranteed teaching authority of the church. They admonish the local bishops for their laxity in dealing with these theologians. Indeed, several curial officials ultimately persuade the pope to "crack down" on these "new theologies" by writing a strongly worded letter to a local bishop. In the papal brief, theologians are reminded that the charism of infallibility extends beyond solemnly defined teachings, although the precise nature and limits of this extension are not made clear. This "crackdown" is cheered in some quarters as necessary for reestablishing the authority of the church. Others, however, claim that such a move simply reinforces the secular view of the church as antiquated and irrelevant.

This scenario is a direct description, *not* of our contemporary ecclesiastical situation, but of the Roman Catholic church of the mid-nineteenth century. The pope is not John Paul II, but Pius IX. The key curial official is not Cardinal Joseph Ratzinger, but Cardinal August von Reisach. The modern theologians do not include among their number Charles Curran, Leonardo Boff or Edward Schillebeeckx, but Ignaz von Döllinger, Jakob Frohschammer and Johannes Evangelist Kuhn. Nevertheless, the similarities between the situation of the church in the mid-nineteenth century and our present ecclesiastical situation are striking. Recent events have too often given rise to statements about the contemporary crisis of authority as if challenges to the church's teaching authority were strictly a contemporary phenomenon. While it is true that our contemporary situation brings with it a particular set of problems and considerations, it is also true that the church's teaching ministry has undergone a long history of change and development, and many of those changes were precipitated by precisely the kind of conflicts which we tend to limit to our own age.

Since the nineteenth century contributions of the Tübingen School and John Henry Newman, there has been, within the Catholic church, an explicit recognition of the development of doctrine. We must not be reticent in admitting that the church's teaching ministry and the conceptions of authority which have supported it have also been subjected to change and development. The present manner of exercising the church's teaching ministry is not identical with that of past eras and it is not likely to be the same as that in future centuries. While recognizing a real, historical continuity of structure in the teaching ministry of the church, this continuity has not negated the manifest diversity in the church's concrete realization of its mission to preach the gospel.

If, as I suggested above, challenges to the authority of the church are not peculiar to the modern age, it is nevertheless true that contemporary challenges to the church's authority have taken on a new character. In today's church, authority is no longer an answer to the questions of the age as it is itself the *question* for our age. After the Enlightenment and the French Revolution, the question of the nature of authority in human society emerged with particular force. Now, since the Second Vatican Council, the church must not only address the question of authority in democratic societies, but it must explore the relationship between authority and community within its own house. Pope John XXIII alluded to this in his homily at the mass celebrating the opening of Vatican II:

> At the outset of the Second Vatican Council, it is evident, as always, that the truth of the Lord will remain forever. We see, in fact, as one age succeeds another, that the opinions of men [and women] follow one another and exclude each other. And often errors vanish as quickly as they arise, like fog before the sun. The Church has always opposed these errors. Frequently she has condemned them with the greatest severity. Nowadays, however, the spouse of Christ prefers to make use of the medicine of mercy rather than that of severity. She considers that she meets the needs of the present day by demonstrating the validity of her teaching rather than by condemnations.[1]

The concrete exercise of the church's teaching ministry, as distinguished from its divine foundations, is not immune to reevaluation. As Pope John and many of the council bishops recognized, the increasing pluralism within the church, with regard not only to theologies but indigenous liturgical and devotional expressions, has challenged monarchical notions of church authority. These notions had presupposed a homogeneous social institution in which universal laws could be effectively promulgated, understood and obeyed. These presuppositions can no longer stand before a developing pluralistic, global consciousness. In today's world the church is being called upon to develop a theology of authority which can be exercised in the service of unity without compromising the legitimate diversity which is the lifeblood of the church.

A broad reexamination of the church's exercise of its legitimate teaching authority cannot be accomplished in a book of this size. Rather, in this book I am interested in calling attention to but one particular aspect of the church's teaching ministry and the authority which undergirds it, namely, the ordinary universal magisterium. This term refers to the ordinary infallible teaching of the bishops, that teaching which occurs when the bishops, while dispersed throughout their local dioceses, nevertheless propose as one body that a particular teaching must be held definitively. This mode of church teaching, as with the church's teaching ministry in general, has a history of change and development which is itself not without some controversy. I hope to offer in this book both an analysis of that history and a proposal for how this particular mode of church teaching might best be understood in the light of contemporary ecclesiology.

In the scenario mentioned above, the nineteenth century papal brief was Pius IX's *Tuas libenter.* In that letter, the term "ordinary magisterium" appeared for the first time in an ecclesiastical document. While the term itself was new, the conviction it expressed—that the consensus of the universal episcopate regarding matters of faith, even when manifested outside of council, was a sure sign of the exercise of infallibility—was an ancient one. Nevertheless, when reformulated in the context of the nineteenth century, with its serious attenuation of the authority of the episcopacy, this ancient conviction would undergo a striking transformation. This new formulation would be found in the documents of Vatican I and in the 1917 Code of Canon Law but would receive little attention in the theological manuals prior to Vatican II. It was only after the Second Vatican Council that this third mode of infallible teaching (distinguished from the solemn definitions of pope or council) would receive new attention, largely due to issues raised in the area of moral theology.

The controversy over the status of the ordinary universal magisterium was instigated by Pope Paul VI's teaching on artificial contraception in *Humanae vitae.* A number of theologians, including several who produced the minority report of the pope's commission on birth control, suggested that the prohibition of artificial contraception had already been taught infallibly by the ordinary universal magisterium. The authoritative status of Pope Pius XI's 1930 encyclical, *Casti connubii,* was considered particularly decisive. The controversy took an unexpected turn when the German theologian Hans Küng admitted that, according to *Lumen gentium* # 25, the minority report was correct in ascribing infallibility to the church's prohibition of artificial contraception. Of course, it was Küng's intent to demonstrate that since, he contended, modern scholarship had persuasively demonstrated the error of the encyclical's teaching, the church's teaching on infallibility itself must be rejected.[2]

Seven years later, theologian John C. Ford and moral philosopher Germain Grisez published an important article in which they contended that the church's teaching on artificial contraception had been taught infallibly by the ordinary universal magisterium.[3] The authors presented a detailed analysis of the conditions for the exercise of the ordinary universal magisterium articulated in *Lumen gentium* #25 and argued that these had clearly been fulfilled in the teaching on contraception. A debate ensued regarding the function and scope of the ordinary universal magisterium. Many theologians feared that this attribution of infallibility to church teaching on contraception would lead to a "creeping infallibility" in which more and more doctrinal positions would be protected from the possibility of legitimate dissent. Indeed, in the recent correspondence between Cardinal Ratzinger and Fr. Charles Curran, the Cardinal Prefect of the Congregation for the Doctrine of the Faith rejected Curran's claim that he was dissenting legitimately from authoritative but fallible church teaching. Ratzinger reminded Curran that the church taught infallibly not only by means of solemn definitions but by the ordinary universal magisterium and he at least implied that some of the teachings from which Curran was dissenting had been so taught infallibly.[4]

I hope to demonstrate that the question of the nature and scope of the ordinary universal teaching of the bishops is a question with profound ecclesiastical and moral implications. How does the church transmit the gospel message and how does it guarantee the veracity of that message? What is the nature of that guarantee? How shall we understand the assistance of the Holy Spirit in the teaching of the church? If the ordinary universal magisterium is the teaching of the bishops when *dispersed throughout the world,* how does the relationship of the bishops to their local churches affect their teaching? Furthermore, how are we to understand the ordinary infallible exercise of the church's teaching office in a pluralistic age which is so much more aware of the historically and culturally conditioned character of all expressions of divine truth?

This book is offered, then, as a modest contribution toward this contemporary reconsideration of the church's teaching authority. It applies to the topic at hand two of the most important ecclesiological developments of the Second Vatican Council: first, the reaffirmation of the episcopacy and the college of bishops as possessing, with the bishop of Rome, supreme authority over the whole church, and second, the reaffirmation of the local church as the place where the universal church is realized through the ministries of word and sacrament.

The first chapter of this book introduces the topic by reviewing the history of the term *magisterium* itself and the church's developing understanding of its authoritative teaching office. In the second chapter I explore the historical background behind the church's first formal articulation of its teaching on the ordinary magisterium, namely, the activities of theologians and bishops which led to Pius IX's *Tuas libenter* and its later articulation in Vatican I's *Dei Filius.*

The next chapter is concerned with the reception of *Tuas libenter* in the Latin manuals, the "approved" theological resource of the church for much of the nineteenth and twentieth centuries. The fourth and fifth chapters explore nineteenth and twentieth century figures who stood outside the manual tradition and either directly considered the ordinary infallible teaching of bishops or helped prepare for what can be called a "paradigm shift" in the theology of the magisterium. This shift was given formal, if tentative, approbation at the Second Vatican Council.

In the documents of Vatican II a new framework for understanding church authority would stand alongside the terms and motifs of neo-scholasticism. The gradual shift, evident in the documents of the council, brought new significance to the formulation of the teaching on the ordinary infallible teaching of bishops in *Lumen gentium,* the Dogmatic Constitution on the Church. The actual formulation of the teaching differs little, in substance, from the earlier formulations in Pius IX's *Tuas libenter* and Vatican I's *Dei Filius,* but the new ecclesiological context in which it is encountered demands new consideration. The sixth chapter, then, highlights the renewed interest which this teaching received in the documents of the Second Vatican Council, the controversies surrounding *Humanae vitae,* and in the 1983 Code of Canon Law.

Having traced the reception and development of the teaching on the ordinary universal magisterium from its official formulation by Pius IX through its treatment in the 1983 code, the seventh and eighth chapters represent both a *status quaestionis* and a tentative proposal toward reconsidering this mode of church teaching in the context of a post-conciliar ecclesiology. With Vatican II we saw an incipient recovery of the ancient *communio* ecclesiology so dominant in the theology of the early church. Chapter 7 draws upon the work of several contemporary ecclesiologists in order to sketch out some of the implications of this ecclesiology. The eighth chapter then concludes by reinterpreting the status of the ordinary universal magisterium within this *communio* ecclesiology.

One of the inviolable rules of writing is to know your audience. There was a time in Roman Catholic scholarship when this was considerably easier than it is today. You either wrote for your fellow academics, for the clergy or for the "person in the pew." It goes without saying that in our contemporary church, particularly here in North America, the flowering of lay ministries and adult education renders impractical this kind of easy demarcation. As I know of no other work which has attempted the kind of historical analysis of the ordinary universal magisterium contained in this book, I would hope that for that reason alone, if not for my own modest proposals, this book might be of some interest to colleagues in the academy interested in Roman Catholic ecclesiology. At the same time, I am convinced that the status of the ordinary infallible teaching of bishops has important implications for all who participate in the church's catechetical ministry, that is, those who bear the responsibility for communicating the gospel message as it has been mediated in the Roman Catholic doctrinal tradition. Much harm has been done by well-meaning priests, catechists and religion teachers who have failed to grasp the import of the varying degrees of authority with which the church proposes its teaching. Finally, this book addresses questions which should be of concern to every Catholic called upon to give an appropriate assent to the teachings of the church.

Yet even beyond the obvious importance of the ordinary universal magisterium is the concern which all Roman Catholics should share in the future of the church. I have suggested that one cannot adequately consider the status of the ordinary universal magisterium without first completely rethinking our view of the church. This rethinking is merely a continuation of the spirit of Vatican II, that is, it is an exercise undertaken with the church and within the church. As the council itself proclaimed in article 6 of the Decree on Ecumenism:

> Christ summons the Church, as she goes her pilgrim way, to that continual reformation of which she always has need, insofar as she is an institution of men [and women] here on earth. Consequently, if, in various times and circumstances, there have been deficiencies in moral conduct or in Church discipline, or even in the way that Church teaching has been formulated—to be carefully distinguished from the deposit of faith itself—these should be set right at the opportune moment and in the proper way.

This book is an attempt to do just that with respect to one very specific yet fundamental issue. If the teaching authority of the Roman Catholic church is in a state of crisis, all Catholics have a stake in restoring the credibility of that authority so that it might better fulfill its mission as "a sign and instrument . . . of communion with God and of unity with all humankind" (*Lumen gentium* #1).

Magisterium in Historical Context

The current use of the term *magisterium,* as referring both to the hierarchy and its teaching activity, is much more recent than is often thought.[1] A brief review of the history of that term will help to situate our consideration of the ordinary magisterium. That history can be divided into three broad historical periods. First is the patristic and early medieval period, second, the late Middle Ages, and third is that period beginning with the Counter-Reformation and culminating in the nineteenth and early twentieth centuries.

Magisterium in the Patristic and Early Medieval Period

There was a fluidity in patristic and medieval usage of the term *magisterium.* In classical Latin the word *magisterium* simply denoted the dignity or office of the *magister. Magister,* in turn, was applied very broadly to anyone designated as a leader in any number of activities, both secular and ecclesiastical. When the early church writers wrote specifically of the teaching ministry of the church, as often as not they would use terms other than *magisterium:* in Greek the teaching ministry was denoted by the term *didaskalos,* and in Latin by the term *praedicatio ecclesiae.*[2]

In the writing of Augustine, and in that of many patristic and medieval authors, *magisterium* carried the general meaning of the authority of one who teaches or commands. It was often applied to God who possessed the true *magisterium* and was then paired with a *ministerium,* the possession of the church. Christ alone was the divine teacher, being greater (*magis*); the church, being lesser (*minor*), was *minister.*[3] Where *magisterium* was applied to the church it had a broader referent than that of teaching authority. St. Gregory wrote of a *magisterium pastorale* and seemed to combine pastoral authority with teaching authority, a combination which Congar finds to be common in early church writers.[4]

This broader usage of the term *magisterium,* evident in the churches of the patristic period and of the early Middle Ages, devolved from an understanding of tradition peculiar to an ecclesiological vision, the broad contours of which endured up to the eleventh century. Yves Congar notes that "for early Christianity, the primary reality is the *ecclesia.*" The emphasis was not on any church structure but on the community of all believers. ". . . [T]he *Ecclesia* is the assembly of the brethren established by an act of the Lord and by his presence in their midst."[5] A study of the early life of the Christian community reveals a profound unity between the hierarchical structure of the church and the communal exercise of all church activities. Even with respect to the role of the episcopacy in handing on and preserving the faith there was a strong conviction regarding the full participation of the laity. Cyprian, for example, wrote of his determination to always consult the priests, deacons and all of the people in preference to making a decision based on his personal opinion alone.[6] While Ignatius of Antioch stressed the constitutive character of the episcopacy for the life of the church, he was also careful to preserve the necessary interrelationship of the hierarchy and the community.[7] This unity of the hierarchy and the faithful was manifested in the liturgical life of the early church and further strengthened in the patristic practice of the participation of the whole local community in the election of bishops.

This ancient ecclesiology yielded a theology of tradition in which a privileged place was given not to the organs of tradition, the hierarchy, but to the object of tradition, the "Living Gospel." It was a priority which likely had its roots in the early baptismal rites of *traditio* in which it was the one gospel of Christ which was being transmitted.[8] Thus Irenaeus of Lyons was able to identify the *regula fidei* with the content of the faith. The bishops were the authoritative witnesses to this doctrinal content and when they were in agreement in witnessing to this doctrinal content they too, however, became a kind of formal rule of faith.[9] Where one does find references to teaching authority, this authority was not viewed in juridical terms but was described as a responsibility for the reception and transmission of the faith. As Congar explained:

The *regula fidei* . . . for the writers of this period [first three centuries], means not the action of the teaching authority, nor a criterion of true belief other than the doctrine itself, but this doctrine handed down to the Church. The bishops, by their agreement, were the sign indicating that a doctrine had always been held and, since this meant that it obviously went back to the origins, that it belonged to the *regula fidei,* that rule which is the same thing as the deposit of faith. This is the position of St. Irenaeus and still that of St. Vincent of Lerins. In this line for ten centuries, popes, bishops, councils, canonists and theologians never ceased to affirm that the role of the members of the hierarchy is to guard and apply the rules received and handed on: the deposit of faith, the dogmas and canons of the councils, the tradition received from the Fathers.[10]

Magisterium was also linked to the *charisma* of the Holy Spirit in the writings of the early church. However, the subject of this charism, this power, was not a particular body of pastors but the church itself. Here we must recall Augustine's primary application of the *magisterium* to God. The church was empowered to exercise God's *magisterium,* but it was clearly attributed first and foremost to God. Furthermore, it was the church as a whole which was the bearer of the living gospel, the tradition, not solely the pastors of the church. The patristic understanding of the authority of the hierarchy was characterized by a twofold openness of the hierarchy to the insights of the whole community and to the word of God itself. The bishops were to be servants both of the word and of the people.

In the third century a number of heretical threats did effect a subtle change in the theology of the episcopacy. The role of the bishop shifted from that of a custodian of the faith to that of an authoritative theological disputant.[11] This led to the development of a synodal structure which proved successful in preserving the church's *communio* in the face of heretical threats. This synodal structure would prepare the way for the larger councils later held to be *ecumenical.* Nevertheless, Athanasius still defended the orthodoxy of the teachings of the Council of Nicea not on the grounds of the council fathers' own authority but on the authority of what was passed on:

The Fathers, in matters of faith, never said: Thus it has been
decreed, but: This is what the Catholic Church believes; and
they confessed what they believed directly, so as to show unmis-
takably that their thought was not new, but apostolic.[12]

It might be thought that this early understanding of teaching
authority would have been lost soon after the Constantinian settlement, with its introduction of imperial offices into the hierarchical
structure of the church. While it is true that the teaching function
was more clearly identified with the bishops in the period between
Constantine and Pope Gregory VII, it is also true that the church
carefully preserved the notion of the bishop's service of both word
and community. The Latin ritual of ordination, for example,
stressed the bishop's duties rather than powers. He was to devote
himself to the scriptures, to prayer, fasting and hospitality.[13] The
personal holiness of the bishop was stressed. We should also note
the consistent situating of the episcopacy *within* the church and not
as itself being the church. The bishops and pastors were considered
variously the *praepositi ecclesiae* and later, with Thomas, the *praelati ecclesiae.* There is no evidence of an application of the term
ecclesia to the bishops alone as we would find in the nineteenth
century.
　　Thus, in spite of the pressures toward a more juridical view of
authority under the influence of the Constantinian settlement Catholicism, from the fifth to the eleventh centuries, maintained both
the transcendent dimension of church authority and its fundamental relationship to the whole *ecclesia.* It was able to do so because
ecclesiology during this period, with the encouragement of monas-
ticism, remained rooted in a spiritual anthropology which always
placed the possessor of church office in a position of servitude
before God and community. If the bishop possessed a particular
dignity as prince of the local community, this was only possible
through God's intervention. The authority of the bishop was understood as ". . . a vehicle of the mystery of that salvation which
God wishes to accomplish in his Church."[14] This ecclesiology
would not allow any juridical identification of the hierarchy itself
with the term *magisterium.*

Magisterium from the Late Middle Ages to the Reformation

Even after the eleventh century, *magisterium* was often employed with respect to the authority not only of teachers but of all who possessed ecclesiastical power. Nevertheless, during the Middle Ages there was a progressive tendency toward the application of the title *magister* to those who were teachers, counselors, or who functioned in some exemplary capacity. *Magisterium,* which applied initially to the authority of those in positions of leadership, would increasingly refer particularly to the authority of the teacher. These teachers in the church, however, were often not the bishops or *praelati* but rather the *doctores* or theologians. Even prior to the birth of the classical universities the *magistri* possessed a recognized authority. Josef Pieper recalls the dispute between King Henry II of England and the Archbishop of Canterbury, Thomas Beckett, in which the king proposed seeking the mediation of the Parisian *magistri,* this a number of years before the formal establishment of the University of Paris.[15] With the birth of the university, *magister* became a fully recognized title given to those who held the position of public lecturer. M.-D. Chenu noted the significance of this new usage:

> Here, again, was something new: that a body of authorized professors, invested with a *licentia docendi* should be given in the Church charge and authority of expounding the revealed truths of faith. To be sure, both in theology and catechesis, there had always been masters acting as adjuncts to the episcopal order. But here it was a question of professors, of a school of men who were professionals in their work, whose energies were devoted to developing a science, and whose juridical status depended on the corporation and was not, properly speaking, a function of the hierarchy. . . . The *magistri* were officially regarded as qualified to discourse on matters of faith and doctrine. Once a question had been disputed, theirs was the office of "determining" a solution that was then accepted as carrying authority.[16]

This usage of the term *magister* was adopted by Thomas Aquinas and others who then distinguished within the church between the office of the "prelate" (*officium praelationis*) or bishop and that of the "master" (*officium magisterii*) or theologian. Elsewhere Thomas distinguished between the magisterium of the pastoral chair (*magisterium cathedrae pastoralis*) and the magisterium of the teaching chair (*magisterium cathedrae magistralis*) thereby granting the bishops a magisterial task, but not granting it to them exclusively.[17] The rise of the university also brought with it a new appreciation for the necessary autonomy of knowledge. In theology this was reflected in the distinction between the *clavis potestatis* and the *clavis scientiae*.[18]

After the eleventh century the term *magisterium* continued to be used not only with respect to the hierarchy but with the *doctores* as well. Nevertheless, important ecclesiological changes occurred during this century which would eventually have a profound effect on the notion of the *magisterium*. Beginning with the pontificates of Leo IX and Gregory VII a slow and uneven movement toward a more juridical view of the church and church authority may be detected. The twelfth century saw a massive gathering of church decretals as canon law began to flourish. Indeed, after Alexander III most popes were themselves canonists.[19] It is the canonist who most insistently presses the question: who possesses what authority and how may it be exercised? This juridical movement would have to compete in the Middle Ages with other more organic conceptions of the church,[20] but the juridical understanding of church authority would become increasingly dominant in the late Middle Ages, eventually becoming a central object of attack by the sixteenth century reformers. Michael Place has described the effects of this juridicization of the church on its understanding of tradition and ecclesiastical teaching authority:

> Whereas the earlier period had understood both the official solicitude of the hierarchical office and the solicitude of the theological community as being in service of a reality (the mysteries of faith) that was greater than both dimensions, the later period saw a growing identification of that reality with the hierarchical office. Rather than serving the truth, the official Church became the organ of the truth which was its possession.[21]

Magisterium from the Counter-Reformation to the Early Twentieth Century

Sixteenth and seventeenth century Catholic thinkers were compelled to defend a gradual accretion of church pronouncements and decrees against the attacks of the reformers. In order to reinforce the authoritative status of these documents it became necessary to more adequately ground the prerogatives of the church in its doctrinal pronouncements. The result was a tendency to identify the *regula fidei* not with the content of the faith as was done in the early church, but, at least proximately, with the hierarchy itself. The growing identification of tradition, and concomitantly *magisterium,* with the hierarchy was further strengthened by the eighteenth century distinction (first made in the sixteenth century by Thomas Stapleton) between the teaching church (*ecclesia docens*) and the learning church (*ecclesia discens*).[22] This distinction, with its rigid separation of the hierarchy from the rest of the faithful, stood in marked contrast to the more organic notion of the church typical of the patristic and medieval periods. Also significant was the urgency which the Roman Catholic church felt in the seventeenth and eighteenth centuries to defend the truths of the faith against not only Protestantism but against various movements within its own house, Jansenism, Gallicanism, Josephinism, and Febronianism.

A particularly significant development in the identification of the term *magisterium* with the hierarchical office of doctrinal teaching occurred in the early nineteenth century when two German canonists, Ferdinand Walter and Georg Phillips, began to develop a tripartite distinction of powers to replace, or at least augment, the traditional distinction between orders and jurisdiction.[23] Phillips in particular was influenced by two prominent Protestant theological themes: the kingdom of God and the threefold office of Christ as priest, prophet and king. Once one saw the kingdom of God as bound up in the person of Christ and saw the church as the manifestation of that kingdom, it was only a short step to applying the threefold office of Christ to the powers of the church. These corresponding powers—teaching, ruling and sanctifying—

were thought to more accurately represent the mission of the church than did the older bipartite orders/jurisdiction schema.

The most significant consequence of this tripartite ecclesiology was the distinct treatment given to the power of teaching apart from that of jurisdiction (ruling) or orders (sanctifying). With the separation of the power of authoritative teaching from those of ruling and sanctifying the ecclesiological foundation was now laid for the identification of the *magisterium* with the hierarchical power of teaching.

This new use of the term *magisterium* could already be found in ecclesiastical documents as early as 1835. There it appeared in Gregory XVI's condemnation of Hermes, *Dum acerbissimas,* in which Hermes was accused of holding positions foreign to Catholic doctrine, revelation and the *magisterium* of the church. In Pius IX's 1849 encyclical *Nostis et nobiscum* he maintained that

> [o]ne cannot rebel against the Catholic faith without at the same time rejecting the authority of the Roman Church. In this authority dwells *the irreformable magisterium of the faith* which was founded by the Divine Redeemer and in which on that account was preserved that which was passed on by the Apostles.[24]

Later, scholastic theologians (e.g., J.B. Franzelin) would combine this new tripartite structure with an emerging ecclesiology which stressed the unity of the human and divine elements within the church, often employing the analogy of the body/soul relationship in which the divine was the soul of the church and the human its exterior form. The result was an ecclesiological synthesis in which the humanity of the church was ordered or guided by the divine and the *magisterium* functioned as the voice of divine truth.[25] This view could hardly avoid attributing the very authority of God to church pronouncements. Leo XIII's use of the term *magisterium* in his 1896 encyclical *Satis cognitum* would betray the influence of this ecclesiology:

> Therefore, Jesus Christ instituted in the Church a living, authentic, and likewise permanent *magisterium,* which He strengthened by His own power, taught by the Spirit of Truth, and

confirmed by miracles. . . . This then, is without any doubt the office of the Church, to watch over Christian doctrine and to propagate it soundly and without corruption. . . . But just as heavenly doctrine was never left to the judgment and mind of individuals, but in the beginning was handed down by Jesus, then committed separately to that *magisterium* which has been mentioned, so, also, was the faculty of performing and administering the divine mysteries, together with the power of ruling and governing divinely, granted not to individuals [generally] of the Christian people but to certain of the elect. . . .[26]

By the end of the nineteenth century, in the writings of Franzelin and others, the gospel, the content of the faith, was reduced to but a remote *regula fidei.* Increasingly, it was the hierarchy which had become the proximate rule of faith. This movement is reflected in the statement of the neo-Thomist, Louis Billot, who wrote: "We ought not to look to that which is believed, but rather to that which guides our belief by proposing the truth to be believed."[27] With Billot the understanding of tradition had shifted from that which was taught to the organs for authoritative teaching. It is not surprising that the term *magisterium* similarly shifted from its original referent, the authority to teach as a witness to the tradition, and came to denote the teachers. *Magisterium* could no longer denote the function of giving witness to tradition, for tradition itself was identified with whatever the *magisterium,* understood now as the body of pastors, taught.

At the same time, the various threats of Gallicanism, Febronianism, Josephinism, and the liberalism emerging out of the French Revolution elicited a reaction which encouraged the centralization of all ecclesial power in Rome.[28] The subject of tradition shifted from the whole church to the hierarchy. Hierarchical authority was, in turn, conceived increasingly as devolving from papal authority. With the pontificate of Pius XII in the mid-twentieth century the notion of the *magisterium* positively excluded the roles of both the faithful and the theologians.[29] It is this movement of increasing centralization of church authority, fruit of nineteenth century ultramontanism, which will provide the immediate context for the first ecclesiastical and theological articulations of the ordinary universal magisterium of bishops.

2

The Ecclesiastical Origins of *Magisterium Ordinarium*

As we noted in the last chapter, the nineteenth century saw a significant shift in ecclesiology. The many ecclesiastical reform movements certainly helped elicit a conservative reaction from Rome. More fundamental, however, was the church reaction to the twin movements of political liberalism and philosophical rationalism. The political liberalism produced by the French Revolution demanded a reconsideration of the relationship between church and state. According to this Enlightenment-influenced political liberalism, no longer was the state to be charged with preserving the harmony of society by assisting in directing its members to their true and final end. This more medieval conception had provided an integral role for the church in assisting the state toward the realization of the final end of both society and its members. Liberalism, however, viewed the state primarily as the protector of individual freedoms.[1] This view made it difficult to maintain a role for the church in society. As Gerald McCool notes:

> The liberal bourgeoisie identified the intellectual and political world view associated with the French Revolution, with scientific progress, political freedom, and cultural maturity. As the century progressed political and cultural liberalism became more widespread among the educated middle classes. It was the driving force behind the revolutions of 1830 and 1848, which seriously threatened the temporal power of the papacy and the continued existence of the Papal States.[2]

This challenge resulted in the church's vigorous reassertion of the necessary authority of the papacy as the guarantor of all church authority. In the eventual theological development of this "ultramontane" ecclesiology, Joseph de Maistre's *Du pape,* a reaffirmation of papal authority in the face of liberalism, and the works of other French traditionalists like Louis de Bonald and Felicité Lamennais, would have a tremendous influence. The rejection of the temporal power of the pope by political liberalism and the tenuous status of the Papal States colored many of the theological events of the century. The necessity for the pope's departure from Rome during the brief Italian Revolution of 1848 left an indelible mark on nineteenth century papal concerns. It was in response to the perceived threats to the authority of the church that a papalist ecclesiology was advocated by the French traditionalists.[3]

The Romantic Restoration of Theology in Early Nineteenth Century Germany

The conservative ecclesiological shift which ultramontanism represented would not have equal influence in all of Europe. Germany was particularly reluctant to cede its ecclesiastical and theological independence to Rome. There the beginning of the nineteenth century had seen the exploration of new paths in theological studies during the years between 1790 and 1840.[4] It was only after 1840 that ultramontanist tendencies began to enter into the German theological world.

Enlightenment rationalism in the 1780s gave way in Germany first to romanticism in which not timeless reason but history, intuition and nature were central, and second, to the idealist philosophical currents of Fichte, Schelling and Hegel. Friedrich Schelling would have the greatest influence on Roman Catholic theology; Fichte's subjective idealism was simply too intra-mental, and Hegel, who was openly critical of Roman Catholicism, offered a philosophy of history which gave too much to necessity in comparison with the rich theogonies of Schelling's systems. Schelling's interests in mythology and mysticism were more amenable to Catholic sensibilities. The influence of his thought on Roman Catholic theology would be particularly apparent at two important centers, Tübingen and Munich.

At Tübingen one can identify two successive generations of brilliant thinkers. The contributions of the first generation belonged primarily to Johann Sebastian Drey (1777–1853).[5] When in

1817 the Catholic seminary at Ellwangen was moved to Tübingen, home of the distinguished Protestant faculty, Drey moved as well. At Tübingen Drey would introduce a generation of students to a new intellectual world which replaced the sterility of eighteenth century rationalism with the dynamism of idealism. He borrowed from Schelling the notions of organic growth, of history as the self-realization of God, and of the primacy of the *idea* as objectified in the finite. He would transpose these insights into Catholic theology and profess the kingdom of God as Christianity's primal *idea*. Drey's protégés formed the second generation of Roman Catholic thought at Tübingen: Johann Adam Möhler, Franz Anton Staudenmaier and Johann Evangelist Kuhn. These figures, particularly Möhler, would continue Drey's interest in the complex interplay of revelation and history.

Turning to the Roman Catholic center in Munich, we must note first of all the creative early presence of thinkers like Joseph Görres and Franz von Baader. Of more direct importance, however, were the later figures present during the years of Munich's declining influence, Martin Deutinger, the systematic theologian, and Ignaz von Döllinger the church historian. Döllinger was clearly one of the most intriguing figures in Germany at the time; his life spanned almost the entire nineteenth century. Döllinger is particularly important for this study as he was a central organizer and participant in the Munich Congress of 1863 which in many ways represented the final gasp of a theological movement which offered the principal alternative to neo-scholasticism in the nineteenth century.

Expansion of Ultramontanism and Neo-Scholasticism in Germany

While a prelude to the ultramontanist program can be detected in the series of papal interventions in theological disputes,[6] the revolutions of 1848 represent an apt dividing line in the history of the nineteenth century.[7] The harsh political realities surrounding the revolutions spelled the death of German idealism. The great speculative systems were often associated with the revolutionary spirit. The political and social upheavals of 1848 led many in Rome to suspect any modern theology, linked as they were with the liberal movements of the age. The calls for a return to scholasticism, which went largely unheeded early in the century were renewed, and this time they received a hearing from important ecclesiastical figures. The neo-scholastic journals *Der Katholik* in Mainz and *La Civiltà Cattolica* in Rome expanded their spheres of influence. Joseph Kleutgen's multi-volume works, *Die Philosophie der Vorzeit* and *Die Theologie der Vorzeit,*[8] presented developed exposés of the errors of the age. Writing from a distance in Rome, Kleutgen would outline the thought of such key German figures as Hermes, Günther, Hirscher and Staudenmaier, and then demonstrate their inadequacies, always concluding to the necessary bankruptcy of any theological approach grounded in post-Cartesian philosophy.

By the middle of the nineteenth century, then, a German theology built on what Döllinger would call the two eyes of theology, philosophy and history,[9] would be pushed to the periphery by a theology which wished to canonize its particular brand of scholastic philosophy and which was fundamentally a-historical in both methodology and content. In the late 1850s and early 1860s the ecclesiastical condemnations became more frequent: Günther in 1857, ontologism in 1861, Jacob Frohschammer in 1862. Not insignificantly, Kleutgen would be involved in each one of these condemnations.[10]

At the same time, Gallican episcopalism, already on the wane, was quickly being suppressed in favor of Roman centralization. Pius IX, who succeeded Gregory XVI in 1846, was eager to facilitate a shift in the locus of ecclesiastical powers away from the local churches and toward Rome. During his reign the role of the bishops decreased and the role of the Roman congregations increased. Nuncios, originally only diplomatic liaisons to governments, became increasingly involved in the internal affairs of the churches in the countries in which they served. The periodic visits of bishops to Rome, a practice which had fallen into disuse, was revived. Appeals by the lower clergy against their bishops to the curia were heard and encouraged. At the same time Pius IX began to appoint bishops whose principal qualifications, as Roger Aubert put it, were a Roman education and a certain "pliability."[11] In 1853 even the much more moderated expressions of episcopalism in France and Germany would be condemned in the encyclical *Inter multiples.* Finally, the 1854 definition of the immaculate conception symbolized, perhaps more directly than any other event, the shift in ecclesiology toward an exaggerated papalism. With the approach of the First Vatican Council, neo-scholasticism would become the approved theological school of the ultramontanist program.[12]

It is from within this framework that we must see Ignaz von Döllinger's decision to invite German-speaking theologians from Germany, Austria and Switzerland to attend a congress in Munich and there attempt to heal the bitter divisions which had developed in German Catholicism.

Tuas libenter and the Origins of "Ordinary Magisterium"

The ordinary magisterium of bishops would find its first formal ecclesiastical articulation in the papal brief of Pius IX, *Tuas libenter,* addressed to the archbishop of Munich. This letter was written in response to the controversial theological congress which took place in Munich in 1863. This section will examine the events which precipitated this papal brief and conclude with an analysis of the understanding of the ordinary universal magisterium reflected in *Tuas libenter* and in Vatican I's *Dei Filius.*

The Munich Congress of 1863

Döllinger and his German colleagues Bonifacius Haneberg and Johannes B. Alzog were motivated largely by apologetic concerns in their theological and historical endeavors. As Aubert notes, they were

> . . . primarily animated by the desire to liberate Catholic intellectuals from the inferiority complex which the flowering of Protestant rationalistic scholarship had given them. They expected to accomplish their aim by suggesting to them to compete with the same weapons and to give them the feeling of complete intellectual freedom, aside from the relatively few questions of dogma.[13]

Döllinger sought in the Munich Congress a rapprochement with the neo-scholastics, thereby effecting a unified front in addressing the demands of the age. In retrospect, however, his efforts were doomed from the start. After the papal nuncio in Munich, Matteo Gonella, became aware of the coming congress he immediately forwarded a copy of the congress invitation to Cardinal Antonelli, the secretary of state.[14] The contents of Gonella's accompanying letter reflected the sensitivities of the ultramontanists and the degree to which all events were interpreted through the lens of a program for the centralization of authority in Rome and for theological uniformity. Gonella's letter reminded the cardinal of the recent controversy in Munich over the work of Jacob Frohschammer.[15] Gonella further remarked on Döllinger's leadership role in convening the congress and linked many of his ideas with those of Frohschammer. The nuncio was also quite critical of the German bishops; he contended that the German theologians were taking advantage of the bishops' reluctance to assert themselves as guarantors of orthodoxy. He then made the following appeal to Antonelli:

> I allow myself to observe, with due submission, how necessary it seems to me that the Holy Father take some opportunity to remind the bishops to be more vigilant over the tendencies of many professors in these universities, who elevate themselves to the status of judges and custodians of true Catholic doctrine and of the way it is to be propagated, while the bishops, who are the real depositories of doctrine, remain silent and permit the younger clergy to imbibe such principles . . .[16]

Gonella's letter to Antonelli drew into the controversy Cardinal Karl August von Reisach, a member of the curia. Reisach had long been a strong supporter of the ultramontane program. One-time archbishop of Munich, Reisach had been a friend of Cardinal Cappellari and did much to develop Munich as a center for ultramontanism. Archive notes for a proposed response by Reisach to Gonella's letter reveal a shared concern for the predilection of German university professors, typified by Frohschammer, for too narrowly circumscribing the doctrinal authority of the church.[17] Reisach also shared with Gonella the conviction that the German bishops were not sufficiently vigilant in the defense of the faith against dangerous thought and recommended to Antonelli a "papal act" which might remind them of their responsibilities.

This correspondence demonstrates that a critical papal response to the congress was planned even before the results of the congress were known.[18] The issues which separated the German university professors from the ultramontanists were simply too great to be bridged. Döllinger's address opening the congress reflected the true size of the chasm between the two approaches. While calling for a synthesis of the historical and neo-scholastic approaches, Döllinger criticized neo-scholasticism precisely for its lack of historical consciousness. He further suggested that the apologetic resources which neo-scholasticism possessed were like "bows and arrows" next to the "canons" of German historical theology.

The actual events of the congress suggest that Gonella and Reisach may have miscalculated the dangers which the congress presented. The opening mass was presided over by Archbishop von Scherr himself and the participants drafted an address to the pope in which they professed their loyalty (they had already recited the Tridentine profession of faith at the opening of the congress) and sought his blessing. Furthermore, many of the suspect German theologians (e.g., J.B. Balzer, Frohschammer and Kuhn) were not in attendance. One resolution passed by the congress must be noted, however, for it reflects a dogmatic minimalism present in the theology of Döllinger and many of the other congress participants. The resolution maintained that while theologians were bound in conscience to submit to the dogmatic decrees of the church (that is, those teachings which had been solemnly defined), they possessed a liberty natural to the sciences in all other questions.[19] Inasmuch as this resolution appeared to reject the ancient belief in the dogmatic significance of the witness of the universal episcopate it became the direct target of the eventual papal response.

Much to the embarrassment of Gonella, the pope sent the requested blessing via the Munich archbishop. After the conclusion of the congress both von Scherr and Gonella separately reported the results to Rome with Gonella again requesting that the pope make a public statement of warning to the German theologians and bishops. The substance of the papal response, *Tuas libenter,* makes it clear that the pope was acting not on the observations of von Scherr but on those of Gonella and the entreaties of Reisach.

Tuas libenter: *The Vatican Response*

There was apparently some initial consideration in Rome of placing the proceedings of the congress on the Index; ultimately, however, the pope settled with sending a letter of admonishment to the archbishop of Munich. In the letter Pius IX praised the participants of the congress for their fidelity but questioned the lack of prior approval by the appropriate ecclesiastical authority. He reminded the archbishop of the recent censures of current ideas which attributed too much to the power of unaided human reason and exaggerated the freedom of the sciences. Clearly the pope intended to repudiate the minimalistic view of the contents of the deposit of the faith reflected in the aforementioned resolution. After commending the congress for affirming the obligation to hold the infallibly defined dogmas of the church, the pope continued:

> We want to persuade ourselves that they do not wish to limit the obligation by which Catholic teachers and writers are bound only to those things which have been proposed by the infallible judgement of the Church as dogmas of faith to be believed by all. And we are persuaded that they did not wish to declare that that perfect adherence to revealed truths which they acknowledge to be absolutely necessary for the genuine progress of science and for the refutation of errors can be had if faith and assent is given only to the expressly defined dogmas of the Church. For even if it is a matter of that subjection which must be given in the act of divine faith, it must not be limited to those things which have been defined by the express decrees of councils or of the Roman Pontiffs and of this Apostolic See, but must also be extended to those things which are handed on by the ordinary magisterium of the Church scattered throughout the world as divinely revealed and therefore are held by the universal and constant consent of Catholic theologians to pertain to the faith.[20]

This passage is the first in any ecclesiastical document to explicitly speak of a *magisterium ordinarium* the teachings of which also demanded the assent of faith.[21] But what is the precise meaning of this new expression?

John Boyle has demonstrated the influence of Cardinal Reisach on the substance of *Tuas libenter,* further showing that Reisach himself was indebted to the thought of the prominent Jesuit neo-scholastic Joseph Kleutgen (1811–83). Many of the theological formulations found in Reisach's memorandum have their source in Kleutgen's *Die Theologie der Vorzeit* and ultimately found their way into *Tuas libenter.*

Kleutgen's own theology of tradition and church authority, though sharing a strong papalism, differed at several important points from that of the prominent theologians associated with the Roman College.[22] He lacked the dynamic notion of tradition maintained by Passaglia and later Franzelin, both of whom were influenced in varying degrees by the Tübingen school. In particular, while Passaglia consistently subordinated the church to the word of God, Kleutgen effectively made the word subject to the church by emphasizing the primacy of the church as the organ of tradition.[23] The church's role as the organ of tradition is treated in volume 1 of *Die Theologie der Vorzeit* in the section on the *Glaubensnorm.*[24] The principal opponent was J.B. Hirscher of the Tübingen school, particularly with respect to his position on the contents of revelation, the rule of faith. This rule was defined by Kleutgen as follows:

> All that (and only that) belongs to faith which God has revealed (i.e., that which is contained in the Word of God, handed on in written or oral form) and which has been offered as such to all by the church for belief.[25]

Hirscher's claim of normativity for the New Testament alone was rejected. Hirscher and others wished to limit the unwritten tradition belonging to revelation to the church's most central creedal statements produced by ecumenical councils, but Kleutgen insisted that the church's teaching authority could not be so limited.

> Others wish to acknowledge as determinations of the church in matters of faith only conciliar decisions. But can they maintain that the fullness of power to judge disputes on matters of faith is given to the church under the condition of a definite form of judgment? Without falling away from Catholicism, can they deny that the church dispersed throughout the world is just as infallible as the church gathered in council?[26]

He remarked that there were numerous teachings of popes and regional synods which were later taught by the whole church as *de fide.* Kleutgen had in mind here a twofold magisterium: one was ordinary and perpetual (*ordentliche und immerwährende*) and the second was extraordinary (*ausserordentlich*) and employed only in specific situations where error threatens the peace of the church.[27] This was expressed in *Tuas libenter's* distinction between that which was taught by ecumenical council or the Roman pontiff and that taught by the church [bishops] dispersed throughout the world.[28]

Kleutgen assumed that virtually all of the facts contained in scripture belonged to revelation. Since most of these facts had never been solemnly defined he maintained that they must have been taught by the ordinary magisterium. Biblical "facts" like the sacrifice of Abraham, Jonah's being swallowed by a whale and the miracles of Jesus and of the apostles all were taught infallibly by the church's ordinary magisterium. But the ordinary magisterium was not limited to biblical facts; it also taught from tradition. Here Kleutgen cited as examples church teachings on hellfire, prayer for the dead and the church's sacraments.[29] While some of these teachings would later be defined, they were taught infallibly, Kleutgen maintained, prior to their solemn definition by the ordinary magisterium.

The Jesuit did recognize that the church might teach a doctrine with a lesser note than that of infallibility. He wrote in this regard of a *Hirtenamt* which applied revealed truth to particular circumstances. This application of revealed truth was not, properly speaking, an exercise in the teaching of the ordinary or extraordinary magisterium but was a matter of applying what was already revealed. In point of fact, the relationship between the teaching office and the pastoral office was unclear in Kleutgen's thought, and indeed was often unclear in the writings of Pius IX.[30] That is to say, that nowhere does one find clear criteria for distinguishing that teaching which is an expression of its pastoral office and that which belongs to the church's teaching and judging office (*Lehramt und Richteramt*).

Finally, Kleutgen noted that the doctrinal certitude of the ordinary magisterium might also be reflected in the unanimous opinion of theologians. While Boyle maintains that Kleutgen had in

mind ". . . only reputable theologians, who may be known by their
being called to fill important posts and by their unquestioned orthodoxy . . . ,"[31] and adds that these theologians were to be only witnesses and not judges of the faith, this qualification did not appear
in the papal letter. The brief simply maintained that an act of divine
faith was owed also to those teachings of the ordinary magisterium
which were held as divinely revealed and which were ". . . therefore
held by the universal and constant consent of Catholic theologians
to pertain to the faith" (*ideoque universali et constanti consensu a
catholicis theologis ad fidem pertinere retinentur*). While Kleutgen
presumed that the unanimous consensus of the approved theologians was another source of doctrinal certitude, *Tuas libenter,* significantly, appeared to connect the exercise of the ordinary magisterium with the consensus of theologians. In fact, based on the
wording of the papal brief, it would seem legitimate to conclude
that where there is no universal and constant consensus of Catholic
theologians the infallibility of a teaching of the ordinary magisterium might itself be called into question.[32] Curiously, this reference
to the universal consensus of theologians will be absent from all
later ecclesiastical articulations of the ordinary magisterium.

Clearly, Kleutgen's elucidation of the ordinary magisterium
found its way into *Tuas libenter* by way of Cardinal Reisach. As we
shall see below, Kleutgen would continue to have an influential
role in the formulation of the theology of church authority in the
second half of the nineteenth century.

The Understanding of the Ordinary Universal Magisterium at Vatican I

Vatican I was unique among ecumenical councils insofar as it
was convened principally for the purpose of reinforcing ecclesial
authority and for rejecting certain theological errors rather than for
combating heresy. Immediately after Pius IX announced in 1867
his intention to convene a council, the division between the ultramontanists and those more sympathetic to a moderate episcopalist
ecclesiology was exacerbated in debate over the coming council.
While most studies have focused their attention on the ecclesiastical politics of these two parties as manifested in the debates regard-

ing *Pastor aetemus,* it is important to note the fundamental unity in ecclesiology of *Dei Filius* and *Pastor aetemus.* Both were, in the main, intent upon reinforcing church authority. *Dei Filius* represented an attempt to reaffirm, specifically, the church's teaching on revelation and faith thought to be under attack by the new theologies.[33]

The understanding of the ordinary magisterium, as first articulated in Kleutgen's theology and in *Tuas libenter,* was solidified in *Dei Filius.* The first draft of that constitution (probably written by Johann Baptist Franzelin) was considered too technical in style and conceptualization and so was sent to the Deputation for the Faith for revision. This earlier schema did not contain any direct reference to the ordinary magisterium, but there were several allusions to a double form of teaching. Chapter 11 of the Franzelin schema, for example, made a distinction between *definitiones* and the *propositio articulorum fidei.* The official *adnotatio* made it clear that this distinction was one between solemn definitions and the profession and preaching of the faith.[34]

The revision of the first schema was accomplished largely by Bishop Martin of Paderborn with the assistance of Kleutgen. In the sixth meeting of the Deputation Bishop Senestrey, an ultramontane, wished a clarification in the text whereby it would be clear that alongside those definitions proposed in response to heresy there existed another form of ecclesiastical teaching which, Senestrey maintained, possessed the same obligatory force. The following passage was then inserted into chapter 3:

> All those things are to be believed by divine and catholic faith which are contained in the Word of God either written or handed on and are proposed by the church for belief either by a solemn judgment or by the ordinary magisterium.[35]

In the commentary on the text Bishop Simor, Primate of Hungary, maintained that the passage was addressed to those who would pretend that only conciliar definitions are the object of an act of divine faith to the exclusion of that which is taught by the unanimous consensus of the church.[36]

When the passage was presented to the 27th and 28th general sessions it was the object of some disagreement. Some bishops found the wording to be too obscure and others simply requested that the whole passage be suppressed. Marc Caudron's study demonstrates the extent to which many of the council fathers had completely misunderstood the import of the passage: Bishop Martinez, for example, thought the expression *magisterium ordinarium* referred to the infallible teaching of the pope as distinguished from conciliar definitions.[37] Consequently, it was necessary for Bishop Martin to explain that it was expressly not the intention of the Deputation to make allusion to papal infallibility (a topic far from settled at that point) but to describe the material object of faith. As an example, Martin cited the teaching of the divine nature of Jesus Christ which, he contended, was taught infallibly by the ordinary magisterium even prior to the definition at Nicea. Here he placed special emphasis on the crucial role of the bishops in this teaching:

> All of you, most reverend fathers, know that before the council of Nicea all the Catholic bishops already believed in the divinity of our Lord Jesus Christ. Before the council not even this dogma was plainly defined or declared. Accordingly, in the time before the council of Nicea this dogma was taught by the ordinary magisterium.[38]

Furthermore, and this may have been crucial to the eventual acceptance of the passage, Martin pointed out that the Deputation was simply employing a concept already expressed by the pope in *Tuas libenter.*

Two significant amendments for this passage were proposed and passed. First Bishop Monzon y Martins wished to specify that the material object of faith was taught *tamquam divinitus revelata.* The addition of this phrase was designed to eliminate any attempt to treat theological opinions and doctrines of faith equally, and in fact was only reinserting a specification which was already present in *Tuas libenter.*[39] Second, Bishop Meurin suggested that to the phrase *magisterio ordinario* be added the words *publico et universali.* The Deputation eventually agreed to the addition of the word *universali,* with Bishop Martin explaining that it was to be added in order to avoid any possibility of interpreting the phrase *magisterium ordinarium* as referring to papal teaching. Thus the final text read:

> All those things are to be believed by divine and catholic faith which are contained in the word of God either written or handed down and are proposed by the Church for belief as divinely revealed either by a solemn judgement or by its ordinary and universal magisterium (DS 3011).

In summary it can be assumed that were it not for Pius IX's prior use of the expression in *Tuas libenter* the passage would likely have been suppressed. Given the two modes of teaching, the fathers understood quite clearly the first form, that of a solemn definition. Here the emphasis was on that of judgment or decision. The ordinary magisterium was essentially defined in opposition to this form of teaching. Yet apart from this negative definition of the ordinary magisterium (a teaching which does not issue from a solemn judgment), the fathers seemed quite imprecise. One must presume that the bishops were aware of the ancient conviction that the universal agreement of the episcopate was a sure sign of the authenticity of a teaching. Evidence from the *acta* suggests that they were less comfortable with its more recent formulation in both *Tuas libenter* and *Dei Filius*. Caudron finds the use of such terms as *propositio, professio et praedicatio, doctrina,* and *praedicat et docet* to describe the ordinary magisterium. In sum, one must conclude that the fathers generally had little understanding of the precise meaning of the expression *magisterium ordinarium.*[40]

After Vatican I, this teaching on the ordinary universal magisterium of bishops would appear only sporadically in ecclesiastical documents prior to the Second Vatican Council. In canon 1323.1 of the 1917 Code of Canon Law the teaching of Vatican I was repeated verbatim and, as with the text in Vatican I, it made no mention of the accompanying consensus of theologians found in *Tuas libenter.* In 1928 Pope Pius XI in his encyclical *Mortalium animos,* would allude to the ordinary magisterium and the circumstance in which it must give way to an exercise of solemn teaching:

> Also, the magisterium of the church—which has been constituted on earth by divine counsel, so that revealed doctrines both might soundly exist for perpetuity and might be given over to the knowledge of the human race easily and safely—although it is exercised daily through the Roman Pontiff and the bishops having communion with him, still it embraces the of-

fice so that, if when it is fitting either more efficaciously to meet
the errors and hostilities of heretics or to impress more clearly
and more subtly the explained main parts of sacred doctrine in
the minds of the faithful, it might proceed opportunely to define something by solemn rites and decrees (DS 3683).

Pope Pius XII, in the Apostolic Constitution *Munificentissimus
Deus,* noted the "strong and firm argument" for the definition of
Mary's assumption which could be drawn from the universal con-
sensus of the ordinary universal magisterium of the church:

> And so from the universal consent of the ordinary universal
> magisterium of the church a certain and firm argument is
> drawn by which the bodily assumption of the blessed virgin
> Mary into heaven is verified . . . to be a truth revealed by God,
> and therefore to be believed by all the children of the church
> finally and faithfully.[41]

This passage was followed by a citation from the First Vatican
Council's teaching on the ordinary universal magisterium in *Dei
Filius.* This view of Pope Pius XII reflects the understanding of the
ordinary universal magisterium found in the writings of many
theologians in the late nineteenth and early twentieth centuries.
One of the most commonly cited examples of the infallible ordinary teaching of bishops was, in fact, the teaching of the church on
the immaculate conception and the assumption of Mary prior to
the solemn definition of those teachings.

These scattered references to the ordinary universal magisterium of bishops must be understood against the backdrop of a
growing process of Roman centralization and with it the accompanying significance of the papal encyclical as a mode of magisterial teaching from the nineteenth century on.[42] Indeed, by the time
of Pius XII's pontificate one could discern a consistent tendency to
identify the ordinary universal magisterium with the ordinary papal magisterium.[43] This theological development will be treated at
greater length in chapters 4 and 5.

Conclusion

In the chief ecclesiastical documents from *Tuas libenter* to *Dei
Filius* we see the convergence of neo-scholasticism and ultramon-

tanism in the exposition of the authority of the magisterium. Kleutgen and Pius IX, two principal figures during this period, shared the same ecclesiological vision. Each in his own way possessed an apocalyptic perspective. In Deufel's biographical section on Kleutgen, he sums up the brilliant theologian's life orientation as one characterized by a profound, boundless pessimism with respect to the modern world. The dread which he experienced in the face of the future was transformed into a "militant engagement."[44] Kleutgen channeled the energies of his early pessimism into an ecclesial battle plan to shore up the shaky foundations of the modern church. For his part, Pius IX

> . . . attached too much weight to prophecies and other manifestations of the miraculous, and tended to see in the political convulsions which involved the Church a new episode in the great battle between God and Satan instead of realistically subjecting the events to a technical analysis.[45]

The apocalyptic vision of Pius IX would direct two nineteenth century developments: an increasing concentration of ecclesiastical power in Rome and a concomitant stress on the charism of infallibility as the guarantor of the Christian tradition.

The a-historical methodology, the influence of static Aristotelian clarity, and the focus on certitude which belonged to neoscholasticism all combined to fuel a suspicion of theological movements which threatened to abandon the Christian tradition before the seductions of modernity. The two eyes of theology invoked by Döllinger, philosophical and historical studies, henceforth were to be employed grudgingly if at all.

Episcopalism in all of its forms was connected with nationalist and republican movements and so was viewed with great mistrust and apprehension.[46] This mistrust in turn produced a restorationist ecclesiology after the ascent of Pope Gregory XVI which sought to consolidate religious authority in the papacy at all costs. The consequent view of authority left little room for theological pluralism or the ancient view of the *sensus fidei* as expressed by the whole church, the *congregatio fidelium*. First with *Tuas libenter,* then continued in the constitutions of Vatican I, ". . . the scope of obligatory doctrinal decisions was excessively broadened, while the field of theological research and debate was drastically reduced."[47]

Yves Congar sees in *Tuas libenter* the attempt of the Holy See to exclude from theology any prolongation of the Gallican spirit. This program required the reaffirmation of authority and the limitation of consensus.[48] Authority was no longer to be understood in relation to the *testificatio fidei* but rather to the *determinatio fidei*. That is, the bishops were not primarily authoritative witnesses of a faith which was first received and then transmitted, but were authoritative judges who articulated and thereby determined the content of the faith. Magisterial authority was now only extrinsically bound to the deposit of faith.[49] The ancient conviction regarding the authoritative status of the consensus of the universal episcopate was subtly transformed in the nineteenth century formulation "ordinary universal magisterium." What was initially a conviction regarding those tenets of the Christian faith which never required solemn definition had become a means of extending the mantle of infallibility to virtually every expression of ordinary teaching. Yet in this extension of the charism of infallibility, the stress was not placed on the deposit of faith itself, but on the teaching office which could effectively determine the deposit. Giuseppe Alberigo has remarked on the significance of this development:

> What remains surprising is the fact that within the brief space of a decade the equation of solemn acts and ordinary acts of instruction was approved by a general council. It represents an innovation with respect to an unbroken tradition of validating the solemnity of such decisions not only because of their exceptional context but also because of the reception and approval they had received in the Church. It was in this way that the Church had sanctioned the definitive nature of such decisions. However, this fact was a remote concern of the majority of the council who seemed to prefer a hierarchical interpretation of the teaching office.[50]

Perhaps the greatest anomaly in this early history of the notion of the ordinary universal magisterium is the fact that, while the term theoretically denotes that teaching of the bishops dispersed throughout the world, this was understood in the context of an ecclesiology which viewed episcopal authority as derivative of papal authority. In a homogeneous church of western European sensibilities, it would not be possible to conceive of the bishops as the bearers of some unique expression of the deposit of faith not available to the pope. The bishops were not vicars of Christ, a title applied to them in the early church, but functionally, vicars of the pope. The international Catholic culture was not given to pluralistic expression: its theology was founded on neo-scholasticism and given quasi-normative status in Leo XIII's *Aetemi Patris* and the language of theological texts and classroom instruction was Latin. As a consequence, a teaching which might appear to further the cause of a Gallican episcopalism, in reality was employed to strengthen the magisterial authority of the papacy. The infallibility of the ordinary universal magisterium effectively meant an extension of papal infallibility.

At this early stage in the history of the teaching on the ordinary universal magisterium, several important questions were left unanswered. First, how does one distinguish the *de fide* teachings of the ordinary magisterium from those which are not taught as divinely revealed? The prevailing understanding of the magisterium was one which was reluctant to acknowledge explicitly the existence of non-infallible teaching by the ordinary magisterium. Second, how does one discern that a consensus among the bishops exists with respect to any given teaching? Third, how does the teaching of the college of bishops differ from papal teaching? In the next three chapters we shall investigate the degree to which theologians prior to Vatican II attempted to respond to these questions and, more generally, the manner in which they interpreted the ordinary universal magisterium as it was articulated in the documents reviewed above.

The Ordinary Infallible Teaching of Bishops in the Neo-Scholastic Manual Tradition

The Latin theological manual tradition, from the *Praelectiones* of Giovanni Perrone in the early nineteenth century to Francis Sullivan's *De Ecclesia* written on the eve of the Second Vatican Council, represents a distinct theological *Denkform*. These manuals were written as seminary textbooks within a broadly neo-scholastic theological framework and they served the education of the vast majority of priests and a good number of bishops, cardinals and Vatican administrators up through the Second Vatican Council. Their authors were referred to by the bishops of the Second Vatican Council as the *auctores probati,* approved theologians who could be trusted as sources of sound theological interpretation of the Catholic dogmatic tradition.[1] Much of what John Gallagher has said in his study of the moral manual tradition holds equally for the dogmatic manuals:

> A theological genre was created which, in the years following the 1879 publication of *Aeterni Patris,* would be largely assimilated into neo-Thomism. Ultimately the neo-Thomist manuals would become the "received tradition," the body of knowledge conveyed to each generation of seminarians in their courses in moral theology. . . . The authority of these writings was not the product of the talents or insights of a particular author, but rather the authority of a self-authenticating tradition. The manuals retain a medieval notion of authority residing in the text and the tradition, rather than in the authority of the author.[2]

This genre had its origins in the Counter-Reformation and the Council of Trent's demand for a more structured seminary education. However, the church of the baroque was dominated by Latin theological tracts which must be distinguished from the manuals by both aim and structure. Following the baroque, in the period from 1750 to 1840 Catholic theological thought was dominated by the Enlightenment. However, by the mid-nineteenth century there was a simultaneous decline of the universities as centers of Catholic activities with an increase in the importance of the seminary. As the church reacted first to the Enlightenment (rationalism and liberalism) and then to its aftermath (romanticism and idealism), the manual tradition emerged with two clear tasks:

> The first was the defense of the Catholic faith against the rationalism and the religious skepticism of the Enlightenment. The second was the presentation of positive Christian revelation in a coherent, unified system that could stand in comparison with the systems of Fichte, Schelling and Hegel without compromising the supernaturality and the unique, historical character of positive Christian revelation.[3]

It will be fruitful, therefore, to review a representative sample of these Latin manuals in order to discern their understanding of the ordinary universal magisterium as a distinct mode of episcopal teaching. While an exhaustive review of all the schools and religious orders is not possible, this chapter will review representative manuals of the Jesuit tradition as reflective of the dominant understanding of the ordinary universal magisterium of bishops prior to Vatican II.

The Revival of Jesuit Theological Scholarship

Soon after the reestablishment of the Society of Jesus in 1814 Pope Leo XII returned the Roman College to Jesuit control; reorganized in 1824, it became a center for theology in Rome. By the 1850s the prestige of its faculty and the neo-scholastic revival brought it fame throughout Europe. The first stage of the development of a Latin seminary manual tradition would transpire at the Roman College through the efforts of the Jesuit faculty. It was a tradition which in the middle third of the nineteenth century could be described as only generally neo-scholastic. Only after Pope Leo XIII's *Aeterni Patris* (1879), which encouraged the return to studies of St. Thomas, was the manual tradition subsumed under the neo-Thomist movements. At that point its influence began to spread far beyond the Gregorian University in Rome.

For this survey of the Jesuit manualists, it will be helpful to break up this review into three periods. The first period surveys those manualists often considered as the "Roman school," beginning with Giovanni Perrone and concluding with Johann Baptist Franzelin. The beginning of the second period is marked by Domenico Palmieri whose work at the turn of the century represented the beginning of a shift away from the influences of the early Tübingen school. The third period includes the works of three Jesuit ecclesiologists, Joseph Salaverri, Timothy Zapelena and Francis Sullivan, who taught at the Gregorian University between 1930 and 1960 and whose manuals were the most commonly used in educating many of the participants of Vatican II.

The Early Jesuit Manual Tradition (1840–1890)[4]

The "Roman school," in its first decades, was relatively open and creative. In fact, it would not be accurate to describe the members of this school as neo-scholastic, if by that one had in mind adherence to one coherent system of the kind championed by the neo-Thomists of the end of the nineteenth century.[5] These theologians were surprisingly attentive to German theology and were conversant with the Tübingen school, most notably with the theology of Johann Adam Möhler. Within this particular Roman tradition we find first in the writings of Giovanni Perrone, Carlo Passaglia and Clemens Schrader, and later in those of Johann Baptist Franzelin the influence of a christological "Mystical Body" ecclesiology which saw the church as the continuation of the incarnation in history.[6] This development gave ecclesiology a more theological grounding than it had received in the juridical treatments of Robert Bellarmine and other writers of the Counter-Reformation. However, by viewing Christ as a kind of exemplar of the church it would become difficult to give due account of the church's human failings. At the same time, these theologians evinced a marked concern for the preservation of papal prerogatives in the face of the incursions of the modern state. What followed was an ecclesiology which was reluctant to accede authority to the local church and understood all ecclesial authority as *de facto* if not *de iure* dependent upon papal authority.

The first influential manual of the Roman school was that of Giovanni Perrone (1794–1876).[7] His early manual was influenced in part by the christological ecclesiology developed in Johann Adam Möhler's *Symbolik* and, to a lesser extent, in his earlier *Die Einheit*. A theological moderate much respected in the Roman congregations, Perrone was an influential member of the commissions responsible for preparing the definition on the dogma of the immaculate conception. Perrone's ecclesiology reflects the restorationist period in which he wrote; the erroneous assertion of the autonomy of reason and the freedom of the individual required a vigorous reaffirmation of the authority of the church.[8]

His *Praelectiones* began, as was common in the manuals, with a *De Vera Religione*. Infallibility was ascribed to the church, not understood as the whole of the faithful but as the universal episcopate in union with the pope.[9] Perrone grounded the college of bishops in the college of apostles, thereby establishing tradition as a source of revelation. The role of the bishop was treated in a section on heterodoxy with a discussion of the bishop's immediate and ordinary authority over his particular flock, an authority which was always subordinated to that of the Roman pontiff.[10] The authority of the universal episcopacy was sustained by Perrone's notion of the "moral person." Those who acted in the name of Christ, first the apostles and then the bishops, were established by Christ as moral persons capable of acting with his authority.[11] In Perrone's earlier writing this notion of the church as a moral person established by Christ was understood in a peculiarly juridical sense. His later writing, however, reinterpreted the concept in the light of Möhler's understanding of the church as an organic living unity.[12] Nevertheless, it was not the church as a whole which Perrone had in mind when he spoke of this unity but the college of bishops. The precise character of this authority was not spelled out in any detail, and more importantly, no mention was made of the responsibilities of the bishop individually or collectively as *magister*.

Turning directly to the tract *De Ecclesia Christi* in the *Praelec-*

tiones, we find no explicit treatment of bishops. In the article on the infallibility of the church Perrone mentioned the church's three offices: *testis, iudex* and *magister,* but with no discussion of the proper subject of these offices. In later manuals it will be common to find the treatment of infallibility generally divided into two sections, treating separately the subject and the object of infallibility. Here it was only the object of infallibility, namely, that which pertained to faith and morals, which was discussed. The subject was presumed to be the church, which, as we saw above, meant the hierarchy.[13]

In the tract *De Romano Pontifice,* the episcopacy was mentioned mainly when Perrone wished to stress that the pope's own authority was episcopal. Episcopal authority was described as that of pastoring, ruling and governing the flock.[14] All other bishops were then subordinated to the pope who was *episcopus episcoporum.* This view would later be enshrined in Vatican I's *Pastor aeternus.*

While the church was said to possess the office of *magister,* and while for Perrone *church* meant the episcopacy in union with the pope, the treatment of this office was quite vague. Although he granted infallibility to the church, his understanding of the pope's relationship to the episcopal college led him to consider the magisterium as if it were the property and function of the pope alone. His manual contained no treatment of the bishops collectively as teachers, and obviously, as this manual predates *Tuas libenter,* there was no explicit mention of an *ordinary magisterium* of bishops. In fact, the word *episcopus* does not even appear in Perrone's consideration of ecumenical councils.[15] One might conclude then that while the ministry of *magister* for the bishops did appear in Perrone's text, it was generally subordinated to papal authority.

Carlo Passaglia's *De Ecclesia Christi,* written in collaboration with Clemens Schrader (1820–1875), continued Perrone's view of church authority.[16] Particularly noteworthy was the explicit application of the *communicatio idiomatum* to the church.[17] Passaglia (1812–1887) and Schrader always spoke of the magisterium as one of the functions of the apostolic college and their successors, never as belonging to the pope or the papacy alone. Schrader, however, would move increasingly toward a more pronounced ultramontane position in his later years. He understood Pius IX's *Syllabus of*

Errors to consist in a collection of dogmatic definitions which he interpreted in a very strict fashion. His spirited support of papal infallibility on the preparatory commission for Vatican I was an indication of his eventual embrace of a pro-papalist position.[18]

The writings of Perrone and Passaglia preceded the papal brief *Tuas libenter* and therefore did not make explicit reference to the ordinary magisterium of bishops. At the same time these members of the Roman school played an important role in sketching the essential lines of development for a theology of teaching authority which would serve as the interpretive framework for later understandings of the teaching authority of the episcopal college. In their work one finds a common concern for order, unity and certainty. These were to be preserved primarily through the teaching authority of the church and in particular in the charism of infallibility.[19] Theirs was a nascent mystical body theology which stressed the continuity between the incarnation and the unity of the human and supernatural in the church.

If Perrone, Passaglia and Schrader sketched out in broad strokes a theology of teaching authority it was in the writing of Johann Baptist Franzelin (1816–1886), more than that of any other nineteenth century figure, that this theology flourished.[20] Franzelin was explicitly concerned with the problem of the transmission of revelation and developed his fundamental theology as a response to the Protestant *sola scriptura* doctrine. He was one of the first manualists to make full use of the tripartite distinction of powers first developed by German canonists.[21] This distinction between the teaching, ruling and sanctifying powers of the church allowed for a fuller treatment of the church's teaching authority.

In Franzelin's *De Divina Traditione et Scriptura* he distinguished between objective and active tradition. Objective tradition referred to the actual content of the faith while active tradition denoted the ecclesiastical organs for the faith's transmission. However, for Franzelin the active sense of tradition contained within it the objective aspect, for the latter could not be preserved without the former. The magisterium (active tradition) was the essential formal aspect of the transmission of the faith which the Protestant church's *sola scriptura* doctrine lacked.[22]

Franzelin further distinguished between an infallibility in teaching which was given to those bishops in communion with but subordinate to the pope, and an infallibility in believing which was given to the whole church.[23] The whole teaching church possessed the charism of infallibility in teaching but while the efficient cause of that infallibility was the assistance of the Holy Spirit, the formal cause was a unity with the pope as head of the church. As Sanks comments, "his emphasis on the papal prerogatives is still in opposition to the Gallican or Febronian position which he seems to find lurking behind every mention of episcopal consensus."[24] While Franzelin admitted that it was wise for the pope to consult the bishops and through them the whole faithful on a given matter, and while he pointed to the necessity for a consensus in the church on all doctrinal matters, he was quick to add that a papal definition was sufficient to create such a consensus, thereby avoiding any hint of Gallican episcopalism.[25]

Franzelin's explicit treatment of the teaching authority of the episcopacy was actually rather undeveloped. Bishops in their pastoring the flock of God and in their ruling the church by a magisterial and jurisdictional power were successors of the apostles.[26] Curiously, Franzelin made little mention of the role of the bishops in ecumenical councils. Of this surprising omission Sanks says:

> What is perhaps most amazing of all is that there is little or no mention of the function of councils (ecumenical or local) as part of the magisterium at all. Various conclusions are possible but the fact that a man who was the papal theologian at a council in session the same year that his major work was published does not discuss the councils as magisterial is astounding. . . . There is no doubt that he considers the bishops in council as exercising the magisterial power, but the relationship of this form of the magisterium to the papal magisterium is treated only so far as to affirm their union with and subordination to the Roman Pontiff. Conciliar theology seems to have held no interest for him.[27]

Franzelin made no explicit reference to the ordinary universal magisterium in the posthumously published *Theses De Ecclesia Christi* and only a passing citation of *Tuas libenter* in his *De Traditione*.[28] Nevertheless, in several passages, most notably in theses V, VIII and IX, he does write of the importance of the consensus of the episcopate as a guarantee of the apostolic faith. His theology of the episcopacy was more developed than that of the earlier generation at the Roman College but more attention was given to the bishops' authority in their individual churches than to their authority as a college. All of the bishops, along with the rest of the clergy and the faithful, constituted the church, though in a manner clearly subordinated to the pope, the visible head of the whole church.[29]

Franzelin's theology continued the development of the ecclesiological trajectory begun by his predecessors at the Roman College. His theology of teaching authority stressed the divine-human character of the church as a continuation of the incarnation, reflecting the influence of the Tübingen school. He emphasized the church's possession of a deposit of truth and grounded that deposit in the charism of infallibility manifested in the witness of the bishops and particularly in the teaching office of the pope.

The Jesuit Manual Tradition (1890–1930)

Beginning with Domenico Palmieri (1829–1909), the manual tradition underwent a discernible shift. The organic conception of the church as the mystical body, so prominent in the writings of Perrone, Passaglia, Schrader and Franzelin, virtually disappeared in Palmieri's manual and those which followed. At the same time, the moderate papalism of the earlier Roman school began to receive much greater emphasis. If the earlier writers understood the college of bishops to be clearly subordinate to the pope, they nevertheless maintained that the charism of infallibility resided in the episcopal college. Palmieri, and those who followed him, presented a theology of teaching authority in which the sure charism of truth was given immediately to the pope and only derivatively to the bishops.

The title of Palmieri's manual on ecclesiology, *Tractatus de Romano Pontifice cum Prolegomena de Ecclesia* reflects the significant shift in the theology of the magisterium after Franzelin.[30] The tract on the church was only a prolegomenon to the treatment of the papacy, the principal subject of the manual. With Palmieri we see perhaps the influence of the dogmatic constitution *Pastor aeternus* of Vatican I on subsequent ecclesiological reflection. "The question about the magisterium that is of prime importance for Palmieri, in contrast to Franzelin and his predecessors, is the question of *who* exercises it."[31] For the earlier manualists the distinction between the ordinary and extraordinary magisterium was of little importance since the two modes shared the common object of infallibility, the faith of the church. Beginning with Palmieri, however, we find in the later manuals distinct treatments of the subject of infallibility with an increasing concern for the differing modes of infallible teaching.

According to Palmieri, when the bishops taught infallibly they did so only because of their communion with the pope.[32] He proposed only one immediate subject of infallibility, that being the pope. The Roman pontiff was the recipient of a special assistance of the Holy Spirit whereas the bishops received the Spirit's assistance only mediately through the pope. In the prolegomenon on the church Palmieri did briefly affirm both the infallibility of the magisterium in general and that of the bishops. He stated explicitly that the bishops taught infallibly not only when gathered collectively but *singuli in suis cathedris.*[33] For Palmieri the whole hierarchy itself was infallible when in communion with the pope. If all the pastors of individual churches were to teach error, the church itself would be in error. However, the exercise of this infallible magisterium did not require the convocation of a synod; it could be exercised with each bishop in his own see, for even residing in their own dioceses the bishops constituted an assembly or *coetum.* Palmieri did not outline, however, what conditions must be met for the bishops to constitute a *coetum.* He concluded his brief treatment on the ordinary universal magisterium with a quotation of the text from *Dei Filius* (DS 3011), but without any commentary.

Palmieri's manual did provide a more extensive theology of the teaching ministry of the bishop, particularly with regard to the ordinary universal magisterium, than did Franzelin and the earlier figures. Nevertheless, he seemed suspicious of episcopal authority, and this suspicion led to a carefully circumscribed juridical treatment of the role of the bishop. Also, unlike Franzelin, Palmieri employed the bipartite orders/jurisdiction schema in which the magisterium was subsumed under the power of jurisdiction.

Published in 1896, Bernard Tepe's (1833–1904) *Institutiones Theologicae in Usum Scholarum* is the first theological manual treated here to be authored by a Jesuit not associated with the Roman College.[34] Nevertheless, Tepe's fundamental ecclesiological perspective differed little from that of Palmieri. If anything he went even further than Palmieri in subordinating the authority of the bishops to the pope.

The day-to-day exercise of the magisterial office was central to Tepe's understanding of the ordinary magisterium. Since Christ promised to protect the church from error, this protection could not be a rare or extraordinary event, for in actual fact the church did not teach only rarely but exercised the teaching office daily. The teaching of the church must be protected in this more "regular" daily exercise.[35] As with Palmieri, Tepe argued for an infallibility of the ordinary magisterium of bishops in union with the pope from the premise that the church itself was infallible:

> The church is the pillar and firmament of truth. But if it were to propose something erroneous as a truth divinely revealed then it would not be the pillar and firmament of truth since then the whole church teaching and learning would lack in truth: the teaching church by proposing error and the learning church by accepting error.[36]

Tepe's theology did make explicit the need for the bishop's daily teaching about revelation to be protected from error, and in this regard went beyond the statements of *Tuas libenter* and *Dei Filius* which did not address the question of *how often* the bishops actually exercise this mode of magisterial teaching. This stress on the quotidian teaching ministry of the bishops will be increasingly common in the manuals from this time on.

The nine-volume manual of Christian Pesch (1835–1925) was first published in the years from 1894 to 1897; it went through numerous editions and was used by seminaries through the 1950s. This manual offered what was by far the most extensive treatment of the magisterium of bishops up to this point. In the section on the active subject of the ecclesiastical magisterium, Pesch devoted twenty-two pages to the episcopacy. According to Pesch, the bishops were not infallible when they taught individually in their own dioceses. Nevertheless, they were "authoritative teachers"[37] and judges of the faith in their capacity as individual teachers. An individual bishop did not define dogma but rather conserved two things: that which had been defined and that which had been handed down. Pesch stressed this strictly conservative role, for he noted that in many other matters the bishop taught only as a private doctor.

Infallibility was not to be extended to the individual bishops because the infallibility of individual bishops was not necessary either for verifying the promises of Christ or for conserving integral Christian doctrine.[38] This was the reverse form of the argument discussed earlier whereby the infallibility of the ordinary magisterium flowed from the necessity of the church as the infallible conservator of truth. Here, on the other hand, the charism was extended only as far as was necessary for the preservation of the church as a whole in truth.

A particularly important contribution of Pesch was his consideration of the possible means by which the bishops dispersed throughout the world might achieve a consensus in church doctrine. This consensus might appear either expressly or tacitly. It appeared expressly when: (1) bishops accepted the decrees of particular councils; (2) bishops, requested by the pope, put forth opinions approaching a conciliar action, as occurred in preparation for the definition of the immaculate conception; (3) bishops proposed doctrine for the faithful in the face of a controversy; (4) bishops offered approval and approbation for books containing doctrinal matter, e.g., catechisms and devotional matter.[39] This consensus was manifested tacitly when bishops knew of doctrine commonly presented in their dioceses and yet did not oppose it, as they were required to do if they deemed such doctrine to be false.[40]

Finally, Pesch offered Matthew 28:20 as a further defense of the infallibility of the ordinary universal magisterium. The emphasis was placed on Christ's promise to be present *all days*. If the promise of the preservation of truth was to be effective in the life of the church, it was insufficient that the charism of infallibility be operative only in the extraordinary exercise of the church's teaching office. The treatment of the topic concluded with a quotation of *Dei Filius* on the ordinary magisterium (DS 3011) and *Tuas libenter* (DS 2879).

The most significant contribution of Pesch was his attempt to develop the notion of an episcopal *consensus* outside of council.

Significantly, he did not offer concrete manners for *achieving* consensus so much as examples of where one would look to try and discern if in fact the bishops were in agreement, e.g., episcopal approval of catechetical material. Yet, in order to verify that the bishops were in agreement on a particular doctrine one would have to review all catechetical materials in all dioceses pertaining to the doctrine in question which individual bishops had approved in order to ascertain that such a consensus did in fact exist. Such a task would be monumental. How could one possibly discover whether every bishop in the universal church knew of a certain doctrine being taught in his diocese and did not oppose it? What if this particular teaching was not taught at all or deemed irrelevant in certain dioceses, perhaps because of cultural differences? Is this an obstacle to a true *consensus?* Pesch's explication of the doctrine of the ordinary universal magisterium may be more helpful for the implicit questions it raised than it is for the clarity it provided.

With the manual of Michael D'Herbigny (1880–1957) we step fully into the twentieth century and meet a second French Jesuit who taught at Rome. His treatment of ecclesiological topics gave evidence of an extensive knowledge of both scripture and the early Christian writers which went beyond the prooftexting tendencies found in some earlier manuals. Within a large section on infallibility D'Herbigny specifically addressed the infallibility of bishops. He defended the teaching that individual bishops were not infallible, providing a list of individual bishops in the history of the church who did, in fact, err. It was only the college of bishops which promulgated doctrine infallibly, both when in ecumenical council and when dispersed throughout the world. It followed that the bishops need not be physically congregated together; it was sufficient that their *concordia* of mind and will be extrinsically manifested.[41] According to D'Herbigny, church practice revealed the possibility for this concord in the correspondence between bishops. In this situation (dispersed throughout the world) the bishops continued to function as if they were in a permanent council of the whole church.

D'Herbigny did offer an important qualification regarding the manifestation of *consensus* among the bishops. If Pesch spoke of "explicit" and "tacit" agreement, D'Herbigny spoke of an agreement which was to be "manifested extrinsically," demonstrating a more cautious approach than that of Pesch regarding the possibilities for this concord or consensus.

The German manualist, Hermann Dieckmann (1880–1928), provided an extensive presentation of the magisterium of bishops in his *De Ecclesia*.[42] His theology of the teaching authority of bishops began with the authority of the individual bishop teaching in his own diocese and then moved to consider the bishops when they constitute a universal magisterium. The German theologian's fuller consideration of the episcopacy considered not only the status of individual bishops but also that of bishops gathered in provincial councils and synods. Provincial councils and synods, Dieckmann claimed, must be clearly differentiated from universal, ecumenical councils. With both the individual bishop and the provincial synod the bishops were authentic teachers but were not infallible. The faithful owed to such teaching a religious and intellectual obedience but not a response of divine faith.[43] While each bishop's ordinary jurisdiction or field of authority was limited to his local church, he retained a relationship to the universal church insofar as the local church was part of the universal church. According to Dieckmann, this relationship is concretized in the bishop's membership in the episcopal college.

The universal magisterium of the episcopal college was exercised in one of two modes: ordinary or extraordinary. In beginning with the ordinary mode Dieckmann departed from previous treatments.[44] The bishops dispersed throughout the world possessed not simply a material consensus but a formal one. This consensus yielded a moral and social bond among the bishops. This same bond and formal consensus existed as well in the extraordinary exercise of the magisterium, where the bishops were physically gathered and united together.[45] Dieckmann did not, however, develop the precise nature of this distinction. He offered no criteria for ascertaining when a formal consensus might exist. How is one to differentiate the formal from the merely material consensus?

The bond between the bishops, and particularly that bond between the bishops and the pope, was constituted through written correspondence, papal nuncios, Roman legates, and by the bishops' visits to Rome—all modes of *commercio frequenti*.[46] Here Dieckmann was more helpful than previous manualists; he provided illustrations of ways in which bishops might achieve this consensus, and various media by which one may look for evidence of episcopal agreement. As with Christian Pesch, who also provided some examples for discerning episcopal agreement, Dieckmann did not consider the enormous difficulties which any serious attempt to ascertain episcopal consensus through these diverse modes would present.

In a concluding section, Dieckmann distinguished himself from previous manualists who were content to quickly conclude with a brief citation from *Tuas libenter* or *Dei Filius.* The German Jesuit went further and actually presented a textual history of the teaching of the ordinary universal magisterium at the First Vatican Council, the first account provided in a Jesuit manual.

In conclusion, this manual contained a relatively thorough explication of the ordinary universal magisterium of bishops. An emphasis on the need for a formal rather than material consensus among the bishops is significant, as is the attempt to adumbrate the way in which a consensus might be achieved by means of written correspondence and episcopal visits to Rome.

The Late Jesuit Manual Tradition (1930–1960)

This review of the ecclesiology of the Jesuit manualists will conclude by returning to the Gregorianum in Rome and three influential Jesuit professors: Joseph Salaverri, Timothy Zapelena and Francis Sullivan. The manuals of these three ecclesiologists will have special significance due to their close chronological proximity to the Second Vatican Council and the likelihood that many of the council participants would have studied these texts in their own theological training.

The first of the three to be considered is Salaverri (1892–1979), who authored the influential *Sacrae Theologiae Summa,* a popular manual used in the 1940s and 1950s prior to the Second Vatican Council.[47] This work contained a relatively extensive treatment of the episcopacy and the magisterium, giving attention to the biblical and patristic roots of the episcopal title and office. Salaverri began his consideration of the ordinary universal magisterium, writing: "The bishops, successors of the apostles, are infallible when, in concord with one another under the Roman Pontiff, they propose to the faithful either in council or outside of council doctrine to be held definitively."[48] This definition was followed by a commentary elaborating on three key phrases in definition. First, by *concordes* he meant that the bishops, in handing on doctrine, were of one opinion among themselves, not only materially but formally; this agreement with each other could be either explicit or implicit.[49] Second, *sub Romano Pontifice* meant that the bishops, when proposing a doctrine, viewed themselves to be in agreement with the teaching of the pope, though this agreement also might be only implicit. Third, by *definitive tenendam* Salaverri identified that doctrine which the bishops taught with the highest level of authority, requiring of the faithful irrevocable assent. This phrase, *definitive tenendam doctrinam,* takes on a special significance in light of the discussions which have transpired since Vatican II regarding the meaning of the phrase *tamquam definitive tenendam* in *Lumen gentium* #25. For Salaverri, only that teaching for which the bishops demanded an irrevocable assent fell under the category of the teaching of the ordinary universal magisterium.[50] It is clear, therefore, that the author wished to restrict the field of episcopal teachings which carry the charism of infallibility.

Salaverri also addressed the vexing problem of verifying the principal conditions for the infallible teaching of the ordinary universal magisterium. First, the concord of bishops could be verified through the bishops' communication with one another and with the pope. The second condition, *sub Romano Pontifice,* could be verified again by communication with the pope. Third, *doctrinam definitive tenendam* could be verified when the bishops put forth doctrine by means of formulas which state the gravity of the teaching and the assent which is obliged.[51] But this attempt at verification raises several questions. How does one verify this communication among the bishops and with the pope? What form does it take? Does the pope always initiate the determination of *consensus* as when Pius IX and Pius XII polled the bishops regarding the definability of the Marian dogmas? We shall return to these fundamental questions later.

Particular attention must be given to the manual of Timothy Zapelena (1883–1962).[52] Its six editions were used at the Gregorian University over three decades. The Jesuit professor continued the practice found in Palmieri and Billot of assuming a bipartite division of powers and situating teaching authority within the context of the power of jurisdiction. Consequently, he held that the distinguishing characteristic of the church's teaching authority was derived from jurisdiction, its power to command assent, whereas the teaching authority of theologians was unable to demand assent.[53] While the theologian's position elicited assent by the persuasiveness of its presentation, the hierarchical teaching authority could command assent by virtue of the authority vested in it by Christ. The response to such teaching was not critical inquiry as with the positions of the theologian, but an assent understood juridically as an act of obedience.

The second volume of Zapelena's *De Ecclesia Christi* was divided into four major tracts: *Tractatus De Episcopatu, Tractatus De Magisterio Ecclesiastico, Tractatus De Traditione* and *Tractatus Dogmaticus De Ecclesia Corpore Christi Mystico.* This volume contained an extended treatment of the episcopacy and the magisterium in separate tracts. This separate consideration reflected a typical theology of the episcopacy in which matters of jurisdiction were emphasized at the expense of the role of the bishop as preacher and teacher. In the tract on the magisterium Zapelena considered the infallible teaching of the college of bishops. His seventeenth thesis proposed that it was in the bishops alone (including of course the pope) that the power of the magisterium dwelled. When they agreed in doctrine with the pope their teaching was infallible, either when gathered in council or when dispersed throughout the world.[54] These bishops could be considered either singly or collegially. When considered collegially, this collegiality might be either partial, as with provincial synods, or integral as when the bishops gathered in ecumenical council. Furthermore, the episcopal college could teach by means of a solemn and conciliar magisterium (*magisterio sollemni et conciliari*) or by means of an ordinary and daily magisterium (*magisterio ordinario et quotidiano*). Zapelena then divided this section into three parts. First, he considered the bishops viewed singly as subjects of a magisterium which was authentic but not yet infallible. Second, he treated the bishops gathered collegially in an ecumenical council as the subjects of a magisterium which was authentic and infallible. Third, he considered the bishops collegially but dispersed as subjects of the ordinary and universal magisterium which was infallible.

Three conditions must be met for either the solemn (extraordinary) or ordinary mode of infallible teaching: (1) there must be an agreement among a majority of the bishops (2) on a matter of faith and morals (3) which was taught with the approval of the head of the college, the pope.[55] The Jesuit theologian further expounded on the ordinary mode of infallible teaching. According to Zapelena, the ordinary universal magisterium of bishops might itself be exercised according to two modes. First was that manner of exercise which occurred when, faced with a controversial matter, the pope condemned an error by his judgment and the bishops adhered to this judgment. In third century Africa Pope Stephen condemned the error which held for the nullity of baptism by heretics or schismatics. History showed, Zapelena contended, that the universal episcopate adhered to Stephen's decision. The second mode of exercise occurred when the bishops actually proposed something as belonging to the deposit of faith. This was proposed to the faithful as something absolutely and irrevocably to be held.[56] The inclusion of the phrase *absolute seu irrevocabiliter tenendam* continued a restriction which we saw earlier in Salaverri's manual and it raised the question of episcopal intention in the act of teaching.

Zapelena was one of the first manualists to recognize explicitly the difficulties attendant upon the verification or discernment of teaching proposed infallibly by the ordinary universal magisterium. He admitted, for example, that the consensus among the bishops and their intention was more easily perceived when the bishops were gathered in council than when the bishops were dispersed.[57] In support of this, he cited the norm of canon law which held that nothing was to be understood as dogmatically defined unless it was manifestly evident as such. Nevertheless, Zapelena maintained, it was still possible to identify that which the bishops taught by the ordinary and universal magisterium. This teaching could be discovered in both the oral and written preaching of pope and bishops, in the approbation of theological manuals and catechisms, in the approbation of theological doctrine which dogmatic and moral theologians have constantly proposed as revealed, in the doctrinal decrees of provincial and national synods and in liturgical documents (following the principle *lex orandi, lex credendi*).[58] This last form is worthy of note as Zapelena was one of the few manualists to remark on the doctrinal role of liturgical texts and practices.

What was the distinction between the extraordinary and the ordinary exercise of the infallible teaching of the bishops? First, the extraordinary magisterium was exercised in one place and not in many places, as with the bishops dispersed throughout the world. Second, the extraordinary magisterium was exercised only rarely whereas the ordinary magisterium occurred regularly (*quotidiani*). Zapelena suggested that conciliar doctrinal decrees were in most instances proclaimed for the purpose of proscribing heretical errors or of checking certain controversies concerning faith and morals. The ordinary magisterium, on the other hand, was concerned for the most part with proposing the deposit of faith and also with expounding doctrines already solemnly defined by papal or conciliar definition. Finally, and this is significant, the extraordinary magisterium was exercised by the bishops personally, while the ordinary magisterium could be manifested through subordinates such as parish priests, theologians or canon lawyers. Zapelena noted the connection made in *Tuas libenter* between the ordinary magisterium of the bishops and the universal consensus of theologians.[59] The suggestion was that while it was the college of bishops which taught authoritatively in exercising the ordinary magisterium, since this was not exercised through a solemn definition it was best discerned by looking to a plurality of sources for ecclesial teaching —pastors, theologians and canonists—and seeking evidence for the episcopal consensus there. Apparently, then, Zapelena concurred with Pius IX's papal brief in indirectly proposing a criterion for discerning the bishops' teaching on a matter—the consensus of pastors, theologians, etc.

To conclude this review of Jesuit manualists we examine the manual of Francis Sullivan. His tract on ecclesiology represents the end of the Latin manual tradition. Originally intended as a two-volume work, Sullivan never completed the second volume as ". . . the demand for Latin text-books had died with the Council."[60] In the one completed volume, the author offered the following qualification for the infallible exercise of the bishops' teaching office.

> Residential bishops alone, in communion with the bishop of
> Rome, possess by divine law the authoritative magisterium in
> the church. Their collegial consensus on matters of faith and
> morals is infallible when they teach either gathered in council
> or when dispersed throughout the world.[61]

The first thing to note is Sullivan's specification that it was the
residential bishops who possessed the infallible magisterium. Implicit in this limitation of the authentic magisterium to residential
bishops was the assumption that the possession of a local church
was essential for participation in the exercise of the ordinary universal magisterium. "The whole Christian church, from the second
century on, acknowledged solely those bishops who were true pastors of their flocks as authoritative doctors of the faith and successors to the apostles in the authentic magisterium."[62] This notion
that the bishop's function as shepherd of a particular flock was
essential for his participation in the authentic magisterium was
unique in the manual tradition and represented an important
development.

With regard to the consensus of the college, Sullivan maintained that such a consensus did not require unanimity; it was
sufficient that the pope and the majority of the members consent.
But how could one verify that a consensus among the bishops
existed with regard to a particular doctrine? Sullivan contended
that there were various modes by which this consensus could be
discerned. First, it could be discerned through the communication
of letters, particularly between the pope and the patriarchs in
which, after his election, there is a mutual communication of their
profession of faith. Second, it could be discerned through synodal
letters with which provincial or regional synods communicated
their decisions to the other churches. Here Sullivan cited the rejection of Pelagianism which first occurred in a regional synod. Third,
it could be discerned through the investigation of pertinent documents, e.g., papal encyclicals, decrees of the Roman congregations,
catechisms approved either by the apostolic see or by the local
bishop, approved theological texts for clerical institutions, etc.
Fourth, this consensus could be discerned through the specific and
direct questioning of the bishops by the pope regarding the possible
definition of a doctrine.[63] This was Pius XII's approach in his 1946

letter *Deiparae Virginis* regarding the assumption of Mary. Aside from the mutual professions of faith of pope and patriarch, few of these means for verifying an episcopal consensus went beyond those offered by earlier writers.

Concluding Observations

The historical period from the reign of Pope Gregory XVI through that of Pope Pius XII was marked by an increase of papal influence in doctrine and ecclesiastical control unprecedented in the history of the church. This influence was evident in the growing identification of the magisterium not merely with the hierarchy but with the papacy. It was within this context that the Latin manual tradition developed.

T. Howland Sanks has employed Thomas Kuhn's paradigm theory[64] to provide a summary of the theology of teaching authority operative in this manual tradition. First, considering the sociopolitical paradigm, Sanks finds a view of church structure dominated by a model of absolute monarchy. Supreme power resides in the pope who then delegates that power. This monarchical structure is preserved by the application of the head/body motif in which the body, which is the church, is juridically subsumed into its head, the pope. The second paradigm embodied in the manual tradition concerns the operative view of authority itself. In the manual tradition authority is a means of order and stability. The lower is subordinated to the higher, and change is viewed with suspicion; it is the source of all disorder and instability. Frequently the magisterium is viewed not as a true ministry of teaching but as an expression of the power of jurisdiction. Doctrine is confused with organization and dogma with canon law. The response of the faithful to church teaching is expressed according to the model of command and obedience.

The third paradigm seeks to identify the dominant understanding of truth. Here the manualists follow the neo-scholastic definition of truth as the *adaequatio intellectus et rei,* the conformity of the knowing mind with the thing known. Truth is "complete, unified, consistent, absolute and immutable from the beginning."[65] It is static and objective, given completely to the church as the "deposit of faith." The revelation of this truth does not depend on argumentation or factual support other than the fact of God's having revealed it.

The manualists' consideration of the ordinary universal magisterium was largely controlled by these paradigms. With some noteworthy exceptions, e.g., Sullivan's manual, the treatment of the episcopal magisterium was generally overshadowed by a more developed exposition of the papal magisterium. The review of the Jesuit manuals offers evidence of the church's reaction from 1850 to 1960 against the many threats leveled against it in the past by Jansenism, Gallicanism, Febronianism, and Josephinism, attacks which often stressed the priority of the episcopacy over the papacy. In many manuals the defense of infallibility was made not on historical bases but on the presupposition of the immutability of the deposit of faith as unchanging truth. The immutability of the faith demanded a similar immutability of the deposit of faith's authoritative conservator, the magisterium. This leads us to three general issues raised by the investigations of this chapter.

An Inadequate Theology of the Episcopacy

The later manuals all took as their starting point the understanding of the ordinary universal magisterium as it was expressed in *Tuas libenter* and *Dei Filius:* the infallible teaching of the college of bishops when dispersed throughout the world. An architectonic analysis of the table of contents for these manuals may be helpful here. While the ordinary universal magisterium is the term given to the teaching of the college of bishops when dispersed, it is rarely treated in the sections concerned with the episcopacy itself. Where there are separate tracts on the episcopacy, and in many of the manuals there are none, the discussion is dominated by demonstrations of apostolic succession and responses to canonical questions concerned with episcopal jurisdiction. The ordinary universal magisterium is generally treated under infallibility, considered as one of the gifts of the church, or in a separate section on the magisterium: a section generally, again with some exceptions, dominated by the papacy.

One important development, however, in the theology of the episcopacy was offered by Sullivan who distinguished between residential and titular bishops, a distinction in keeping with ancient tradition: only residential bishops participate in the ordinary universal magisterium. He is the first among the manualists reviewed here to explicitly address the bishop's possession of a local church as a necessary condition for the ordinary universal magisterium. While he does not develop this, one can ask whether embedded within this requirement is the recognition that the bishop does not teach solely, or even primarily, as the pope's representative but as the representative and shepherd of the local community. This raises the possibility that the bishops, as pastors of local communities, have access to expressions of the faith of the church which do more than repeat papal teaching. That this distinction does not appear until Sullivan's work on the eve of Vatican II suggests the extent to which the manual tradition interpreted the doctrine of the ordinary universal magisterium from within a papalist paradigm. This paradigm was unable to appreciate the unique contributions of the bishops who teach simultaneously as pastors of local churches and as members of the episcopal college.

Sullivan's qualification further highlights another area of ambiguity, whether the bishop's teaching ministry is grounded in orders, jurisdiction, or something else. We saw in our review that while some manualists preferred the bipartite orders/jurisdiction schema, others adopted the later tripartite teaching/ruling/sanctifying schema. If the teaching ministry is grounded in orders, then possession of a local church cannot be a requirement for participation in the ordinary universal magisterium. If it is grounded in jurisdiction and not orders there is the danger of reducing the proclamation of the gospel to canon law and the juridical demand for obedience. It is reasonable to conclude then, that if the consideration of the church's teaching on the ordinary universal magisterium is scant in the manual tradition, this is due at least in part to an underdeveloped theology of the episcopacy.

The Relationship between the Pope and the Episcopal College

Where the manual treatments went beyond a simple citation of *Tuas libenter* and *Dei Filius* they often stressed the concord which must exist between the bishops and the pope. The proper relationship between bishops and pope was the *sine qua non* for any further consideration of the ordinary universal magisterium. The formulation of this theme is telling. The issue is not the agreement within the college of bishops, a college which includes the bishop of Rome as its head. Where the subject of infallibility is discussed, the manualists will opt for one of two approaches. In the first they posit two inadequately distinct subjects of infallibility: the pope and the college. In the second, while one may speak of differing subjects, there is in reality only one true subject of infallibility, the college of bishops, but the manualists go on to maintain that that college is always sufficiently represented by the head alone, without any consultation. Franzelin's claim that a pope's solemn definition creates an episcopal consensus demonstrates this tendency. That is, the pope, as head of the college of bishops, always represents in his teaching the whole college. The manuals often give the impression that papal teaching, in and of itself, assumes that consensus which must always exist between head and body. The manuals do not view the pope as the head of the collegial body in virtue of his office as bishop of Rome. Rather, they presuppose the ecclesiology common to the Pian popes in which it is the bishops who derive their authority from the pope.

Lack of Theological Clarity

The lack of clarity in the manual tradition's exposition of the ordinary universal magisterium becomes more apparent when we focus on two aspects of the ordinary teaching of bishops: intention and consensus. Both Zapelena and Salaverri add the specification that the infallible teaching of the ordinary universal magisterium must be proposed as definitively or irrevocably to be held. This raises the question of the intention of the bishops in proposing a particular teaching. Do the bishops intend a particular teaching to be held definitively, or do they teach a particular theological position, even at times in unanimity, to be "safe" but with the intent that this position be open to revision and change?[66] A related problem is that of verification. How does the church ascertain the intent which underlies any given teaching of the bishops? This, in turn, brings us once again to the problem involved in producing an adequate criteriology.

The question of the achievement and verification or discernment of episcopal consensus first appeared in the manual of Christian Pesch at the turn of the century and was treated in every Jesuit manual reviewed here published after 1920. Dieckmann and Salaverri maintain that the bishops' consensus must be formal and not merely material, though Salaverri confuses matters somewhat when he suggests along with Pesch that this formal consensus may be either implicit (tacit) or explicit. D'Herbigny, on the other hand, writes that this consensus or concord must be manifested explicitly. But what constitutes a formal rather than a material consensus? This would appear to bring us back to the question of intention raised above.

How is the consensus achieved and verified? The manuals do seem to recognize that the infallible teaching of the ordinary universal magisterium of bishops is manifested in a plurality of forms and expressions. This composite list taken from the manualists suggests the different modes of expression within the ordinary universal magisterium:

1) episcopal and papal correspondence,
2) episcopal and papal preaching,
3) documents from provincial synods and their acceptance by the bishops,
4) bishops' proposal of doctrine in the face of controversy,
5) episcopal visits to Rome,
6) the interaction between bishops and papal nuntios and Roman legates,
7) liturgical documents,
8) bishops' approbation of: catechisms, theological manuals, the consensus of theologians,
9) bishops' response to papal solicitation regarding the definability of a doctrine.

What the manualists generally do not address is the difficulty in evaluating this plurality of teaching forms with an eye toward discerning an episcopal consensus. This verification would be no easy matter. What degree of unanimity would constitute a consensus? How does one consider the position of the significant number of bishops whose correspondence or approbation of catechetical materials may not reveal a specific position on a particular teaching? Is silence to be construed as consent? Must the possibility of a subtle coercion be taken into account? What role does historical approbation play? Must the bishops of every age have taught this particular position for it to be considered an expression of the ordinary universal magisterium?

Many of the manualists stressed the essential identity between the teaching of the college of bishops in the ordinary and extraordinary mode, thereby minimalizing the problems inherent in the verification of consensus in the ordinary mode. Dieckmann and D'Herbigny stressed the moral bond between the bishops which exists whether they are dispersed or gathered. Zapelena alone admitted that discerning a consensus among the bishops dispersed throughout the world was a much more difficult matter than when they are gathered in council. The Jesuit recognized that it was precisely this difficulty which represents one of the principal distinctions between the ordinary and extraordinary magisterium. A proper appreciation of the difficulties inherent in the ordinary mode requires a much more realistic appraisal of the assistance of the Holy Spirit in the church and its relationship to human freedom. The manualists displayed little sensitivity to the historically conditioned character of the church in its cooperation with the Spirit.

Another difficulty concerns Salaverri's proposal that certain formulae be used to explicitly identify the theological note[67] to be attached by the bishops to the particular teaching. Presumably this formula would not be a solemn definition but the identification of a teaching already taught by the church. Left unanswered, however, is the means by which such a proposal is produced, and the appropriate note determined. If it is produced by some synod or commission, does this not become simply another form of the extraordinary magisterium? We shall return to many of these questions again later.

This chapter has examined the understanding of the ordinary universal magisterium in the influential Latin manual tradition, the principal theological resource in seminary education for over a hundred years. This survey has confirmed the strength of papalist theologies of teaching authority. The focus on papal authority engendered by a number of political and ecclesiastical factors throughout the nineteenth century would become more pronounced after the attention given to papal authority at Vatican I. This focus on the papacy rendered difficult any comprehensive development in understanding of that mode of church teaching which the manualists themselves considered the more ordinary and regular form of ecclesiastical teaching. The most important lacuna, however, was an adequate consideration of the problems inherent in verifying episcopal consensus.

The Latin manualists, as influential as they were, were not the only theologians writing theology in the late nineteenth and early twentieth centuries. Chapters 4 and 5 will offer a consideration of theologians writing during this same period but outside the manual genre.

4

Nineteenth Century Ecclesiologies

The preceding chapter explored a genre of theological literature noted for its clarity and precision of thought. In the next two
chapters we will turn to theologians outside the manual tradition;
their work differed greatly from the manualists in both tone and
scope. These theologians added new perspectives to the development of a theology of teaching authority.

For years it was a commonplace to divide Roman Catholic
theology in the second half of the nineteenth century into two
camps. According to this schema the first, the neo-scholastic tradition, maintained a clear hegemony in Catholic theology and its
practitioners, often with papal approval, laid sole claim to orthodoxy. The second movement, known as modernism, was viewed as
the implacable enemy of the church because of its systematic rejection of revelation and grace as distinct supernatural realities and its
stress on a historical relativism often confused with dogmatic relativism. However, this rigid historical dichotomy has now been rejected. Today neo-scholasticism is increasingly appreciated as a
generic term for a number of different theological schools which
shared several basic scholastic philosophical premises. Modernism,
on the other hand, is understood today as in many ways a heresy
without adherents. It had become the potter's field for those theological positions which did not receive neo-scholastic approval or
which began from different philosophical and historical premises
than did neo-scholasticism. In this chapter we will review four different theologians whose thought reflects this more fluid state of
affairs inasmuch as they resist easy classification: John Henry Newman, Matthias Scheeben, Herman Schell and J.M.A. Vacant.

While influenced in varying degrees by neo-scholastic commitments and the manual tradition, the four theologians considered in this chapter reflect the diversity of Catholic thought in the
nineteenth century. Matthias Scheeben stands in closest proximity

to the manual tradition and yet the sheer sweep of his system, his pneumatological perspective and his organic ecclesiological vision, demand a separate consideration. Similarly, the German Herman Schell was certainly well-versed in neo-scholastic theology and yet he demonstrated an eclectic vision which refused to be bounded by the neo-scholastic philosophical commitments. While J.M.A. Vacant, too, quoted the manualists he nevertheless displayed an historical appreciation typical of his French heritage and a certain philosophical naiveté which further precludes his treatment within the neo-scholastic paradigm. Finally, John Henry Newman, more than the other three, developed his ecclesiological vision in a world almost totally isolated from the theological currents of the continent; not surprisingly, his work betrays his relative ignorance of neo-scholasticism. All of these theologians were in varying degrees familiar with the manual tradition and occasionally referred to it in their writing.[1] Nevertheless, in each case their own work evinced an independence of thought and creativity which distinguished them from the manualists and the neo-scholastic heritage.

John Henry Newman (1801–1890)

Ever since the Second Vatican Council, which Pope Paul VI referred to as "Newman's Council,"[2] there has been a burgeoning of Newman studies. This development has been furthered by the numerous conferences in 1990 dedicated to the centennial of Newman's death. This study cannot pretend to supplant the fine studies of Newman's ecclesiology which have been published over the past two decades, but nevertheless it will be necessary to review the basic lineaments of his ecclesiological vision as it relates to questions of magisterium.

Newman lacked what Jeremy Miller calls "a clear ideological parentage."[3] If this enabled Newman to construct a theology which was bold in its originality, it also prevented him from engaging many of his contemporary theologians on the continent and contributed to his rather negligible influence on the life of the nineteenth century church. He never produced the great synthetic theological system of which the German Catholic theologians of the nineteenth century were so fond. Rather, Newman the apologist preferred either historical forays into the life of the early church or apologetic tracts responding to a particular issue, crisis or attack on his person.

The Dialectical Character of Human Inquiry

Newman has often been portrayed as prone to contradiction and equivocation, but this may have been due less to any inconsistency than to Newman's fundamental commitments to a view of intellectual inquiry not unlike a kind of mathematical calculus. For Newman, intellectual inquiry functioned as a self-correcting mechanism which achieved its end through a dialectical consideration of the various boundaries and limits within a given field of inquiry. Our capacity to give assent to something as true depends on a subtle and complex process by which we employ various "instruments of discovery," weighing and adapting the plurality of internal voices and considerations. This dialectical process is an essential component of Newman's "illative sense," the ability to achieve assent by means of processes which transcend the capacities of formal logic.[4] It is Newman's term for the subtle interaction of intellect and imagination in weighing a myriad of probabilities which cumulatively bring one to the possibility of definitive judgment regarding the truth of an idea. This process, which requires the balanced interplay and coordination of numerous partners, is in fact the linchpin of Newman's ecclesiology.

Newman's Theology of the Magisterium and His Organic Vision of the Church

Newman's writings on church teaching authority brought together two central themes, the primacy of the individual conscience and the organic character of the Christian community. The activity of the illative sense in the religious or moral sphere was what Newman called conscience and it referred to our capacity to come to religious assent. Yet the conscience was limited by original sin and was therefore subject to distortion and error. For that reason human conscience had need of revelation as an indispensable aid. Edward Miller remarks that

> [a]ccording to Newman, God reveals a message that conscience can follow, and the church is the historical bearer of the mes-

sage, indeed, its oracle. The church is the social embodiment of revelation aiding the task of conscience to do God's will, and as such it is in the world counteracting social sin.[5]

For Newman the church was fundamentally the bearer of revelation. This concern for the dynamics of the revelatory function of the church was evident throughout his career. We see this concern in the writings of his Anglican years, from his earliest work on the Arianist controversy up through his *Via Media,* and later in his Catholic career, especially in *An Essay on the Development of Christian Doctrine* and *On Consulting the Faithful.* The church was "the pillar and ground of truth" whose principal task was to bear witness to the gospel of Jesus Christ.[6] In his earlier writings, seeking as he was to articulate the *via media* of Anglicanism, the early fathers were understood to have possessed a special authority within the tradition-bearing body of the church. As Newman continued his studies this position became increasingly untenable. The authority of the early fathers resided in their role as witnesses to the faith, but how was the authenticity of their witness to be determined? This question led Newman first, in the *Via Media,* to the indefectibility of the church and eventually to Roman Catholicism and ecclesial infallibility as the necessary guarantor of that indefectibility.

Newman's commitment to infallibility assumed, however, that this infallibility was seated in the entire church. He maintained that, as a matter of historical fact, infallibility had been exercised in various ways: through solemn papal pronouncements, through solemn pronouncements of the bishops when gathered in council, and by the whole of the faithful.[7] The infallibility of the faithful was a theme developed in Newman's famous essay *On Consulting the Faithful.* Originally published in the *Rambler* (1859), a lay English Catholic journal founded by Lord Acton among others, the essay sought to defend a prior Newman editorial aside in which the author suggested that the bishops might consult the faithful on certain topics of local concern. Newman suggested that the precedent was both ancient, sound and already in evidence in the preparation for the definition on the immaculate conception. The reaction to this brief observation was so great that Newman felt compelled to offer a more systematic response.

One can contrast Newman's view of infallibility evident in this essay with that of his principal antagonist in the *Rambler* affair, Dr. John Gillow:

> It turned out that the two men disagreed over the way the Church's infallibility was to be understood. They agreed that the whole Church was infallible; in practice, however, Gillow conceived of infallibility only insofar as it was a prerogative of the bishops that they exercised in the definition of doctrine. Newman, on the other hand, felt that infallibility has to be considered first as the prerogative of the whole Church in its behalf, and only secondly as the special function of the magisterium in its teaching role.[8]

Newman possessed an organic vision of the church in which its various component elements, e.g., the hierarchy, the laity, the *schola theologorum,* all functioned in witnessing to the faith *per modum unius:*

> I think I am right in saying that the tradition of the Apostles, committed to the whole Church in its various constituents and functions *per modium unius,* manifests itself variously at various times: sometimes by the mouth of the episcopacy, sometimes by the doctors, sometimes by the people, sometimes by liturgies, rites, ceremonies, and customs, by events, disputes, movements, and all those other phenomena which are comprised under the name of history. It follows that none of these channels of tradition may be treated with disrespect; granting at the same time fully, that the gift of discerning, discriminating, defining, promulgating, and enforcing any portion of that tradition resides solely in the *Ecclesia docens.*[9]

This leads us to a consideration of two of the principal components in Newman's organic view of the church: the *sensus fidelium* and the *schola theologorum.*

The Sensus Fidelium

Just as within the believer there is an instinct or *phronema* for the truth, so such an instinct exists within the church of Christ. This *phronema,* an impulse for the truth provided by the Holy Spirit, resides in the *sensus fidelium.*[10] Newman by no means invented the notion of the *sensus fidelium* yet, as we shall see, in *On Consulting the Faithful* he clearly developed a particularly historical and organic understanding of the concept. In his earlier work on the Arian controversy he had already come to the conclusion that a large body of the bishops at the time of the Arianist threat had, as a matter of historical fact, failed to preserve the faith of the church, a task which then fell to the laity, to the *sensus fidelium.*[11] From this he concluded that the magisterium could not have sole responsibility for the preservation of the church in truth. The faith of the whole church has played a significant role in the task of witnessing to the faith. Newman maintained that this in no way undercut the authentic teaching authority of the magisterium. It has always been a belief of the Roman Catholic communion, Newman insisted, that the whole faithful were infallible in matters of belief. Consequently it was only natural to "consult" the faithful, not in search of their opinion on a matter, nor their advice or counsel, but only in regard to the simple fact of their belief:

> Doubtless their advice, their opinion, their judgment on the question of definition is not asked; but the matter of fact, viz. their belief, *is* sought for, as a testimony to that apostolical tradition, on which alone any doctrine whatsoever can be defined. In like manner we may "consult" the liturgies or the rites of the Church; not that they speak, not that they can take any part whatever in the definition, for they are documents or customs; but they are witnesses to the antiquity or universality of the doctrines which they contain, and about which they are "consulted." (emphasis is Newman's)[12]

It was Newman's commitment to the organic interaction among all the church's members and the dialectical movement of the church as it proceeds in the way of truth which prevented him from setting the *sensus fidelium* and the magisterium in opposition. Miller has identified three key moments in Newman's conception of the interaction of the magisterium and the faithful in witnessing the faith. First there is the *articulation* of the faith. "The community attempts to put into linguistic form some aspect of the inner faith constituting it." These forms are obviously diverse and would include liturgical expressions, local customs, pieties and devotions. The second moment then follows as a period of *pedagogy:*

> Those in the church charged with the office of public . . . teaching must discern what is to be taught. They can only look within the community (its Scriptures, its traditions, its theological developments, the laity's *sensus fidelium*) for the meaning of a doctrine, since church teaching is not the prophetic inspiration of new truths. Teachers, be they a council, a pope, a diocesan bishop . . . pray for the guidance of the Spirit in order to discern the *mind* of the church faithfully. (emphasis is Miller's)[13]

The final moment is the period of *reception* in which the teaching reenters the community. At this point alone can the *sensus fidelium* be said to offer a judgment whereby the community either recognizes or does not recognize its own faith in the particular teaching.

Newman was quite insistent that his elaboration of the role of the *sensus fidelium* was not original with him. In the *Rambler* essay he recounted at some length Giovanni Perrone's treatment of the *sensus fidelium* in his work on the definition of the immaculate conception. He concluded that they were in substantial agreement.[14] Curiously, Newman employed, approvingly, Perrone's analogy of the seal and wax. The Roman theologian maintained that the faithful bore within them the truth much as wax bears the image made upon it by a seal (the magisterium). This view of the *sensus fidelium* would seem to be strengthened by Newman's occasional use of distinctions between active and passive infallibility, *ecclesia docens* and *ecclesia docta.* Yet upon closer reading it is clear that Newman's understanding of the infallibility of the faithful went beyond Perrone and the strictly passive role which the latter theologian attributed to the infallibility of the laity. Perrone viewed the *sensus fidelium* primarily as a means of justifying a dogmatic position which lacked historical support, as was the case with the definition on the immaculate conception. Newman on the other hand, clearly saw the *sensus fidelium* as participating more integrally in the tradition-bearing function of the church.[15] The faithful do not simply echo or reflect the teaching of the magisterium, rather they themselves give witness to the faith; the teaching office determines and expresses definitively the content of that witness and the faithful assimilate and make their own the teaching expressed by the *ecclesia docens.*

The Schola Theologorum

This dialectical process, the to and fro movement of the hierarchy and the faithful, may be expanded to include another component in the life of the church, the *schola theologorum.* Once again it was Newman's historical studies which led him to the prominent role played by the universities and schools in the Middle Ages. There, as we saw in the first chapter, the doctors of the church played an integral and often determinative role in doctrinal disputes. Newman suggested that the doctors and theologians were "the regulating principle of the church."[16] It was the *schola* which must determine the extent and exactness of papal and conciliar definitions.[17] Newman had always appreciated the sacramental character of dogmatic pronouncements, that is, their inevitably imperfect articulation and communication of supernatural truths.[18] It fell to the *schola,* therefore, to ascertain that which was definitive, the precise scope and meaning embedded within a particular pronouncement. Newman expounded on this task in an 1875 letter:

> Some power . . . is needed to determine the general sense of the authoritative words—to determine their direction, drift, limits, and comprehension, to hinder gross perversions. This power is virtually the *passive infallibility* of the whole body of the Catholic people. The active infallibility lies in the Pope and Bishops —the passive in the *"universitas"* of the faithful. . . . [O]n the other hand the *Schola Theologorum* is one chief portion of the *universitas*—and it acts with great force both in correcting popular misapprehensions and narrow views of the teaching of the active *infallibilitas,* and, by the intellectual investigations and disputes which are its very life, it keeps the distinction clear between theological truth and theological opinion, and is the antagonist of dogmatism. And while the differences of the School maintain the liberty of thought, the unanimity of its

members is the safeguard of the infallible decisions of the Church and the champion of faith. (emphasis is Newman's)[19]

The *schola* participates in the third moment of *reception* in which the entirety of the faithful receives, interprets and assimilates church teaching. The free discussion among theologians would allow that which was central in the church's dogmatic teaching to emerge. Yet the *schola* has a broader task than merely interpreting church teaching. Newman wrote:

> Further than this, since its teaching is far wider than the apostolic dogma which is *de fide,* it protects it as forming a large body of doctrine which must be got through before an attack can be made on the dogma. And it steadies the opinion of the Church, embodying tradition, and hindering frequent changes. And it is the arena in which questions of development and change are argued out. And again, if changes of opinion are to come, and false interpretations of scripture, or false views of the dogma, to be set right, it prepares the way, accustoming the minds of Catholics to the idea of the change, and preventing surprise and scandal. . . . Without it, the dogma of the Church would be the raw flesh without skin; nay, or a tree without leaves; for as devotional feelings clothe dogma on the one hand, so does the teaching of the *schola* on the other. Moreover, it is the immediate authority for the practical working and course of the Church, e.g. what are mortal sins, what venial, what are the effects of the Mass, what about indulgences, etc., etc.?[20]

The *schola* not only interprets solemn definitions but itself embodies central elements of the tradition of the church. It further mediates church teaching then, in the practical realm of Christian living.

Conclusion

In this selective review of Newman's writings on ecclesiology we have consistently returned to one theme which was central to his understanding of church teaching authority, the organic character of the church. The romantic metaphor of the *organism* served Newman's purpose in demanding the healthy interaction of the various component parts of the church.[21] To the degree that one component was either underdeveloped or neglected the whole church suffered. Newman stressed the roles of the *sensus fidelium* and the *schola theologorum,* not because he saw them as substitutes for the authority of the magisterium, but because they were ancient components in the life of the church which had been neglected in the post-Tridentine epoch.

This brings us to a curious lacuna in Newman's ecclesiology, a developed theology of the episcopate. He certainly did not completely ignore the place of the bishops in the church. In his historical writings he returned time and again to the example of Athanasius and stressed the inseparability of the bishop's task as an authoritative conveyor of truth and his personal moral character.[22] The episcopacy was not only one of the *instrumenta traditionis* but, along with the papacy, it offered the authoritative witness to the faith and alone possessed an active infallibility. Nevertheless, when Newman wrote of the episcopacy's teaching authority he seemed to share with the manual tradition a view of the bishops as extensions of papal authority. The magisterium consisted of the pope and bishops and, excluding his explicit treatment of the definition on papal infallibility, he seldom felt the need to distinguish between the college of bishops and the papacy. What was of concern for Newman was not the distinct modes of magisterial teaching but the relationship of the magisterium to the other participants in the life of the church, namely, the theologians and the laity.

It is nevertheless somewhat surprising that Newman never wrote in any detail on the ordinary universal magisterium. He certainly was aware of *Tuas libenter;* the final chapter of his *Apologia* was written in part in response to a request by Lord Acton that he comment on the implications of the papal brief. His interest in the First Vatican Council would surely have brought the treatment of the subject in *Dei Filius* to his attention. As Dulles has remarked: "If Newman had systematically pursued this theme [the ordinary universal magisterium] he might have come closer than he did to the concept of collegiality as taught by Vatican II."[23]

In spite of this oversight, Newman's ecclesiology provided several important contributions to a theology of teaching authority which will have no small bearing on a contemporary theology of the ordinary universal magisterium. If Newman neglected a consideration of episcopal collegiality, he nevertheless anticipated in substance the "people of God" and "*communio*" ecclesiologies and the dynamic interaction of all the component parts of the church. This represented an implicit rejection of the centralization of church teaching authority in favor of a recovery of the multiplicity of the *instrumenta traditionis*. More importantly, his ecclesiology suggested that while the bishops were the authoritative teachers of the faith, their teaching was inextricably bound to the faith of the whole church to which they were to give witness. On this count Newman prepared the way for later reflection on the bishop's relationship to his local flock. Finally, Newman intimated that episcopal teaching might best be discerned in the beliefs of the whole faithful and in the teachings of the theologians. This will obviously be the case particularly where the bishops have not defined a particular teaching solemnly.

Matthias Scheeben (1835–1888)

Like Newman, Matthias Scheeben[24] is difficult to classify as a theologian. He cannot be placed with his contemporaries at the Roman College, but his broadly neo-scholastic orientation distanced him from the Tübingen school as well. Theologically, Scheeben was always an outsider, suspicious of wholesale commitments to any one school of thought. His theological program sought a middle way between the paths taken by his colleagues at both Rome and Tübingen. His theology represents an ambitious attempt to transcend neo-scholasticism by employing patristic and idealist thought.[25] Scheeben undertook an extensive study of the Greek fathers, influenced as he was by the Tübingen school's return to the patristic sources. Some scholars have even written of Tübingen as "the preliminary school for Scheeben's work."[26] His emphasis on the living and the organic clearly supported this observation. At the same time, Scheeben studied under Joseph Kleutgen who provided him with a foundation in neo-scholastic theology and encouraged the study of St. Thomas.[27] Nevertheless, his theology was considered sufficiently suspect to elicit a recommendation by Kleutgen that his *Dogmatik* be suppressed.[28] Like Kleutgen, however, he viewed the idealist philosophies of the first half of the century with some suspicion.

Yves Congar has recognized Scheeben's work as one of the

more creative endeavors in nineteenth century ecclesiology.[29] One distinctive aspect of Scheeben's ecclesiology is his consideration of the church within the fundamental mysteries of the Christian faith: eucharist, incarnation and Trinity. Not surprisingly, Scheeben viewed the church itself as mystery.[30] He developed what could be described as a pneumatological ecclesiology, often describing the church as a kind of incarnation of the Holy Spirit.[31] Here he followed Aquinas in considering Christ as the head of the church and the Spirit as its soul.[32] This emphasis on the mystical was applicable not only to the being of the church but to its very organizational structure. The church, even in its juridical and hierarchical structure, was animated by the Holy Spirit.

It would be inaccurate to see Scheeben as advocating the kind of papalism typical of many of the manualists; nevertheless, according to Eugen Paul, Scheeben did pursue a "moderate ultramontane position."[33] No disinterested observer of the Vatican Council, Scheeben wrote many articles defending the definition on papal infallibility, founding the journal *Das okumenische Concil* [*sic*] for this very purpose. He stressed the limited and essentially dependent character of episcopal authority, grounded in the limited jurisdiction of the bishop, in contrast with the unlimited and independent powers of the pope.

Scheeben's consideration of the teaching authority of the bishops began with the episcopal body's origin in the college of apostles and was followed by a contrast of the respective powers which obtain for each body. In spite of the distinctive membership of the two bodies (the body of apostles and the body of bishops) the college of bishops as a body shared the same charism of infallibility which was possessed by the apostles. While the plurality of witnesses (the bishops) considered individually were not absolute and infallible, the consistent testimony of the totality of witnesses could and must be absolutely authoritative and infallible.[34] This testimony must be infallible because otherwise the purpose of the authority bestowed upon the witnesses, the universal possession of the true faith, failed not just partially and relatively but rather universally and absolutely.

> It (the testimony of all of the bishops together) *can* be infallible and in fact is infallible because the illuminating and lifegiving

effectiveness of the Holy Spirit upon the individual witnesses
cannot possibly be frustrated in all of them together . . .[35]

This argument for the infallibility of the college of bishops
shares with many of the manualists the contention that the church
must be protected from error in its ordinary and daily teaching.
Scheeben, however, following his more pneumatological approach,
credits the necessity of infallibility to the infrustrability (*Unvereitel-
barkeit*) of the power of the Spirit alive in the church. He further
posited that absolute authority and infallibility were present in each
collective manifestation (*Gesamtmanifestation*) of the whole episcopate in which the universal testimony of the members, the sovereign judgment of the pope and hence the fructifying and guiding
efficacy of the Holy Spirit united and collaborated together. He
does not, however, outline the possible forms and criteria for verification regarding this *Gesamtmanifestation.*

Scheeben did offer an important clarification regarding the
infallibility of the episcopal college. This infallibility was not attributed to the whole college materially considered, that is, simply to
the entirety of the individual members. Rather, it was applied to
the whole college only considered formally, that is, to the college
considered in the light of the head of the college, the principle of
unity and leadership for the whole.[36] This distinction between the
teaching body of the bishops considered materially and formally
appeared in the writings of several of the manualists in chapter 3,
but Scheeben's treatment goes beyond the manualists in positing
that the teaching body functioned as a body, considered formally,
not merely with the pope's consent but only under his directing
influence. This is but the first of several examples of the dominant
role of the pope in Scheeben's consideration of the teaching office
of the episcopate.

While it is possible for Scheeben to speak of a twofold infallibility ascribed to both the whole body of bishops and to the pope, he
accentuated the unity of this infallibility, noting that in the gospels
Christ was able to give full authority for teaching at one place to all
the apostles, and at another place to Peter alone. This represented
an effective "fusion" (*Verschmelzung*) of the two subjects with the
practical result that the bishops as members of the body were subsumed under the head.[37] This was a variation on the theory that in

the pope and the episcopal college one found two inadequately distinct subjects of infallibility. For Scheeben the infallibility of each subject possessed its own proper end. The infallibility of the pope was necessary for preserving the unity of church teaching. The infallibility of the bishops, on the other hand, was necessary primarily to make clearer the assistance of the Holy Spirit insofar as the judgment of the pope was attested to by all the organs of the Holy Spirit.[38] As Wilhelm Bartz has noted, for Scheeben

> [t]he witness of infallible faith of all the bishops dispersed throughout the whole world has its central home in the infallibility of the pope, from whence it radiates with an increased force, and the infallible approbation given by the episcopate to the infallible *ex cathedra* decision of the pope not only assures for the latter a promulgation requiring a universal adherence, but still effects the perception in an impressive fashion that it was born with the assistance of the Holy Spirit.[39]

So Scheeben conceives of the infallible authority of the bishops primarily as a visible approbation of papal teaching.

In a difficult exposition, Scheeben considered the ordinary magisterium in his treatment of the rule of faith. He first noted that there was a sense in which one could speak of the unity of all the faithful as the fullest and most concrete manifestation of the law of faith. This, however, was not properly speaking the law of faith itself but rather the expression or symbol of that law. Scheeben—much more than many of his predecessors—sought to provide a more integral place for all of the faithful in his reflections on tradition and the preservation of the church in truth. He developed the distinction between the active infallibility of the teaching body of the church and the passive infallibility of the learning church. Nevertheless, it was the constant action of the teaching apostolate of the church (the bishops) which enabled it to possess the proximate and immediate rule of Catholic faith. "This rule is clearly located only in the teaching authority of the teaching body of the church, by virtue of which this teaching authority can and ought to promulgate the Word of God as law of faith."[40]

In the same section Scheeben evaluated the then current tendency among some (a likely reference to Möhler and the Tübingen school) to speak of a "consciousness" of the church with regard to the rule of faith. While this was patent of a correct reading, it was a phraseology, he warned, which was susceptible to error. A correct understanding of the consciousness of the church as the rule of faith could not forget that this rule was always public and therefore was always expressed by the public authority of the church, its hierarchical teaching body.[41]

In the *Dogmatik* the German theologian further considered Vatican I's teaching on the ordinary magisterium. He noted the significance of the council fathers' decision to attribute to the ordinary magisterium the same significance as that of a solemn judgment. With regard to the particular manner and form in which the rule of faith is promulgated, he offered the following exposition:

> Because on the one hand the Word of God, which is communicated and given witness to by the organs of the apostolic teaching body, always enters as something completely determinate and permanent in the church and demands an obedient faith, and on the other hand the communication and testimony of the same Word aims necessarily at the generation of such a faith, in this way the promulgation of the law of faith comes to pass ordinarily *ipso facto* through the ordinary and universal exercise of the teaching and preaching office . . . or, which is the same, through the living teaching tradition. According to this, where in fact and universally a particular teaching is decided by the entire teaching body and is being taught universally as the Word of God, there too is the obligation to believe this teaching, *ipso facto* universally promulgated. The law of faith appears in the church first in the form of a law of custom ("*Gewohnheitsgesetz*") and this is precisely its ordinary and at the same time inherent ("*angeboren*") form.[42]

Scheeben claimed that the teaching of the ordinary universal magisterium promulgated the law of faith in the form of a law of custom. He did not elaborate, however, on the precise form which such laws of custom might take. The acts of the extraordinary magisterium were normally reserved only for instances where there existed an obstinate conflict or an occasional eclipse of the teaching of the faith (*Verdunkelung der Glaubenslehre*). These rare occasions demanded an explicit formulation. This extraordinary expression of the law of faith was more determinate and tangible than the first and, since it was better able to bring about and secure the rule of faith according to the particular circumstances, it enjoyed a certain priority.

Scheeben's work represented the development of a pneumatological ecclesiology begun by the Tübingen school which was certainly an advance over the standard juridical treatments of the baroque and the work of his contemporaries at the Gregorian. In comparison with the neo-scholastic manuals, his theology stood out because of its incorporation of patristic, mystical and romantic-idealist elements. If the church was infallible in its teaching authority, this was not simply due to Christ's institution of the church, but to the church's animation by the Spirit.

Turning to Scheeben's specific treatment of the teaching authority of the bishops, however, one must admit the overriding influence of a pronounced papalism; it stressed the pope as not just the head, but the initiator, source of unity and driving force behind the teaching apostolate of the college of bishops. This was particularly evident in his distinction between the witness of the teaching body of bishops materially considered, and formally considered as brought together by the leadership of the pope. Scheeben consistently employed the body metaphor in his ecclesiology. Accordingly, it was the head which possessed complete control and leadership of the body and could even serve as a kind of proxy for the body. This led to a consideration of the bishops as teachers whose chief responsibility was to follow the lead of the pope and to echo papal teaching.

Finally, notice must be taken of what was not considered by Scheeben. There is a conspicuous absence of any treatment of the achievement and verification of the consensus of the bishops. As was noted above, Scheeben offered no consideration of the precise character of the *Gesamtmanifestation* of the bishops. The German theologian was more interested in the teaching body as an instrument and organ of the animating presence of the Spirit than he was in the concrete realizations of this teaching body and the consequent problems and difficulties which these concrete realizations raised. Perhaps this was inevitable from a theologian of grace whose themes of mystery, organism and sacramentality did not lend themselves to concrete considerations of the place of papal legates, provincial synods, and episcopal correspondence as evidences of

episcopal consensus. If Scheeben's theology of grace was characterized by a sharp distinction between the two realms of the natural
and supernatural, his ecclesiology separated the human from the
divine in the church. He understood the animating presence of the
Spirit to be so infrustrable as to completely overwhelm all practical
difficulties and human exigencies attendant on a human church.
Scheeben's ecclesiology was prone to a downplaying of the historical dimension of the church and an absolutizing of the institutional
as the organ of the Spirit.[43]

Herman Schell (1850–1906)

Herman Schell[44] was an important, if little known Catholic
apologist writing in Germany at the end of the nineteenth century.
Of the theological age leading up to Schell, Bernhard Welte wrote:

> This tension between orthodoxy and creativity, between scho-
> lasticism and the thinking subject permeated the entire period.
> And yet there were still some original, independent and great
> figures. If the most prominent name in this period is John
> Henry Newman, in Germany the most significant is Herman
> Schell. . . . One recalls that both of these men were pushed to
> the edge of church and theology in their time. And neither
> Schell's theological impulses (an alternative to modernism) nor
> the magnificent and more influential thoughts of Newman
> were appreciated and absorbed by the schools and figures of
> theology at that time.[45]

Schell produced a theology which synthesized Aristotelian,
idealist and patristic strains as he sought to interpret numerous
theological and cultural issues of the late nineteenth century. His
theology was particularly notable for its attempt to relate Roman
Catholicism to the modern culture of the last third of the nineteenth century. He was well equipped to take on the challenges of
modernity which Roman Catholic theology faced, for his extensive
education brought him into contact with many of the great schools
and great thinkers of his age.

Schell's theological vision was marked by a determination to
engage contemporary culture and science as the only hope for the
necessary renewal of Roman Catholicism. Freedom and progress

were ideas which must be integrated into Catholicism if it was to survive. These concepts were not without their dangers but Schell contended that they were the essential tools for the human journey toward truth. In keeping with this call to renewal Schell made three concrete pastoral suggestions.[46] First, he invoked the general priesthood of all baptized and called for a more significant place for the laity in the church. Second, theology should be permitted free development, avoiding the ghetto tendencies often found in seminary theology. At one point Schell caricatured Rome's understanding of freedom by comparing it to the trivial freedom of a caged bird.[47]

Third, Catholicism should try to achieve, not simply a peaceful coexistence with culture, but should try actively to influence it. It was largely in service of this renewal that he so strongly criticized ultramontanism for putting forward an authoritarian church which was fundamentally world-denying. Schell's program for the renewal of Catholicism did not receive an appreciative hearing in Rome and by 1900 most of his major works had been placed on the Index.

Turning to his ecclesiology, we find evidence of the Tübingen school's influence in his understanding of the church as "the essential form of the kingdom of God."[48] Schell posited a church vitalized by the Holy Spirit which possessed both interior and exterior aspects of religious and social life. Unlike the Tübingen school, however, Schell rejected the view of the church as the continuation of the incarnation. Rather, Schell wrote of a covenantal relation between God and the church. He clearly placed the hierarchy at the service of the activity of the Spirit such that in its teaching office the hierarchy must be understood not to control revelation but to witness to it authoritatively:

> The assistance of the Holy Spirit is not, in any case, a replacement for the necessity which is incumbent upon the church teaching office to employ at any given time all the means for the human recognition of truth, but rather the divine assistance operates as it wills to, above all through that which is mediately and immediately called forth in human efforts.[49]

As the soul of the church, the illuminating presence of the Holy Spirit led the church to truth mediately through the teaching office of the church, but immediately through its particular assistance in each soul. Schell was intent here, not in replacing the external revelation offered through the church with some private illumination, but rather with overcoming the harsh division between the teaching and the learning church.

In his consideration of the teaching office of the church Schell preferred the tripartite schema, identifying the offices of ruling, teaching and sanctifying, over the more traditional bipartite orders/jurisdiction schema.[50] His treatment reveals a cautious avoidance of reducing the teaching office to juridical determinations. Schell understood the bearers of the church's infallible teaching office to be the pope and the bishops gathered with the pope in ecumenical council. The pope was the organ of unity ruling the whole church; the council was the organ of living communion. Conspicuously lacking, however, was any consideration of the infallible teaching of the bishops when dispersed throughout the world.

Schell's treatment of the papacy recalls the spiritual anthropology which provided the foundation for the theologies of teaching authority in the first millennium. He characterized the relationship of the pope to both God and the community as one of service. The pope always acted as head of church within the church and not over it.[51] He did support the Vatican definition on papal infallibility but warned against identifying the dogma of papal infallibility with a "curialism" which understood all truth as coming to the church only through the pope. Equally rejected was an "episcopalism" which held that all papal teaching was infallible only with the approval of the episcopate. Rather, the church was infallible as a teaching and hearing church. "It is in accord with the organic character of the Body of Christ that it is guided and ruled not purely through one organ, but rather through the interplay of two organs by the animating Spirit of truth."[52] It is this concern for an ecclesiastical system of checks and balances, reflecting Schell's fear of the centralization of teaching authority in the church, which led him to call for a more dynamic interplay of the college of bishops and the pope.

Schell's theological perspective has been included in this chapter, in spite of his surprising silence on the ordinary universal magisterium, because his theology represented an important step away from the papalist ecclesiologies dominant in his time. While continuing the Tübingen tradition which stressed the organic and pneumatological character of the church, Schell distanced himself from a view of the church as a continuation of the incarnation. His ecclesiology anticipated the work of Yves Congar in the positive place given to the laity and to his characterization of the church's relationship to God as a covenantal relation. This covenantal relation in turn demanded a view of the assistance of the Holy Spirit which carefully avoided a mechanistic stress on an efficient or instrumental causality in favor of a view which appreciated the Spirit's cooperation with human endeavor.

J.M.A. Vacant (1852–1901)

J.M.A. Vacant,[53] a professor of fundamental and dogmatic theology at the French seminary in Nancy, wrote what appears to be the first theological monograph to focus exclusively on the ordinary magisterium of the church, *Le Magistère ordinaire de l'église et ses organs.*[54] Because of the unprecedented attention which this volume gave to the question of the ordinary magisterium, it merits an extended analysis.

Vacant understood the ordinary universal magisterium to be closely associated with the fundamental mission of the church to teach all the nations. He recalled that the foundation of the church's faith rested on the ordinary universal magisterium before there were any solemn definitions by councils or popes. On this matter he cited the teachings of Ignatius of Antioch and Irenaeus of Lyons who both held that the teaching of the bishops in preserving the apostolic faith was the sure rule of faith. With the development of ecumenical councils out of the earlier regional synods, an emphasis was placed on the solemn judgments of councils. But according to Vacant this never superseded the infallible teaching of the bishops when dispersed throughout the world.

The Ministers Who Serve as Instruments
of the Ordinary Magisterium

In the second chapter of Vacant's work on the ordinary magisterium the author considered the ministers who served the ordinary universal magisterium as its organ or instrument. This theology was itself placed within the context of the Pauline image of the church as the mystical body of Christ. Within the mystical body were established a head and a college of bishops who were charged with communicating Christ's life to that body. By the power of the Holy Spirit these ministers were to be the light of the world:

> All the divine gifts come to us therefore from the hands of the episcopate. If the church is the mystical body of Christ, the bishops united to the pope are as the soul and substantial form which vivifies this body, by virtue of Jesus Christ whose place they take here below.[55]

Here we find a contrast to the ecclesiology of Scheeben and Schell who, unlike Vacant, wrote of the Holy Spirit rather than the hierarchy as the soul of the church. Vacant followed the analogy of the body to suggest that the "church taught" (*L'Eglise enseignée*) was related to the hierarchy as the sense organs were related to the soul. The "inferior ministers" and the laity participated in the magisterium insofar as it was delegated to them as a kind of auxiliary to the episcopate. These might participate in the teaching church but they would not possess infallibility in and of themselves. Nevertheless, the writings of canon lawyers and theologians, for example, could, by having received episcopal approbation, be instruments of the ordinary magisterium of the bishops. One could even include the laity as instruments of the ordinary magisterium, as when parents receive implicit permission to provide Christian education for their children.[56] All these are expressions or echoes of the teaching of the episcopate. The infallibility which all believers possessed was infallible only insofar as it was the teaching of the bishops. Since the plurality of those who might echo the teaching of the ordinary magisterium (e.g., pastors, laity, theologians) must all be in harmony with the teaching of the bishops, it was not necessary, Vacant claimed, to consider all the voices in determining episcopal teaching. It would be sufficient, for example, to consider the constant and universal teaching of the fathers of the church or of the theologians—as Pius IX pointed out in *Tuas libenter*.[57] The surest source for discerning the teaching of the bishops would be the creeds of the faith whose catholicity was accepted by all, as with the Nicene

Creed, Apostles' Creed, Athanasian Creed, and, Vacant added, the catechism of the Council of Trent.

The Ordinary Magisterium's Modes of Expression

Having discussed the various instruments which serve the ordinary magisterium, in the third chapter Vacant explored the manner in which the ordinary magisterium was expressed. The French theologian considered three kinds of teaching: expressed, implicit and tacit. The "expressed" teaching of the church could be offered by either solemn judgment or by the ordinary magisterium. The ordinary magisterium might be exercised through the preaching of missionaries, the teaching of catechists, the writing of apologists, etc. As guardian of doctrine, however, the church must be able to distinguish the sacred from the profane, that which is of faith from that which is of mere opinion, that which is obligatory from that which is free. Vacant admitted the difficulty involved in making these distinctions.[58] He admitted further that often in church teaching there were elements of human origin intermingled with that which formed the body of divine doctrine. Church teaching has often assimilated into it that which it has gained from the profane sciences. These elements could appear in the expression of church teaching. This was the case in Jesus' use of parables, in Paul's use of human imagery and in Aquinas' use of Aristotle. The question was: how do we discern the unity in teaching which found expression in such diverse human forms?[59] Vacant looked to the development of church teaching in the early centuries of the church in which less fortunate expressions of doctrine were replaced by those witnessed to by the fathers of the church for their orthodoxy. The fathers and the doctors of the church played an important role in certifying the pedigree of certain formulations. The writings of these figures carried particular weight because of their proven love and fidelity to church tradition.

> The care with which all these venerable writers have displayed the faith of the church and the approbation which they have received from it requires that their writings be regarded as expressing the teachings of the church's ordinary magisterium.[60]

This authority, however, was not necessarily to be attributed to each of their teachings taken individually, but rather to the whole of their teaching. Thus, if a teaching of a particular father were not to be found in a number of the fathers and theologians it might not be considered an expression of the ordinary magisterium. Put positively, the unanimous agreement of the fathers or authorized theologians regarding a particular teaching was to be viewed as an indubitable sign (*signe indubitable*) that the teaching belonged to the ordinary magisterium.[61]

Vacant next turned to the second form of infallible teaching of the ordinary magisterium, that which was taught *implicite.* This teaching was embedded in the discipline, worship and conduct of the church. Again invoking the organic nature of the church as modeled on the interdependence of the human body, Vacant maintained that the safeguarding of the doctrine of the faith required true morality, discipline and worship without which the revealed teaching could be neither preached, believed nor respected. For this the assistance of the Holy Spirit must be extended to ecclesiastical legislation.[62] Recalling what was said earlier about those who served as instruments of the ordinary magisterium, Vacant proposed that, just as the Holy Office served as an instrument of the ordinary magisterium in expressing papal teaching, so the Congregation of Rites might serve implicitly as an instrument of the ordinary magisterium. Even the conduct of the faithful, Vacant added, might in some way echo the teaching of the ordinary magisterium:

> All the functions of the supernatural life which are exercised in the mystical body of Christ, under the action of the government of the legitimate pastors, become therefore permanent manifestations of the doctrine of the Savior. . . . This teaching is before our eyes, in all the works of the church, in its discipline, its liturgy, its institutions, its religious orders, its temples and its monuments, in the devotions and the practices of charity, of zeal or of the piety of children, in its history, in the life of the saints which it places over its altars, in the life of humble Christians who are docile in voice, in civilization, the morals, the language, the arts of the people whom it has educated.[63]

Finally, Vacant added that in addition to the teaching of the ordinary magisterium which was expressed and which was implicit, the church also taught *tacite.* This referred to the status of a teaching prior to its being explicitly taught in response to certain theological controversies. For example, what was the status of the church's teaching on grace and justification prior to its expression in the teaching of the Council of Trent? Vacant claimed that such teaching was not developed prior to that which occasioned its expression, but nevertheless had been taught tacitly by the ordinary magisterium.[64] The church was a living and growing body which grew not only in membership but in the development of the formulations which were contained in its doctrine.

The Obligations which the Ordinary Magisterium Imposes on the Substance of Doctrine

The author addressed the question whether a proposition of the ordinary magisterium was sufficient to demand our adherence. Some clear sign that the doctrine had been taught infallibly by the ordinary and universal magisterium was needed. This evidence could be found in the universal adherence of the faithful who in their unanimity always echoed the teaching of the bishops. However, this sign was not always so easily discernible. Thus another important source for discerning the obligation which a teaching carried could be found in creeds, professions of faith and catechisms. These catechisms, like the catechism of the Council of Trent or the various diocesan catechisms, had as their goal, not the publication of theological opinion, but that which was the faith of all. One should assume, in general, that what was taught by the catechisms was an expression of the ordinary universal magisterium. Furthermore, one could find the implicit teaching of the ordinary magisterium in the activity of the church. Vacant held that the acts of the church, as expressed in the liturgy and in devotions, for example, were sanctioned by the infallible deposit of the faith. He offered the example of the adoration of the eucharist which would be idolatry if Jesus Christ were not fully present in the host; it was therefore necessary that the teaching of the real presence be an infallible teaching of the church.[65] However, if there was not a clear and necessary relationship between the legitimacy of a particular church practice and a given doctrine, then it should not be assumed that this practice indicated a teaching of the ordinary universal magisterium. His example for this situation: the cult rendered to the Sacred Heart of our Lord could be justified and explained without the necessity of admitting that the heart is the organ of passion in the human person.

Vacant returned in this chapter to the teaching of the fathers and theologians; their unanimity offered further evidence of the teaching of the ordinary magisterium. Here, Vacant warned, it must be remembered that the fathers and theologians taught in this capacity, not as private doctors but as witnesses to the tradition. He was not willing to provide a numerical figure which would suffice for the moral unanimity of the fathers and theologians but noted that the number should be more considerable when the teaching considered was opposed by some of the respected fathers and theologians of the time.

> In effect, in order that a truth be proposed to our faith by the church, it is not sufficient that it be really found in the tradition, it is still necessary that one see it clearly; now, if serious and orthodox theologians do not see it, this is a sign that the obligation to accept this truth is not manifest, and that it is not affirmed by the moral unanimity of the authors.[66]

Vacant admonished certain German theologians who attempted to limit the number of truths of the faith in order to make the Catholic religion more amenable to its critics. While their motives were laudable, many "weapons and treasures" of the faith were lost. Yet he insisted that his general rule must still hold: the rejection of serious (*grave*) orthodox theologians was sufficient to demonstrate that a doctrine was not proposed for our faith. His only elaboration, however, on what constituted a serious and orthodox theologian was to say that they must fully understand the rules of faith and desire to follow them.

Vacant turned to one final question in this chapter. While it is clear that the ordinary magisterium has taught matters which have been held since the beginnings of Christianity, and matters which have been taught by solemn judgment, is it possible for the ordinary universal magisterium "to create for us new obligations in matters of doctrine, to render certain a point which up till then had been doubtful, or better, to render a truth of catholic faith that which had been only certain"?[67] After an extended review of the historical interplay of the ordinary magisterium with the church's solemn judgments, Vacant concluded:

> The ordinary magisterium can elucidate an idea which was originally obscure, doubtful or free, and can render it certain and obligatory to the point that the contrary proposition will merit all the notes less severe than that of heresy; but that up to now, it does not appear to have transformed any doctrine, even one which is certain, into a dogma of faith, and that would be difficult to accomplish.[68]

Vacant's argument rested on a distinction between the dogma of the faith which could be taught by the ordinary universal magisterium, and a defined dogma which could only be taught by solemn judgment. The note of heresy could only be attached to a teaching which rejected defined dogma, and not to undefined dogma taught by the ordinary universal magisterium. The French theologian maintained that for the assignment of such a negative theological note (heresy) it was necessary that the given dogma be taught with the clarity which could be offered only in a solemn definition. Using the example of the dogma of the immaculate conception, Vacant noted that prior to its solemn definition no theologian regarded that teaching as a dogma of Catholic faith. Nevertheless, this teaching was taught by the ordinary universal magisterium and by numerous popes, but never as a dogma of Catholic faith prior to its formal definition.

The Doctrinal Authority of the Majority of the Bishops Dispersed

The French seminary professor next turned his attention to the central component of the ordinary universal magisterium, the authority of the pope and bishops. According to Vacant, the principal sign of the episcopal college was its submission to the sovereign pontiff.[69] Infallibility pertained to the successors of those apostles who were in faithful submission before the successors of Peter. But what of a case in which the bishops who were in union with the pope did not form a majority? Could a majority of bishops teach contrary to the teaching of the pope? Vacant responded that when one referred to the majority of the Catholic episcopate, that meant, by definition, the bishops in union with the pope. Christ did not promise infallibility to schismatic or heretical bishops. Vacant based his conclusion on an understanding of episcopal ordination in which it was not episcopal consecration but the delegation of jurisdiction which gave the bishop the authority to teach.[70] The author refused to resolve the question whether this jurisdiction came immediately from Christ or from the pope, for it was universally agreed, he held, that whatever the case the pope did have the power to restrict and regulate jurisdiction. Therefore, no bishop could put before the faithful as obligatory any doctrine which did not, at least implicitly, have papal assent.

Vacant has raised a fundamental question in the understanding of the ordinary magisterium: what must the relationship be between the pope and the bishops on this matter? He admitted that it was possible for the bishops to put forward a teaching about which the papacy had been silent. In this instance, the silence was to be viewed as approbation. However, he then proposed a case in which the pope might impose a truth for the assent of the church which up until then had been open to discussion. He insisted that, regardless of their prior disposition on the matter, the bishops must immediately teach this truth as obligatory. No episcopal teaching act could ever contradict the clear teaching of the pope.[71] In sum, Vacant concluded that there were two principal signs for the ordinary universal magisterium: first that there be a majority of bishops who teach the particular doctrine and second that those bishops be in union with the pope on the matter. These two conditions, Vacant insisted, will always go hand in hand.

The Particular Role of the Sovereign Pontiff

Finally Vacant turned explicitly to the place of the papacy in the ordinary universal magisterium. We saw already in the last section that he had accorded to the papacy a significant role in the teaching of the episcopal college. Drawing upon the clear rejection of Gallicanism in the First Vatican Council and the council's claim that papal teaching was infallible in itself, he considered whether this infallibility was given to the papacy only in the case of papal solemn judgments or whether it applied to the ordinary papal magisterium as well.

Clearly the pope participated in the ordinary universal magisterium as head of the episcopal college. But was the relationship between the ordinary magisterium of the episcopate in union with the pope and the ordinary papal magisterium similar to that between the solemn judgments of ecumenical councils and the solemn judgments of the papacy?[72] Vacant answered in the affirmative. The pope did personally exercise an infallible ordinary magisterium expressly in the teaching of doctrine, implicitly in church discipline and the liturgy and tacitly by maintaining the rule of faith. The French theologian noted that what separated solemn judgments from the teachings of the ordinary magisterium was, after all, not the authority, which was the same for both, but only the form of the teaching. He offered as an example of the infallible ordinary papal magisterium the *Syllabus of Errors* (1864). Whenever it was evident that a pope proposed a teaching as a rule for the daily teaching of the bishops, as was the case with the *Syllabus,* then that teaching was to be understood as a kind of non-solemn, *ex cathedra* teaching.[73] In this instance, while the exterior conditions which characterized a solemn definition were lacking, the papal act could nevertheless be accepted as a definitive, infallible papal act.

According to Vacant, the pope also taught infallibly in an implicit manner. This was accomplished through the papal promulgation of ecclesiastical laws which governed church discipline and worship, for church doctrine was to be found in both of these areas.[74] Finally the pope possessed an infallible ordinary magisterium in teaching tacitly, through the maintenance of the rule of faith in the various delegated organs, the patriarchs and metropolitans, the local synods and the Catholic universities, all of which teach with his approbation. Thus when Vacant spoke earlier of the unanimous teaching of the theologians, this teaching could be considered a teaching of the ordinary magisterium only insofar as it received at least the tacit approbation of the pope.

In concluding this treatment of the ordinary papal magisterium, Vacant considered whether the definition of papal infallibility at Vatican I included the exercise of the pope's daily and ordinary teaching. Here Vacant admitted that the conciliar definition did not expressly speak of the infallibility of the pope outside of solemn judgments, but that his infallibility could be so extended as a theological conclusion. There was nothing to prevent the conditions for an *ex cathedra* definition from being realized in the teachings of the ordinary papal magisterium, for there could never be a disagreement between the pope and the episcopal college. It followed that if one wished to discern the teaching of the ordinary magisterium it might be easier to look to the teaching of the pope, to which all bishops must conform, than to seek out the many views of the bishops; in other instances the reverse might be true.

Conclusion

Vacant's treatment of the ordinary magisterium was remarkable in a number of respects. First, he developed, more than did previous figures, an appreciation for the plurality of modes of manifesting the teaching of the ordinary universal magisterium. He recognized the various ways in which catechists, priests, theologians and the church as a whole could be said to participate, in some manner, in the ordinary magisterium. Second, he explicitly connected the teaching of the ordinary universal magisterium with tradition, and in turn stressed objective tradition as reflected in the monuments of tradition, the fathers of the church, the great theologians and even the liturgy. In his consideration of the necessary unanimity required among the fathers Vacant displayed a subtle appreciation for the complexity of the matter. He maintained that the unanimity must be clearly evident; in essence, a lack of clarity on the matter should be a sign that the teaching was not taught by the ordinary magisterium. He also gave considerable weight to the opinions of the theologians on the matter, given that their orthodoxy was not in doubt.

Vacant's claim that the ordinary magisterium could not declare a teaching heretical reflected a cautious respect for the lack of clarity found in the teaching of the ordinary magisterium; while it possessed the same authority as solemn judgments, only a solemn judgment could define a teaching and only a solemn judgment could determine that a teaching was actually heretical.

All this reflected an awareness of the complex character of this mode of church teaching. He readily admitted that human and therefore conditional elements often found their way into church teaching in ways which made it quite difficult to differentiate the human and conditional from that which belonged to revelation.

However, he seemed more aware of the problems at the level of expressed or explicit teaching than of the yet more difficult problems connected with the implicit and tacit teaching of the ordinary universal magisterium.

Vacant's treatment of the college of bishops and their relationship to the episcopacy was more reflective of the regnant neoscholastic ecclesiology of the late nineteenth century. Writing in the wake of the First Vatican Council's teaching on the universal jurisdiction of the papacy, Vacant reflected the then current tendency to understand episcopal jurisdiction as functionally delegated from the papacy. Although he claimed to be avoiding the question whether episcopal jurisdiction came from the pope or Christ, by granting an excessively broad reading of the pope's right to limit and regulate that jurisdiction Vacant blurred the essential distinction between an ordinary and a delegated power of jurisdiction. Not surprisingly then, his theology of the pope's role as head of the episcopal college gave little place for the contributions of the body, the remainder of the episcopal college. Moreover, it is one thing to maintain that for a teaching to be taught by the ordinary universal magisterium the bishops must be teaching in union with the pope; it is another to claim that the college consists only of those bishops who agree with the pope. Vacant seemed to hold the latter opinion and thereby maintained that the pope and whatever bishops agreed with him on a particular teaching effectively constituted a moral unanimity of the college of bishops. This position would seem to render moot the role of the episcopal college. This intuition was confirmed in Vacant's claim that the pope alone, apart from the college, possessed an infallible ordinary papal magisterium.[75] It is remarkable, coming from a theologian who wrote a major work on Vatican I's *Dei Filius,* that he completely ignored the significance of the council's explicit addition of the word *universale* to the ordinary magisterium, an act intended to make it clear that the council fathers were referring to the college of the bishops and not to any ordinary papal magisterium.

A final comment must be made regarding Vacant's rejection of the possibility of the ordinary universal magisterium condemning a position as heretical. This would be difficult if not impossible, he contended, because the ordinary magisterium did not, and apparently could not, define dogma. The French theologian has brought to light, perhaps unintentionally, a certain paradoxical dimension in the church's teaching on the ordinary universal magisterium: it does not "define" dogma yet it teaches doctrine "definitively." Both are protected from error by the charism of infallibility but only one is a defined proposition the denial of which constitutes heresy.

Vacant's work highlights what has become the fundamental difficulty in conceptualizing the ordinary magisterium, namely the question of collegiality. The understanding of the ordinary universal magisterium by virtually every theologian examined in this book follows inexorably from their theology of the episcopacy and the episcopal college. The prominence of papal authority in most of the ecclesiological tracts of the late nineteenth and early twentieth centuries made it difficult to posit any teaching authority for the episcopal college apart from the task of echoing papal teaching.

In the next chapter we will explore the thought of two of the more influential ecclesiologists of the twentieth century, Charles Journet and Yves Congar, with an eye toward discerning signs of a more developed theology of the episcopacy which might provide an adequate foundation for understanding the role of the ordinary universal magisterium in the teaching ministry of the church.

Early Twentieth Century Ecclesiologies

In chapter 3 we investigated the reception of *Tuas libenter* in the dominant neo-scholastic manual tradition and discovered that the ordinary universal magisterium received strikingly little attention in the manuals. When space was devoted to the topic, there was scant consideration of what must be considered the most significant difficulty associated with Pope Pius IX's teaching, the problem of verifying when the church has taught infallibly in its ordinary teaching. In chapter 4 we broadened our survey to consider theologians who wrote outside of the manual tradition. There we found a greater consideration of the topic, particularly with Scheeben and Vacant. However, in spite of their helpful considerations of the topic, both ultimately suffered from an insufficient theology of the episcopacy. Indeed even Newman, for all his many contributions to Catholic ecclesiology, gave surprisingly little attention to a theology of the episcopacy. In this chapter we will continue our review of Catholic theologians who developed their thought outside the manual tradition by turning to two twentieth century figures who devoted considerable attention to the episcopacy in their theology, Charles Journet and Yves Congar.

Charles Journet (1891–1975)

Charles Journet[1] has been described as the most profound ecclesiologist of the first half of the twentieth century.[2] Though writing within a neo-scholastic milieu, Journet influenced numerous theologians and ecclesiastical figures, not the least of whom was Pope Paul VI.[3] Journet's ecclesiological project was nothing less than an ontology of the church which creatively synthesized patristic, medieval, scholastic and neo-scholastic sources. His massive study of the church[4] had as its internal structure an exploration of the church according to the four Aristotelian causes. The first volume, *The Apostolic Hierarchy,* is of immediate interest for this study.

Journet understood the hierarchy to be the efficient cause of the church.[5] Here the author has taken the Tübingen school's understanding of the *church* as the continuation of the incarnation and replaced the church with the *hierarchy.* If Jesus Christ, the incarnation of the Word, was the first mediation of God's grace, the hierarchy was a second, subordinate, and therefore only instrumental mediation. Through Journet's theology of the hierarchy he brought together both an incarnational theology and a metaphysics of causality.[6] His analysis of the episcopacy assumed the bipartite orders/jurisdiction schema. Consequently, he grounded the church's teaching authority in the power of jurisdiction. This teaching authority contained within it three tasks, each of which corresponded to three different kinds of divine assistance. In the first instance there would be an absolute assistance given to the hierarchy in preserving the propositions of revelation. This absolute assistance is, of course, infallible for "the least inexactitude here would be a catastrophe." [7] The second task is not one which determines what is or is not revealed but is concerned rather with the proper adaptation and application of church teaching to the lives of the faithful. This will be carried out in the canonical and disciplinary actions of the teaching church. Here there are two "species" of assistance possible. The first offers a prudential assistance which will be considered "prudentially infallible" insofar as it guarantees the prudence of each disciplinary or canonical decision. The second kind of assistance will also be prudential but fallible insofar as the prudence of each decision will not be guaranteed, though the general orientation of the decisions will be. The final task is to assure the temporal conditions necessary for the church's continued existence in the world of politics and culture. This task is accompanied by a kind of "biological assistance" which is also infallible but only in a very general sense in which the continued existence of the church must be assured.

While the bishop possessed the plenitude of the power of order, his power of jurisdiction was limited and much more dependent on the pope. "The jurisdictional power is 'proper' both in the pope and the bishops. It descends from the pope, who possesses it as its source, to the bishops, who possess it as a proper power no doubt, but derivatively." [8] The bishops' power of jurisdiction was in fact nothing but a kind of refraction of the papal power. Reflecting a view of the relationship between the local and universal church common to many neo-scholastic treatments of the subject, Journet maintained that "the particular churches are portions of the universal church." [9] It followed, then, that the particular jurisdiction of the local bishop and the universal jurisdiction of the papacy would be bound up together. So severe was Journet's emphasis on the universal jurisdiction of the pope that he found it necessary to explain, following Cajetan, why the church was called the body of Christ and not the body of Peter.

It is true that in addition to their particular jurisdiction the bishops did exercise a universal jurisdiction as a college, but this universal jurisdiction was, in actuality, only a participation in the papal jurisdiction.

> But, besides this particular jurisdiction which they possess as *properly* theirs, the bishops, taken as a college, in virtue of their close union with the Sovereign Pontiff, participate in the universal jurisdiction proper to the Pontiff. . . . In other words, the power to rule the universal Church resides first of all in the Sovereign Pontiff, then in the episcopal college united with the Pontiff; and it can be exercised either singly by the Sovereign Pontiff, or jointly by the Pontiff and the episcopal college: the power of the sovereign Pontiff singly and that of the Sovereign Pontiff united with the episcopal college constituting not two powers adequately distinct, but one sole supreme power—considered on the one hand in the head of the Church teaching, in whom it resides in its wholeness and as in its source, and on the other hand as at once in the head and in the body of the Church, to which it is communicated and in which it finds its plenary and integral subject.[10]

At this point Journet turned his attention to the episcopal college's exercise of the ordinary universal magisterium. By virtue of the consent which they receive, at least tacitly, from the pope, the college of bishops may teach infallibly though dispersed throughout the world. Journet then considered two related questions.

First, he responded to Vacant's claim that the pope might be, through his personal teaching, an organ of the ordinary universal magisterium. While he agreed with Vacant that an at least "prudential infallibility" could be attributed to the ordinary teaching of the pope, an "absolute infallibility" required that it be the expressed will of the pope and that it be clearly manifested that he wished to teach infallibly. In this situation, Journet concluded, the *ex cathedra* conditions for a solemn judgment would seem to have been met.[11] Second, with regard to the infallible teaching of the episcopal college, Journet inquired as to the signs for recognizing the true episcopal body. The most important sign, he responded, must be the college's communion with the sovereign pontiff. Beyond that Journet followed Vacant in resisting the attribution of a sure sign to a simple majority of the bishops, unless one qualifies that as a majority of bishops possessing jurisdiction, for such a majority could never be in disagreement with the pope. Journet resisted Vacant's position that such a situation (disagreement between the pope and the majority of bishops) would be strictly impossible but he held that it would be "highly unlikely." In the end, Journet seemed to be suspicious of the possibility of the ordinary universal magisterium effectively preserving the unity of the church and suggested the gathering of the bishops in an ecumenical council was more effective for this purpose.

Journet's study of the church represented one of the most ambitious ecclesiological projects of the twentieth century. Nevertheless, it suffered from several serious shortcomings.[12] His stress on the ontological or metaphysical dimensions of the church led to an a-historical consideration of the life of the church. One might simply compare Vacant's extensive development of the monuments of tradition as expressions of the ordinary magisterium to Journet's more formal treatment. For Journet, the incarnation of the Word in the church throughout the ages was merely the timeless extension of the trinitarian processions through the instrumental mediation of the hierarchy. One finds little awareness of the dynamic development of church teaching and ministries in the church's history. The rigorous application of an efficient causality to the hierarchy all but excluded any contributions by other sectors of the church, like the theologians or the faithful. As O'Meara remarked: "The employment of instrumental causality explains why the theological process of learning, reflecting, and then teaching is never mentioned, and why the non-juridical realm of orders and sacraments is absent." [13]

In his presentation of the ordinary universal magisterium Journet did not pursue any developed classification of the various assistances given to episcopal teaching and he completely passed over the vexing question of how the bishops were to achieve a consensus and how that consensus was to be discerned by the faithful. This oversight may be a consequence of his understanding of the activities of the hierarchy as governed by an instrumental causality. Journet ignored the distinction in Aquinas between an instrumental causality which possessed no real autonomy and was most often attributed to inanimate objects, and a true secondary causality which possessed a real autonomy in which God as the primary cause did not subsume the secondary cause but worked through the activities proper to the secondary cause. By considering the hierarchy according to the category of instrumental causality, Journet was unable to attribute to the hierarchy its own proper, human processes in its activity. It was then difficult to ask the question of how, historically, the college of bishops actually came to a consensus, nor was it possible to attribute any role for the theologians or the laity. As O'Meara points out however, "[w]hat is wonderful about conscious, free and active creatures is not that they are recipients but that they are agents, not that they are links in a chain or tubes in a pipeline, but that they are acting persons—with the gift of causality." [14] The result of Journet's ecclesiological approach is a subtle fideism in which the motive for belief is the instrumental causality of the hierarchy. Here we are close to Billot's identification of the *regula fidei* with the magisterium. It is perhaps the result of an exclusive grounding of the teaching office of the church in jurisdiction with the inevitable legalistic and juridical approaches which must follow. The assistance of the Spirit through human interaction, dialogue and inquiry is simply never considered.

Journet's ecclesiology, in many ways, suited and reflected the papacy of Pius XII. As with Pius XII, he provided no meaningful place for theological inquiry and encouraged a process of centralization of teaching authority in the papacy which reduced the bishops functionally to vicars apostolic, or ecclesiastical delegates. It is, finally, an ecclesiology which will be challenged at the Second Vatican Council through the reappropriation of the ancient principle of collegiality and the theologies which flow out of that principle.

Yves Congar (b. 1904)

In the history of Catholic theology in the twentieth century, two figures stand out: Yves Congar and Karl Rahner. But while Rahner would achieve his greatest influence in the years after Vatican II, when his works began to be translated from German into English and other languages, Yves Congar[15] was particularly influential in the decades immediately prior to Vatican II. His greatest service to the church came not in the form of a sweeping philosophical and theological system, as with Rahner, but rather in the form of meticulous historical research which paid close attention to the rich diversity present within the Christian tradition of both East and West. He studied with equal seriousness the works of Augustine and the Cappadocians, John Scotus Eriugena and Maximus the Confessor, Thomas Aquinas and Gregory Palamas, Martin Luther, John Calvin and the Council of Trent, Aleksei Khomiakov and Johann Adam Möhler, Karl Rahner and Karl Barth. His work illuminated the cultural and historical matrices through which the gospel was realized in each historical epoch and geographic locale. He stressed that the perduring reality of the gospel and of the church could only be discovered through a serious consideration of these cultural and historical forms and limitations. Committed as he was to the unity of the church, one can find underlying virtually all of Congar's work an attempt to distinguish the essential from the non-essential, Tradition from the traditions, the one reality of the gospel message from the plurality of cultural and historical forms, the necessary requirements for unity from the myriad possibilities for diversity.

The Ecclesiological Vision of Yves Congar

Before turning to Congar's theology of teaching authority we must briefly review his dominant ecclesiological commitments. Almost from the beginning of his theological career Congar had reacted to an overly juridical conception of the church as a *societas perfecta.* This conception, originally informed by Aquinas' more fundamental notion of the church as the *congregatio fidelium,* had come to denote a reality conceived as static, independent, grounded in the hierarchy with clear lines of authority and possessing a deposit of power and truth to be employed or revealed as necessary.[16] This static and juridical view of the church neglected the eschatological and historical dimensions so dominant in the ecclesiological writings of the New Testament and early church. In his historical work Congar recovered an ancient view of the church understood as mystery and grounded in both the triune life of God and the sacramental life of the people.[17] This appreciation for the mystery of the church led the early writers to eschew rigid definitions of the church in favor of rich biblical metaphors: "the people of God," "the new Israel," "the body of Christ," "the bride of Christ." Congar discovered a careful patristic balance between the church's divine and human dimensions: it was both visible and invisible, historical and eschatological. It was at the same time the bride of Christ, thereby stressing the transcendence of God and the human servanthood of the church, and the body of Christ, highlighting the church's sacramental character. He was therefore wary of treatments of the church which had allowed the divine to eclipse the human. As Congar wrote:

> For the Church, and the apostolic succession in the Church, God's link with its activity is no more than a covenant relation, but it is enough to secure the unerring character of the Church (Matt. 16:18), its indefectibility in that which bears specifically upon the substance of the covenant. . . . Certain presentations of the idea of a "continued Incarnation," according to which, as the Church is Christ's body so its mouth would be Christ's own, and all that it says would come from Christ, fail to take sufficient account of the difference that exists between a hypostatic and a covenant union. In the first case *all* the actions of the Man-God may be predicated of God and thus bear an absolute guarantee. In the second we have a "mystical" body, which is also the Bride and keeps its own individual subjectivity before Christ its Lord.[18]

The French Dominican's recovery of the eschatological dimension of the church is evident in this dialectic between structure and life,[19]

Witnesses to the Faith

identity and non-identity which is present in all of his works. The church must never lose its "already-but-not-yet" character.

In his writings after the council Congar would give increasing attention to the images of the church as people of God and as a messianic people. Before the council, however, it was the church as *communio* which received most of his attention.[20] This image brought together the mystery of the triune God as a *communio* of divine persons and spiritual anthropology's view of the human person as realized in communion with others and with God. The church as *communio* incorporates, therefore, the horizontal and vertical dimensions of the church. The church becomes a communion of persons as it opens itself up to a participation in the life of the triune God. This theme echoes the Pauline image of the church as a *koinonia* and is in continuity with the ancient eucharistic ecclesiology of the early church which understands the church as constituted in the celebration of the eucharistic liturgy.

For Congar, the image of the church as *communio* served as a corrective to an excessively hierarchical conceptualization. Put to service in the Dominican's ecumenical work, the image of the church as *communio* allowed him to view church unity not according to a strict canon of uniformity but as that which is realized in the diversity of the churches maintaining a *communio* with one another.[21] Most importantly for our purposes, the image of the church as *communio* provided the basis for a theology of the episcopacy which grounds the bishop in the local church and its eucharistic life.

Congar must also be credited with challenging the Latin tradition's at times excessively Christo-monist orientation. Drawing on the Eastern fathers as well as such nineteenth century figures as Möhler and Scheeben, Congar held that if the church was grounded in the triune life of God then ecclesiology must incorporate the missions of both Son and Spirit, for while the Son instituted the church it was the Spirit which continued to constitute and animate it.[22] The Spirit is the soul of the church and its principle of unity. It is the Spirit which forms a gathering of individuals into a true *communio*. This role of the Spirit, Congar has written, is what separates Aquinas' view of the church as a *congregatio fidelium* from that of William of Ockham. For Ockham the church was a simple aggregate of individuals, whereas Aquinas recognized that through the Spirit these individuals were bonded together and became a new relational entity, modeled on the relational life of God.

The Role of the Hierarchy

Congar never questioned the necessary place of the hierarchy in the life of the church. In fact, in his earlier writings his work reflected traces of the pyramidical model of the church in which it was the hierarchy which constituted the church.[23] But as Congar's writing progressed, he moved further away from this pyramidical model in favor of a circular model in which all ministries, including the hierarchical ministries, were situated within the community and existed for the service of the community.[24] Congar writes that

> [t]here exists a hierarchic fact, but this hierarchic fact situates itself entirely in the fraternal union of the baptized. . . . There is a work of the diaconate which consists in building the Body of Christ: it is incumbent on all Christians. The role of functions or ministries is to organize Christians with this work in view. From this view of the hierarchic functions within the baptismal community derive the three following consequences that concern our subject: 1) The hierarchy, the Pope himself, is not above the community, but in it. . . . 2) He is a baptized person, qualified by the essential conditions of Christian existence, who is eventually constituted in a position of authority. In that case, not only does he remain a Christian and must, as such, pray, convert himself to the Gospel, love, etc., but his attribute of Christian qualifies his function of authority itself. . . . 3) In these conditions, finally, we must lay stress on this point, which is decisive in the heading of authority and of obedience: the superior and the subordinate pursue and serve the same good. . . . Thus without denying its obligations, obedience assumes an aspect of cooperation, of coresponsibility and, therefore, to some degree, of dialogue. . . .[25]

J.-P. Jossua has described Congar's view of the church not just as a communion, but as a "structured communion" in which the hierarchy plays a particular role in structuring and ordering the interrelationships of all the members.[26] Here we see again the interplay in Congar's ecclesiology between structure and life. Louch describes this dialectic:

For the Church to be truly and fully herself the *ex officio* and the *ex spiritu* have to come together. Only with co-operation on all levels, all working together and each fulfilling his function, can the fullness of truth and communion be achieved. Although there will always be tension between them, spirit and form, inspiration and authority cannot be set in opposition.[27]

In his essay, "The Hierarchy as Service," Congar looked to the gospel accounts of authority understood not only as power but as service to the church:

We must get back to the true vision of the Gospel: posts of authority in the Church do indeed exist; a real jurisdictional power does exist, which the shepherds of God's people receive from Christ in conformity with the order which Christ willed and instituted (at least in its essential lines). But this power exists only within the structure of the fundamental religious relationshp of the Gospel, as an organizational element within the life given to men by Christ, the one Lord and the one Head of his Body, for which each is accountable to all the rest according to the place and measure granted to him. So there is never simply a relationship of subordination or superiority, as in secular society, but always a loving obedience to Christ, shaping the life of each with all and for all, according to the position which the Lord has given him in the Body.[28]

Thus while Congar accepts the necessity of an authority within the church, and believes that this authority resides primarily in the hierarchy, he continually emphasizes that the exercise of this authority occurs in and for the whole church.

Congar's Theology of the Magisterium

Congar's historical work, as we saw in chapter 1, led him to a much broader and richer view of the magisterium than was common in the period in which he wrote, a period typified by the papalist and juridical view evident in Pius XII's *Humani Generis*. The Dominican's own view may be analyzed in terms of form, and function.[29]

For Congar the form of the magisterium is realized in the

principle of collegiality. This notion developed as a result of his consideration of the biblical principle in which all members of the church have a necessary part to play in the life of the whole. He was also influenced by the slavophile movement and the Russian Orthodox idea of *Sobornost,* the fundamental organic unity of the church. Collegiality, for Congar, thus applies first of all to the life of the whole church.[30] This implies, of course, that the whole faithful in some way participates in the teaching of the church, though without compromising the unique role of the hierarchy. Congar is certainly in sympathy with Newman's understanding of the *consensus fidelium* and its contributions to the transmission of church teaching.[31] He maintains that while the faithful cannot juridically "validate" a particular teaching, within a communal conception of the church in which the hierarchy functions within the community, the faithful must "receive" a doctrine and make it their own. In doing so they offer something positive to the formulation of that teaching. There exists then, in Congar's view, a kind of *conspiratio fidelium et pastorum.*[32]

This extension of the principle of collegiality to the whole faithful is not, however, developed any further after the publication of *Jalons.* His later writings will focus primarily on episcopal collegiality.[33] Congar's theology of episcopal collegiality is built upon the inseparability of the bishop's membership in the episcopal college and his pastoral responsibility to a local church.[34] The Dominican's view constituted a rejection of both a theology of the episcopacy which emphasized consecration into a particular *ordo,* and a theology which stressed the liturgical leadership of a particular community (*jurisdictio*). A bishop participates in the episcopal college *as* a pastor of a particular church. This theology of the episcopacy presupposes that the local church is a manifestation rather than a "part" or "portion" of the universal church. The local does not precede the universal, neither is the local a mere subset of the universal; rather, the local church is the full (*plenary*) manifestation of the universal church.[35]

This understanding of collegiality is first and foremost a manifestation of the church as *communio* which has the Holy Spirit as its animating principle. Thus, while not negating juridical considerations, Congar has stressed that the college's juridical status is dependent on a more fundamental reality.

The acid test for any understanding of collegiality is the relationship between pope and bishops. As we saw with the manualists, this relationship was often so conceived as to preclude any true collegiality in favor of an absolute papal monarchy. More often, however, we saw the theory of two inadequately distinct subjects of infallibility, viz., the episcopal college and the pope. Congar favored a view which posited one subject, the episcopal college, which in turn admitted of a duality of exercise. In this view papal exercise represents merely a "personalizing" of the episcopal college.[36] According to Congar, then, when the pope pronounces *ex cathedra* it may be distinguished juridically from an exercise of the episcopal college but not theologically. This view has profound ecclesiological consequences insofar as it makes the episcopal college (which includes the bishop of Rome as its head) the starting point for a consideration of any exercise of magisterial authority rather than the papacy.

Congar, perhaps influenced by Newman, reconceives the function of the magisterium from the task of defining to that of witnessing, witnessing to the gospel of Jesus Christ.

> The teaching authority has gladly been "defining," above all since Pius IX, and that was accompanied by an over-estimation of this very office, by an absurd abuse of the category of what is "infallible." Today we are brought back to more evangelical authenticity: the witness of the Word of God must dominate over any pretension to define. . . . To bear witness to Jesus Christ, the Incontestable One, and His gospel would be the most efficacious way through which authority, while forgetting itself, would re-discover itself.[37]

Congar is wary of a view of church teaching, regnant since the Council of Trent's espousal of the two-source theory of revelation, which sees the magisterium as a distinct source of revelation. One might recall Billot's view that it was the magisterium itself which was the *regula fidei*. In response to this perspective, much of the French Dominican's historical work was intent on demonstrating the early church's understanding of the *regula fidei* not as the hierarchy but as the gospel message itself. Thus dogmatic definitions, however much they participate in and further the development of dogma, are never completely the production of something new, but rather are simply an intensified expression of the more fundamental task of witnessing.

Congar and the Ordinary Universal Magisterium

It is in his consideration of tradition's subject that Congar briefly considers the ordinary universal magisterium.[38] Congar writes that it is the whole church that is the subject of tradition, yet this whole church is not without structure, a structure intended by Christ to preserve the word of God as transmitted from generation to generation. Within this structure each part—laity, theologians, hierarchy—has an indispensable role to play. Infallibility, which is given in the first instance to the whole church as an assistance in the preservation of the gospel, is exercised by the hierarchy according to two complementary modes: ordinary and extraordinary. Through its infallible teaching the church bestows on the various material elements of objective tradition (that which has been received) their formal value as the rule of faith.

Congar begins by distinguishing between the ordinary magisterium and the ordinary *universal* magisterium, a distinction introduced at Vatican I. While the former referred to the bishops teaching either individually or as a regional group and did not possess the charism of infallibility, the latter concerned only the common teaching of all the bishops and was infallible. "That which the episcopate would hold unanimously and in communion with the Roman See as a truth pertaining to the faith must be considered as actually pertaining to it." [39] The French theologian notes however, that the unanimity of the bishops is not in itself sufficient; they must be agreed that what is held is a matter of faith:

> If a point was held with the same unanimity as probable or near to the faith, or risky, etc. it must be considered as being such. But a teaching of this type not being irreformable, it would remain permissible to highlight another point of view for good reasons in respect of the ecclesiastical peace.[40]

This restriction appears to have the same intent as Salaverri's *definitive tenendam:* to limit the exercise of the ordinary universal magisterium solely to those teachings which the bishops hold as irrevocable.

With Vacant, Congar understands the ordinary universal magisterium as manifested either expressly or tacitly. Thus it may be expressed in preaching, catechisms, synodal letters, doctrinal vigilance, diocesan synods or particular councils. Beyond this, however, he has little to say regarding the means for achieving and discerning the unanimous teaching of the bishops in and through these plurality of forms, nor does he explain what any concrete criteria for moral unanimity might be.

Elsewhere Congar criticized the gradual movement between the pontificates of Pius IX and Pius XII to extend the infallibility of the ordinary universal magisterium to the ordinary papal magisterium.[41] Paul Nau, for example, continued the view first proposed by Vacant that it was a mistake to limit papal infallibility solely to *ex cathedra* solemn judgments. The crux of his argument was that one must not confuse a diversity of forms of papal teaching with the authority of that teaching. If one were to limit papal infallibility strictly to those papal teachings which fulfill the criteria of an *ex cathedra* judgment, then all other papal teachings would be regarded as nothing more than the opinions of a private doctor.[42] According to Nau "it is one thing to limit the case where the conditions for a solemn judgement can be verified, it is another thing to limit the authentic modes of presentation of the rule of faith to a solemn judgment alone." [43] While Vatican I did not explicitly speak of the infallibility of the ordinary papal magisterium, Nau admitted, it did not exclude it either. Nau's view demonstrates a common assumption which saw infallibility as the only possible means by which the Spirit could preserve the church in truth. Commenting on this unfortunate approach, Congar says:

> There has also existed a true inflation of the category of infallibility as if, between the infallible truth and error, there did not exist an immense domain of partial truth, of probable certitude, of research and approximations, or even of the very precious truth not protected from the risks of human finitude.[44]

Congar finds fault with those who would employ the ordinary universal magisterium in the service of extending the mantle of infallibility over all church teaching. Those who promote this approach have mistakenly assumed that infallibility is the only instrument at the church's disposal for teaching the truth of the gospel.

Concluding Observations

As with Newman, Schell and Journet, Congar has surprisingly little to say directly about the ordinary universal magisterium. Nevertheless, there is much in his ecclesiology which has an indirect bearing on the infallible ordinary teaching of the bishops. A summary of his contributions will provide an opportunity to consider briefly the works of the six figures studied in the past two chapters.

Models of the Church: Hierarchy *or* Communio?

Newman, Scheeben, and Schell all accentuated the organic reality of the church and the interrelationship of its various parts. Although all admitted a privileged role in the transmission of church teaching to the hierarchy, this role was to be exercised within the church and not above it. This organic model, which has its roots in the Tübingen school, would be adopted by Congar. The French Dominican, however, employed the *communio* metaphor in order to stress not only the organic interactions within the church, but the interdependence of the various members comprising the body of Christ. Congar brought with the image of *communio* an appreciation for the place of the local church as one pole in the life of the church which had not found the same stress in the Tübingen school. This understanding of the church as *communio* stands in contrast to the more pyramidical and hierarchic ecclesiologies of Journet and, at times, Vacant—for Vacant, too, viewed the hierarchy as the efficient cause of the church and described the pope and bishops as the soul of the church.

These two ecclesiological models, the one hierarchic and the other organic and communal, yield differing understandings of the teaching authority of bishops, and consequently, of the ordinary universal magisterium. The hierarchic model assumes that all power and truth flow from the papacy to the episcopacy. The authority of the college of bishops is rooted in papal authority and the teaching of the bishops will follow the lead of, and echo, papal teaching. The hierarchy's relationship to the faithful in general, and the bishops' relationship to their respective local churches in particular, will be that between the teacher and the one taught. With this model (as Vacant noted) the teaching of the pope would be the surest sign of the universal teaching of the bishops.

In Congar's model of the church as *communio* the power to teach authoritatively does not flow from the top down. Here Congar, much like Schell, sees the pneumatological conditioning of the church as preserving a tension between institution and charism. Both elements are necessary for the life of the church. This view of the church further yields a theology of the magisterium grounded in the principle of collegiality. Against Journet, Congar contends that the fundamental locus of ecclesiastical authority in the church is not the papacy but the episcopal college. Papal authority is always a collegial authority. The importance of this shift cannot be overemphasized. Where most of the manualists, Journet, Vacant, and at times Scheeben, considered episcopal authority as devolving from papal authority, Congar has claimed that even when the pope teaches *ex cathedra* he does so as the bishop of Rome. As head of the episcopal college the pope *personalizes* the authority of the college in a solemn papal definition. Congar rejects the conception of papal headship popularized by the medieval Franciscans, particularly Bonaventure and Thomas of York, which employed a Pseudo-Dionysian notion of hierarchy in which the lower is subsumed by the higher as the *"primus hierarcha."* [45] As did Herman Schell a half century earlier, Congar maintains that it is not necessary to so conceive of papal headship that the pope bears no meaningful relationship to the college. Rather, it is reasonable to assume that the bishop of Rome's fellow bishops do indeed possess resources which add to those of the pope. Collegiality is rendered meaningless if the pope possesses, independent of the bishops, all the resources available to the episcopal body. The head is not a proxy for the body. Congar's conception of papal headship then, reconceives the teaching of the episcopal college as something other than an authoritative echoing of papal teaching. The flow of authority does not start with the top of the pyramid (the pope) and move downward, neither does it start at the base of the pyramid and move upward. Rather the power resides, first in the church itself, laity and clergy, then, most visibly, in the college as a whole. The bishops may not be viewed as mere delegates of the pope, but neither may the pope be understood as solely a spokesperson for the bishops.

The Task of the Magisterium: Witnessing or Defining?

We saw in the manualists a tendency to interpret the teaching ministry of the pope and bishops such that the hierarchy itself, rather than the gospel it preached, became the rule of faith for the church. This led to an excessively a-historical understanding of revelation and its mediation in scripture and tradition. Newman was one of the first nineteenth century figures to question this view and posit the nature of the teaching ministry of the hierarchy as a witnessing to the faith of the whole church. Later, Herman Schell also insisted that the hierarchy functioned in service of the activity of the Holy Spirit. Despite the hierarchy's privileged role, it did not control revelation but was revelation's authoritative witness. Congar's view of collegial authority as the form of the magisterium develops the view of Newman and Schell further. He, too, views witnessing to be the principal task of the magisterium. As he has often stressed, the magisterium, while possessing an undeniably creative and productive dimension, does not bring forth in its teachings "new revelations," however much its teaching may be a development of what was only implicitly contained in revelation. The bishops give witness to the faith of the church which they have received and which they are bound to transmit. As Congar noted, the bishops' membership in the episcopal college is closely aligned with their pastoral mission as head of a local flock. It follows then that their task of witnessing to the gospel will be informed by their relationship to their local flock. The gospel to which they give witness as a college will be expressed in ways influenced by the incarnation of that gospel in the local churches.

The Assistance of the Holy Spirit

Ancient tradition had generally distinguished between the *inspiration* and the *assistance* of the Holy Spirit. While the authors of scripture were indeed *inspired* by the Spirit, the church teaches only with the Spirit's *assistance.* This distinction had, since the

Council of Trent, however, become increasingly blurred. Scheeben, for example, in spite of his organic vision of the church, ultimately succumbed to an overly mechanistic conceptualization of
church teaching as produced by the hierarchy according to a kind
of instrumental causality. When Scheeben defended the infallibility of the episcopal teaching body, his argument was based on the
infrustrability of the Holy Spirit, yet without considering the question of any real human causality. This approach was expressed in
its most developed from in the work of Journet whose whole ecclesiology was dominated by an analysis of the church in terms of the
four Aristotelian causes. Journet's view precluded any real consideration of human causality in the authoritative teaching of the
hierarchy.

Newman's writing, on the other hand, reflected a more
nuanced appreciation for the problems involved in conceptualizing the role of the Spirit in the development of church teaching and
the protection of the church from error. His consideration of the
illative sense as a complex dialectical process of coming to religious
assent found its ecclesial analogue in the church's development of
dogma. He recognized a certain unpredictability in the development of dogma which was due in no small part to the integral role
which the human processes of discernment played in the development of church teaching. While the Spirit might, in certain instances, be able to protect the church from error, that did not mean
that the timing and precise form of a dogma's development would
not be affected by the limitations of human processes. Newman's
treatment implicitly rejected any understanding of dogmatic development which assumed that an authoritative hierarchical magisterium peremptorily defined whatever it wished whenever it
wished.

As we saw above, Herman Schell rejected the conception of
the church as a continuation of the incarnation in favor of one in
which the church's humanity was bound to Christ in a covenantal
relation. Consequently, Schell, like Newman, was much more willing to attribute a real causality to the human dimension of the
church; the assistance of the Holy Spirit does not replace the human means and resources for recognizing the truth but works
through human capabilities and limitations. This concern to preserve the integrity of a free human causality in any theology of the

assistance of the Holy Spirit, already evident in Newman and Schell, would find new emphasis in the thought of Congar. He also warned against employing the hypostatic union as a model for the interrelation of the human and divine in the church precisely because it was prone to an elevation of the divine at the expense of the human. This more subtle theology of the assistance of the Holy Spirit, found in Newman, Schell and Congar, demands caution in ascertaining what has and has not been taught with the infallible protection of the Holy Spirit. It is a caution which Newman proposed even in the case of defined dogma. While none of these authors explicitly said as much, it is not unreasonable to assume that even greater caution would be warranted in the case of undefined dogma taught by the ordinary universal magisterium where the processes for the formation and formulation of such teaching is considerably more complex that those involved in solemn definitions.

Criteria for the Recognition of the Teachings of the Ordinary Universal Magisterium

How does one discern or recognize those teachings which have been taught infallibly by the ordinary universal magisterium? Here it is Vacant rather than Congar who offered the most developed treatment of this question. While Vacant's pronounced papalism was evident in his suggestion that papal teaching was the surest sign of the infallible teaching of the ordinary magisterium, elsewhere in his work he seemed to admit the difficulties involved in this task of discernment. Vacant was aware that as the teaching of the bishops in the ordinary magisterium was not solemnly defined, it would have to be discerned in a plurality of sources. The surest sources were of course the ancient creeds, catechisms and the teachings of the fathers. With regard to the teachings of the fathers, near unanimity was required; where a respected father offered an opposing view, the majority supporting the view would have to include a relatively greater number of witnesses. For example, were a teaching to be found in the writings of ten church fathers with none in opposition, that unanimity might be viewed as sufficient to demonstrate the obligation to an assent of faith to the given teaching. But where a church father could be found to disagree with a particular teaching, far more than ten would need to be found explicitly attesting to the teaching in order to constitute a sufficient moral unanimity.

Vacant did view the unanimous adherence of the faithful as a sign that the teaching in question had been taught infallibly, but he admitted that ascertaining that universal adherence was a difficult matter. More helpful, however, is Vacant's contention that the unanimity of orthodox theologians be viewed as a sign of an infallible teaching. In fact, Vacant went so far as to insist that where respected theologians were not in agreement regarding a particular teaching, the obligation to accept the teaching as taught by the ordinary universal magisterium did not exist. Vacant, then, posited a role for the theologians which is not unlike that of Newman's *schola theologorum.*

In conclusion, it should be obvious that, with the exception of Journet, whose treatment of the church teaching authority and the ordinary universal magisterium possessed affinities with the manualist tradition, the theologians treated in the past two chapters have made several important contributions toward the construction of a coherent contemporary theology of the ordinary universal magisterium. While Vacant succeeded, in part, in offering an adequate account of the ordinary universal magisterium, his project was ultimately compromised by an excessively papalist view of church authority. The lack of any extensive consideration of the topic aside from that of Vacant remains surprising. The most plausible explanation may be that the period which we have reviewed was dominated by a general theology of teaching authority which subsumed all church teaching into papal teaching and viewed all papal teaching as, at the very least, practically irrevocable. In such an environment there would be little incentive for developing criteria for ascertaining what was and was not taught infallibly. That incentive would soon come in the form of two epoch-making events in the life of the church which occurred within the same decade: the commencement of the Second Vatican Council and the promulgation of Paul VI's encyclical, *Humanae vitae.* It is these two events and the subsequent reconsiderations of the nature and limits of church authority which we must address in the next chapter.

6

Vatican II and Beyond

Writing to a young Anglican clergyman in 1871 concerning Vatican I's treatment of papal infallibility, John Henry Newman commented:

> Another consideration has struck me forcibly, and that is, that, looking at early history, it would seem as if the Church moved on to the perfect truth by various successive declarations, alternately in contrary directions, and thus perfecting, completing, supplying each other. Let us have a little faith in her I say. Pius is not the last of the popes. The fourth Council modified the third, the fifth the fourth. Men were alternately (i.e. were called) heretics. Look at the history of Theodoret. The late definition [on papal infallibility] does not so much need to be undone, as to be completed. It needs *safeguards* to the Pope's possible acts—explanations as to the matter and extent of his power. I know that a violent reckless party, had it its will, would at this moment define that the Pope's power needs no safeguards, no explanations; but there is a limit to the triumph of the tyrannical. Let us be patient, let us have faith, and a new Pope, and a re-assembled Council may trim the boat. (Emphasis is Newman's)[1]

Clearly Vatican I's one-sided stress on the papacy left a dangerous ecclesiological vacuum which the reign of the Pian popes all too readily filled. Yves Congar, commenting on the results of Vatican II, remarked that if there was one thing that surprised him, it was that

> for the first time the church has formally defined itself. The preceding councils spoke of the sacraments and the priesthood (Trent), and of the primacy of the pope (Vatican I): they did not formulate a complete ecclesiology. The First Vatican Council had intended such a project, but it was interrupted without

113

having been able to conclude and its work, however positive, was limited to the affirmation of the primatial function and led to a certain unilateralism if not a certain disequilibrium.[2]

Thus, Newman's prescient observation would be vindicated some ninety years later with the convocation of the Second Vatican Council, a council which indeed undertook the task of "trimming the boat" by attending to the unfinished agenda of Vatican I, the development of a theology of the episcopacy. This chapter will explore then, Vatican II's theology of the episcopacy and its implications for an understanding of the ordinary universal magisterium. This will require an analysis of the precise conciliar formulation of this teaching in the Dogmatic Constitution on the Church, *Lumen gentium.*

Within a decade of the close of Vatican II, the publication of Paul VI's *Humanae vitae* raised important theological questions regarding the authoritative status of that encyclical's teaching on birth regulation. As the theological discussions which ensued gave a prominent place to Vatican II's formulation of the teaching on the ordinary universal magisterium, special consideration must be given to these debates as well. Finally, this chapter will look to the 1983 Code of Canon Law for further evidence of the current theology of the ordinary universal magisterium.

Lumen Gentium and Episcopal Collegiality

The chapter on the hierarchy,[3] situated in the final schema after the chapter on the people of God, was the most hotly contested of the chapters in the debate on the constitution. So many were the questions and disagreements that the council secretariat felt compelled to divide the text into 39 separate parts in order to facilitate the discussion of specific phrases and sentences. The discussion elicited a deluge of over a thousand amendments. Many of these were offered by a block of some 300 bishops who constituted a persistent minority opposed to the final schema's treatment of the collegiality of both the apostles and the bishops. In the first draft of the schema episcopal collegiality had been treated at the end of the chapter, largely with regard to ecumenical councils. The revised text, however, gave the concept a more central place, but by doing so, highlighted apparent difficulties in reconciling Vatican I's teaching on papal primacy with the claim to the episcopal college's supreme authority. The council bishops were aware of the need to avoid placing the papacy and the episcopal college as rivals; the presentation must reflect their organic union.

A particularly controversial passage in the third schema understood episcopal consecration to confer the offices of sanctifying, teaching and governing. This stood in opposition to the commonly held position prior to the council that only the power of orders was conferred at consecration. The power of jurisdiction, which would include the power of governing and the power of teaching, was generally thought to be conferred by a canonical mission from the pope. The full import of this passage becomes clearer when in article 22 the bishops defined membership in the episcopal college: ". . . one is constituted a member of the episcopal body by virtue of sacramental consecration and by hierarchical communion with the head and members of the body." Together, these texts indicate the clear intent of the majority of the bishops to bind more closely the powers of orders and jurisdiction and to stress that the fullness of episcopal powers was conferred not by the pope (though the regulation of the exercise of powers was subject to papal authority) but by consecration and admission into the episcopal college. For the minority group of bishops this more sacramental approach could not be easily reconciled with the positions put forward at Vatican I. The views of these bishops were reflective of the neo-scholastic and ultramontane ecclesiology which had achieved dominance under the Pian popes.

What was at issue was not papal primacy vs. episcopal collegiality but two competing views of collegiality. The first view, held by the minority, reflected juridical concerns and viewed the church functionally as one universal diocese—the pope was bishop of the whole church and the college of bishops functioned as the universal bishop's "presbyteral college." The second position was grounded

in a nascent *communio* ecclesiology[4] which resisted Roman centralization and saw the universality of the church preserved in the
episcopal college. Evidence of this view can be found in *Lumen
gentium* #22:

> The collegial nature and meaning of the episcopal order found
> expression in the very ancient practice by which bishops ap-
> pointed the world over were linked with one another and with
> the Bishop of Rome by the bonds of unity, charity, and peace;
> also in the conciliar assemblies which made common judg-
> ments about more profound matters in decisions reflecting the
> views of many. The ecumenical councils held through the cen-
> turies clearly attest this collegial aspect. . . . This college, insofar
> as it is composed of many, expresses the variety and universal-
> ity of the People of God, but insofar as it is assembled under
> one head, it expresses the unity of the flock of Christ.

The deep rooted fears of the council minority led to one of the
most controversial actions of the council, the attachment of a *Nota
Explicativa Praevia* to the final text of the dogmatic constitution.
This *Nota* was never formally approved by the council fathers nor
was it ever clearly explained that the document was originally intended only as a response of the theological commission to numerous *modi* put forward by the minority bishops. The quasi-formal
status which it received was much resented.[5] While the *Nota,* properly read, adds little to the constitution itself, the intention was
clearly to assuage the concerns of the minority with respect to possible misunderstandings of the teaching on episcopal collegiality.

The *Nota* consisted of four parts. The first rejected the notion
of a "college" understood as a group of equals who delegate authority to the president. Rather it was defined as "a stable group whose
structure and authority is to be deduced from revelation."[6] The
second part sought to clarify the question of membership in the
episcopal college. For many of the bishops, grounding college
membership in episcopal consecration represented a dangerous in-
novation which departed from the traditional association of membership with the reception of a canonical mission from the pope.
The theological commission thus sought to reassure the minority
by distinguishing between an "office" (*munus*) and a "power" (*po-*

testas) and claiming that while the three offices were received at consecration they required some canonical or juridical determination to become powers "ready to go into action" (*ad actum expedita*). This section of the *Nota* also observed that the council had explicitly spoken of a "hierarchical communion" in order to affirm the necessity of a concrete, hierarchical structure for the ecclesial communion. The third part attempted to bring a certain clarity to the question of the relationship between the bishops and the pope within the episcopal college. This represented, at best however, only a brief nod toward the thorny question of reconciling the council's ascription of full and supreme authority to both pope and college. The *Nota* appeared to defend the theory found in the manualists in which there are two inadequately distinct subjects of supreme church authority: the pope and the college of bishops. Finally, the fourth point distinguished between the college's permanent existence and its activity. While the college exists permanently, not just when gathered in council, its "strictly collegial action" must be seen as occurring only at intervals.[7] However, neither the *Nota* nor the dogmatic constitution itself ever defined the meaning of this evidently technical expression. We shall have reason to return to this text later.

The notion of collegiality proposed in *Lumen gentium* represented a victory for the vast majority of the bishops who wished to give balance to a pre-conciliar ecclesiology grounded in a one-sided reading of Vatican I's *Pastor aeternus*. The majority saw in this view of episcopal collegiality the opportunity to overcome almost a century of Roman centralization; it would encourage the canonical recognition of episcopal conferences and provide a foundation for greater freedom in the ecumenical movement through its implicit recognition of the legitimate richness embedded in the diversity of the local churches. At the same time, however, it must be recognized that the council's articulation of episcopal collegiality betrayed some serious ecclesiological problems, foremost of which was an inadequate grounding of the episcopal college in the universal church as a communion of churches. This is evident in *Lumen gentium* #22's consideration of the requirements for membership in the episcopal college; while its stress on the sacramental over the juridical represented a significant improvement, the lack of any explicit connection with the pastoral charge of a local church soli-

Witnesses to the Faith

dified a view of the bishop as primarily a member of the episcopal college and only secondarily as a shepherd of a local flock.

The Council's Teaching on the Ordinary Universal Magisterium of Bishops

Lumen gentium #22 declares that both the pope and the episcopal college possess full and supreme authority over the whole church. The supreme authority of the episcopal college can be exercised in an ecumenical council, but that same power can also be exercised while the bishops are dispersed throughout the world, provided that "the head of the college calls them to collegiate action, or at least so approves or freely accepts the united action of the dispersed bishops, that it is made a true collegial act."[8]

The magisterial exercise of this collegiality is outlined in article 25:

> Although the individual bishops do not enjoy infallibility, they can nevertheless proclaim Christ's doctrine infallibly. This is so, even when they are dispersed throughout the world, provided that while maintaining the bond of communion among themselves and with Peter's successor, and while teaching authoritatively on a matter of faith or morals, they concur in a single viewpoint as the one which must be held definitively.[9]

Several points must be made regarding the precise phrasing of this text. One key change made in the amended text of the second schema replaced the phrase "collegial bond" with the present "bond of communion."[10] The intention here was apparently to leave aside the question whether an act of the ordinary universal magisterium must be a "strictly collegial act." Nevertheless, Karl Rahner has maintained that it follows as a theological conclusion from what was said previously in article 22 that the exercise of the ordinary universal magisterium must be considered a strictly collegial act. In his commentary on *Lumen gentium* Rahner writes:

> . . . [I]f one simply accepts the intrinsic logical connection between this doctrine and that of Article 22, one is bound to

affirm that in effect this text presupposes that the infallible act of the ordinary magisterium is a strictly collegiate act. An infallible doctrinal act, outside a council, is certainly an exercise of the supreme authority of the Church. But speaking of such an act, Article 22 says that it is only possible as a truly collegiate act. No doubt the Constitution intends to leave the question open, as has already been said. . . . But in any case, the text seems to speak of an active and collegiate exercise of the supreme teaching authority of the college as such ("it teaches"; "it agrees on the same doctrine"—*convenire*), so that the infallible act of the ordinary magisterium of the whole episcopate must be taken as a collegiate act. And this is true even if the act is of a very informal nature, and even if the intention of teaching the doctrine explicitly is not present.[11]

The confusion arises, in part, because of the *Nota's* statement that while the college itself exists perpetually, strictly collegial activity occurs only at intervals. Francis Sullivan has noted:

If one holds that the ordinary magisterium of the bishops, even as infallible, is a permanent or habitual form of activity, then, in the sense of the *Nota Praevia,* one would have to conclude that it is not a *strictly* collegial action. But even in accepting that conclusion, I do not see how it could be denied that, even if it lacks some juridical formality required for a *strictly* collegial action (as the *Nota Praevia* understands the term), it necessarily has a *truly* collegial character, since only the college as such can be understood as the subject of this infallibility.[12]

Rahner and Sullivan have highlighted the problematic character of the qualification of a collegial action by the Latin *stricte.* If by a *"strictly* collegial action" the *Nota* intended collegial actions for which there exist clear juridical norms, as with episcopal synods, "true" collegial action nevertheless cannot be limited to these juridical forms if the college exists permanently. Confusion arose because the *Nota* attached a juridical qualification of collegiality to a document which employed a non-juridical, sacramental-organic view of collegiality.[13] According to this organic view, the activity of the ordinary universal magisterium occurs not at intervals, but, as even the manualists understood, in the concrete daily life of the bishops and the church, in the liturgy, in preaching, catechesis, etc. Understood juridically, however, this ongoing activity will always be secondary, derived from some other magisterial act. It would be, in Rahner's terms, an "*anamnesis*" of some "strictly collegial act" (e.g., the promulgation of a creed, catechism, synodal statement).[14] As the *Nota* never provided any clarification of what constitutes a "strict collegial act," it may be legitimate to question the usefulness of this qualification of collegial activity. Since the individual bishops are not as individuals themselves infallible, but only as a college, it is evident that the exercise of the ordinary universal magisterium must be fundamentally collegial, whatever juridical note be attached to it.

Michael Schmaus has defined a strictly collegial act as one in which "the pronouncement of the bishops evidently expresses a viewpoint in which the total body concurs."[15] Yet he admits that this hardly solves the problem, for there are no norms to govern the recognition of such acts outside of council. If the act is to be realized through some kind of vote or polling, what degree of unanimity is required? Schmaus suggests simply that the college may have to create its own norms in deliberation on a particular teaching. He then considers whether the regular teaching office which is proper to all bishops is to be considered an exercise in collegiality.

> Formally, this does not seem to be a collegial act in the proper sense, since every bishop teaches as the individual shepherd of a local church. In practice, however, the conformity of the teaching as it is set forth in catechisms, in sermons and the like, amounts to the same thing as a collegial act. When the popes (Pius IX, Pius XII, for example) before defining certain doctrines, have questioned the bishops, the answer of all the bishops can be understood as a collegial act.[16]

Joseph Komonchak has also made the observation that the "bond of communion" must be understood as a formal condition for participation in the episcopal magisterium not as a description of the actual exercise of that authority. In other words, a bishop may be in communion with the other bishops and the bishop of Rome and still disagree with them on a particular matter. That a bishop must maintain the "bond of communion" means simply that the bishop must not be schismatic or heretical, not that the bishop is required to agree with the pope and the rest of the college on all matters.[17] This is reflective of a tendency within the constitution to situate the pope within the episcopal college, albeit as its head. Along this same line, Heinrich Fries has drawn attention to the phrase *cum Successore Petri* which is utilized in *Lumen gentium* in place of the more common *sub Romano Pontifice*.[18] The shift in wording reflects again the council's commitment to a subtle reconception of the relationship of pope and bishops and the intent, as much as possible, to situate the pope within the college.

There is a general agreement among the theologians cited here that while the conciliar text is itself ambiguous in places, the overall intent of the council bishops was to situate the bishop of Rome within the episcopal college and to stress the supreme authority which this college possessed. From this perspective the qualification of collegial activity put forward in the *Nota* by the theological commission must be understood as a necessary compromise intended to quell the fears of the minority bishops: at the same time it must be admitted that this qualification seems to work at cross-purposes to the overall thrust of the third chapter of *Lumen gentium.*

Returning to the text of *Lumen gentium* #25, the next key phrase, *res fidei et morum docentes,* replaced the *in revelata fide tradenda* of the amended second schema.[19] The concern expressed by several bishops was that the earlier phrase restricted the scope of infallible teaching to that which was strictly revealed. The text was then amended with the broader phrasing in order to leave open the possibility of the so called "secondary object of infallibility" (that which does not belong to revelation but which either pertains directly to revelation or is necessary for the preservation of revelation; e.g., the teaching on the canon of the Bible). At the same time, this extension of the scope of infallibility was coupled with an amendment intended to restrict its application, thus the crucial qualification that the dispersed bishops taught infallibly only when united in judgment that the teaching was "to be held definitively" (*tamquam definitive tenendam*).[20] "Hence not every doctrine taught unanimously by the whole episcopate is of itself infallible, even when it deals with faith or morals or intends to do so."[21]

Theologians Like Rahner and Sullivan believe that this qualification was intended to preserve the very important distinction between commonly held opinions which may have survived for extended periods of time without notable dissent, and beliefs which the church has taught *irrevocabiliter*. Sullivan justifies his position by citing the pre-conciliar manual of Salaverri which first used the phrase *tamquam definitive tenendam* and understood it to mean teaching proposed as irrevocable.[22] Unfortunately, the conciliar statement does not elaborate on how one might determine when the bishops do intend to teach a doctrine as something to be held definitively. But J. Robert Dionne, while in sympathy with the reading of this phrase by Rahner and Sullivan, finds the text itself to be ambiguous. He has suggested that there are at least seven possible meanings for *tamquam definitive tenendam*. These might be grouped in two categories: the first set of meanings assumes that such teachings are taught irrevocably or as pertaining to the substance of the faith; however, Dionne also suggests a second group of meanings in which these teachings are held as merely *theologice certum* or as teachings no longer considered open for discussion. He further insists that it is hermeneutically inappropriate to assume, as does Sullivan, that Salaverri's understanding of *tamquam definitive tenendam* is the meaning intended by the council bishops. It is this ambiguity, he concludes, which has created serious difficulties:

> Unless the bishops are actually polled, it may be impossible to determine over the short haul (and the short haul may entail a couple of centuries) just what is happening. That is to say, the *tamquam definitive tenendam* . . . is rather ambiguous, for some bishops may be holding and teaching papal doctrine according to one of the first two meanings [namely, as something to be held irrevocably or as pertaining to the substance of the faith], others according to the last four [all of which allow the teaching less than irrevocable status].[23]

Dionne proposes that this ambiguity might be overcome by adding the phrase *ad fidei substantiam spectantem,* thus making explicit the restrictive meaning which Sullivan and Rahner assume.[24]

Vatican II certainly provided more clarity than previous ecclesiastical documents in its articulation of the ordinary universal magisterium. However, as this analysis has demonstrated, the council's formulation did not escape the difficulties which have endured in the tradition's formulation of this teaching since *Tuas libenter*. Its attempt to provide a basic criteriology for the recognition of this mode of magisterial teaching would meet with several important tests in the next two decades, tests which all revolved around the controversial papal encyclical on birth regulation, *Humanae vitae*.

The Theological Discussion of *Humanae Vitae* and the Application of *Lumen Gentium* #25 to the Encyclical

During the Second Vatican Council the pope requested that the bishops not address the thorny question of birth regulation. It was his intention to create a papal commission charged with exploring the question in depth. That commission, with a membership which included bishops, theologians and laity, was created after the council and returned two reports to the pope. The majority report advocated a change in current teaching, citing changing historical circumstances which necessitated a reconsideration of the church's current teaching and warned of the serious consequences to the credibility of the church's teaching office if such a change were to transpire. As is well known, the pope chose to follow the counsel of the minority report and in 1968 Pope Paul VI issued what was to be his last encyclical, *Humanae vitae*. The controversy which followed is well documented; among the various responses to the papal teaching, we are especially interested in one particular response which advanced the view that the church's teaching on contraception had already been taught infallibly by the ordinary universal magisterium. This view already had been suggested tentatively by several theologians prior to the council,[25] but the position would find a most surprising advocate later in the Tübingen theologian, Hans Küng.

Hans Küng's Unfehlbar? Eine Anfrage *and the Critique of Karl Rahner*

The debate on infallibility took a new turn with the controversy surrounding the publication in 1970 of Hans Küng's *Unfehl-*

bar? Eine Anfrage.[26] In that book Küng contended that the church's teaching on infallibility was both historically and philosophically untenable. His approach was to demonstrate church teachings which had been taught infallibly but which have been subsequently proven false. Toward this end, he used as a paradigmatic case, Pope Paul VI's teaching on the sinfulness of artificial contraception as proposed in *Humanae vitae.* Since, he maintained, this teaching was proposed infallibly and since the consensus among theologians is that this teaching is false, the church's teaching on infallibility must itself be false. However, Küng did not suggest that it was Pope Paul's teaching on the prohibition of artificial contraception in *Humanae vitae* which was itself infallible; that is, he was not proposing the possibility of an infallible ordinary papal magisterium. Rather, he suggested that Paul VI was swayed by the minority report's contention that this teaching had already fulfilled the conditions for an infallible teaching of the ordinary universal magisterium of bishops. Küng concluded that Pope Paul was not persuaded by the majority report, but rather found compelling the minority report's claim that the consistent teaching of the church since Pius XI's *Casti connubii* was irreformable. Küng put a lot of weight on the position and argumentation of the minority report since the report's position was the one which Pope Paul adopted. But what exactly was the argument of the minority report?

In brief, the minority report refuted the majority's application of the notion of the development of dogma.[27] According to the minority, an examination of the circumstances surrounding *Casti connubii* established that the arguments to which Pope Pius XI responded were not substantially different from those being proposed at present. Changing historical circumstances simply were not determinative. If one was advocating a change in the church's position this left only one other alternative: the determination that Pope Pius XI erred in *Casti connubii.* Now this was not an impossibility; the church's error in the Galileo affair was commonly acknowledged by theologians. Did *Casti connubii* represent another Galileo affair? The minority report concluded to the negative. For where the Galileo matter was a relatively peripheral doctrinal controversy, Pius XI, and following him, Pius XII, had condemned the use of artificial contraception "under the pain of eternal punishment."[28] To admit error in this matter was to admit that the church had seriously misguided thousands of Catholics in a serious matter of morals. Furthermore, the minority report offered considerable documentary evidence demonstrating the consistency with which the church had taught the sinfulness of artificial contraception. The minority report was, in fact, indirectly appealing to the infallibility of the ordinary universal magisterium:

> The truth of this teaching stems from the fact that it has been proposed with such constancy, with such universality, with such obligatory force, always and everywhere, as something to be held and followed by the faithful. Technical and juridical investigation into the irreformability and infallibility of *Casti connubii* . . . distracts from the central question and even prejudices the question.[29]

The very universality of the teaching demonstrated that it had already been taught by the whole church infallibly.

Küng found the argument of the minority commission persuasive. When he examined the conditions contained in *Lumen gentium* #25, he concluded that they had been fulfilled in the church's teaching on contraception. The bishops had been in agreement on the question of contraception for at least one and a half centuries, they were teaching authoritatively not as private doctors, the doctrine being taught pertained to faith and morals, and as the prohibition was taught under pain of eternal punishment, it was obviously taught as a doctrine to be held definitively.[30] Having concluded in favor of the infallibility of the prohibition against artificial contraception in accord with the conditions set forth in *Lumen gentium* #25, Küng was then in a position to employ the consensus of moral theologians against the teaching of *Humanae vitae* in order to discredit the church's whole teaching on infallibility.

The Tübingen theologian's book sparked an enormous controversy and much of the attention was drawn to his treatment of the infallibility of the teaching on contraception. Karl Rahner was among the critics. An article in *Stimmen der Zeit* commenced a somewhat acrimonious debate between Rahner and Küng; the Jesuit assailed Küng's conclusion that the teaching on contraception had been taught infallibly.[31] He exposed what he believed to be the basic flaw in Küng's argument: the assumption that because the minority report claimed the infallibility of this teaching, (1) Paul VI must have accepted the argument of the minority report since his conclusion coincided with theirs, and (2) that the minority report's ascription of infallibility to this particular teaching in itself made that teaching infallible.[32] With respect to the first point, Rahner contended that Küng had overlooked the significant fact that Paul VI did not employ the minority report's line of argument in *Humanae vitae*. In fact, Küng has placed the whole weight of his argument on a presupposition regarding Paul VI's response to the minority report which is unsubstantiated. There is no evidence for assuming that the pope accepted the minority report's argument in its entirety. Furthermore, even if the pope was in sympathy with the minority report's line of argumentation, Küng failed to recognize the possibility that the pope might have considered the minority report to be less than compelling and therefore chose to take a more modest and prudent approach, one which did not preclude further development on the matter.

Rahner also challenged Küng's assumption that the argument of the minority report itself was valid. One of the key difficulties with the minority report's line of argument was its assumption that a simple consensus among the bishops on a doctrinal matter was a sufficient condition for the infallibility of ordinary teaching. This ignores the import of the *tamquam definitive tenendam* qualification in *Lumen gentium* #25. Rahner noted that many church teachings have been taught unanimously by the bishops, but not explicitly *as irreformable*.[33] One cannot conclude that a general teaching of the church, proposed without serious dissent, is for that reason alone irreformable. In Küng's response to Rahner's critique, the Tübingen theologian claimed, consonant with the contention of the minority report, that the fact that the church taught the sinfulness of contraception "under pain of eternal punishment" fulfilled the demands of the *tamquam definitive tenendam* condition.[34] Yet this is by no means self-evident. In the moral life, the church has often been faced with the responsibility of teaching without absolute certitude on matters which may have serious moral consequences for the believer. One might argue, for example, that the church's earlier teaching on the licitness of slave-ownership might have had equally serious consequences for the believer. The rigid division of church teaching into two distinct categories, infallible teaching and mere theological opinion which Küng's view suggests, is inadequate. In most instances church teaching will be reckoned as more authoritative than mere opinion, but less authoritative than that of infallible or irreformable teaching. The Küng/Rahner debate brought to the fore the real difficulties involved in applying the Second Vatican Council's teaching on the ordinary universal magisterium. Rahner's response to Küng aptly highlighted the crucial significance of the *tamquam definitive tenendam* condition in any attempt to assert the irreformability of a teaching based on the unanimous witness of tradition.

It goes without saying that Hans Küng's perspective on the church's teaching on contraception remains somewhat peculiar. He wished to assert that the church's teaching fulfilled the criteria for infallible teaching of the ordinary universal magisterium only so that he might disprove the validity of infallibility itself. This perspective led to a rather skewed consideration of the question. Rahner himself observed:

> Accordingly, I must say in all honesty that it is incomprehensible to me how Küng can assert so quickly and so apodictically that the teaching against artificial birth control was a dogma of the ordinary magisterium before Paul VI. Please excuse me for having the impression: In order to prove his thesis, Küng is happy over every church teaching that can be shown to be false and at the same time and with any probability can be established as "defined dogma" in any form whatsoever.[35]

However, Küng was not the last to claim that the prohibition of contraception had been taught by the ordinary universal magisterium.

Germain Grisez and John C. Ford

Eight years after the publication of Küng's book John C. Ford and Germain Grisez, a moral theologian and a moral philosopher, published an article in *Theological Studies* in which they advanced an argument not unlike that of Küng, but with quite a different intention.[36] More than did Küng, Ford and Grisez offered a detailed analysis of the pertinent text in *Lumen gentium* #25. They claim to find in that article four specific conditions which function as a criteriology for determining the teaching of the ordinary universal magisterium. They then maintain that the prohibition of contraception has satisfied these four conditions.

The First Condition: The Subject of the Ordinary Universal Magisterium

The authors contend that in the exercise of the ordinary universal magisterium the bishops need not act in a "strictly collegial manner." Yet, as with the *Nota Explicativa Praevia,* they do not define what they understand a "strict collegial act" to mean. Their point, apparently, is that the teaching of the ordinary universal magisterium need not be seen as one distinct act, as is the case with a statement of a universal synod.

The Second Condition: The Object of the Ordinary Universal Magisterium

Grisez and Ford conclude that there is nothing in the conciliar documents which would preclude specific moral norms from being included in the expression "faith and morals." Indeed they find warrant for their position in the following statement of *Gaudium et spes* regarding the regulation of birth:

> Relying on these principles, sons of the Church may not undertake methods of regulating procreation which are found blameworthy by the teaching authority of the Church in its unfolding of the divine law.[37]

From this they conclude that the conciliar bishops believed themselves to possess a teaching competency in moral matters.

The question, however, is much more complicated than Ford and Grisez admit. First, few question the church's competency to teach on moral matters in the manner demonstrated in *Gaudium et spes.* The church is certainly able to guide the faithful in the moral life and is given the assistance of the Holy Spirit in the exercise of its authoritative magisterium precisely for this task. But can the church teach *infallibly* on moral matters and, more importantly, if so, does this pertain to all moral matters? Or, as the question has most commonly been posed, are all the precepts of the natural law a proper object of infallible teaching? For Ford and Grisez the answer is clear: in *Lumen gentium* #25 the object of the infallible magisterium is explicitly not limited to questions of faith but is extended to the moral life as well. This includes concrete moral norms.

The phrase *fides et mores* has a long history in Catholic tradition. Piet Fransen has demonstrated that since the time of Trent the phrase has been employed to assert the church's right to guide the Christian in the moral life. The expression was primarily concerned with moral discipline rather than moral principles.[38] This reading is confirmed by the famous *relatio* of Bishop Gasser, spokesperson for the *Deputatio de Fide* at Vatican I. In response to a proposal to replace the phrase "moral matters" with the phrase "principles of morals" Bishop Gasser responded that principles of morals may belong to a natural morality of goodness and do not necessarily pertain to revelation.[39] According to John Mahoney, Bishop Gasser's response was motivated by a desire to avoid clarifying for the council fathers the precise meaning of *mores*. He further contends that this "skirting of the issue" on the part of Bishop Gasser has contributed in no small degree to the contemporary confusion on the matter.[40] Sullivan has furthered this argument from tradition by highlighting the significance of a particular deletion of a passage found in the schema on the church offered by the preparatory commission at Vatican II. The original text defended the church's prerogative to teach infallibly in interpreting the natural law. It is Sullivan's contention that the deletion of such an important claim reflected the council members' unwillingness to commit themselves to this prerogative.[41]

Admittedly, since the sixteenth century it has not been unusual for Catholic theologians to teach that the entirety of the natural law belonged to revelation.[42] In the nineteenth century, Joseph Kleutgen would claim that the natural law belonged to revelation and therefore could be taught infallibly by the church:

> It is beyond doubt that the church is just as infallible in the teaching of morals as in the teaching of the faith. Thus, to be sure, it cannot err when, for example, it pronounces a statement to be unlawful or determines what the divine law pre-

scribes for a valid reception of a sacrament. Because both the
positive law and the natural law is contained in revelation, the
teaching of morals also belongs to the teaching of the faith and
the infallibility of the church in its explanation can be derived
from its teaching authority. . . .[43]

For most contemporary theologians it is accepted that insofar
as the natural law does belong to revelation it is the proper object of
infallible teaching, but for these same theologians it is no longer
self-evident that the whole of the natural law in fact belongs to
revelation.[44] Clearly many concrete moral norms, such as the prohibition of contraception, cannot be found in scripture and are not
formally revealed. Could they, however, belong to the secondary
object of infallibility, that is, to teachings which while not formally
revealed are both closely connected to revelation and are necessary
for its safeguarding? This is the claim of Ford and Grisez.

We do not assert that the norm [on contraception] is divinely
revealed. This question is one from which we have prescinded.
Our position rather is this: if the norm is not contained in revelation, it is at least connected with it as a truth required to guard
the deposit as inviolable and to expound it with fidelity.[45]

Ford and Grisez attempt to demonstrate the manner in which
this teaching is connected to revelation by citing biblical condemnations which are analogous to the prohibition of contraception. If
the story of Onan (Gen 38:9–10), for example, cannot be considered directly as a condemnation of contraception, nevertheless it
bears a sufficiently close relationship to the church's condemnation
of contraception to sustain the contention that the teaching on
contraception is at least connected with revelation. The authors,
however, have provided no compelling argument for the church's
teaching on contraception being *necessary* for the preservation of
revelation. It is not sufficient that a matter be *useful* for the defense
of revelation, it must be *necessary* for revelation's safeguard.[46]

While this complex issue cannot be treated fully here, there is
serious reason to question whether such an argument can be made
for any concrete moral norm. A close examination of the character
of specific moral norms suggests that they depend for their intelligi-

bility to a large extent on changing social, political and interpersonal contexts. These norms are often not derived in a purely deductive fashion from first principles but may arise inductively in a more complex personal and existential mode. Consequently, while universal norms, or the Thomistic *principia per se nota,* may belong to the object of infallible teaching, the same cannot be said of specific moral norms.[47]

The Third Condition: The Required Universality and Unanimity of Episcopal Teaching

Lumen gentium #25 states that it is necessary for the exercise of the ordinary universal magisterium that the bishops be united in judgment that a teaching is to be held definitively. According to Grisez and Ford this condition does not demand a mathematical episcopal unanimity of the kind which could be broken by the dissent of one bishop. Rather, it refers to a moral unanimity the exact requirements for which the authors do not outline. Neither is the universality of the teaching demanded here rendered null by a present lack of consensus among the bishops on a matter such as the condemnation of contraception.

> What is once infallibly proposed must always afterword be accepted with absolute assurance of its truth. Once the truth about what Christ commanded has been proclaimed infallibly, every opinion incompatible with it must always afterward be excluded from gaining true normative force for the faith and life of the Church with which Christ remains forever.[48]

In other words, as long as the conditions for the teaching of the ordinary universal magisterium have been met in the past, any subsequent lack of consensus among the bishops is irrelevant. But what is required concretely for this universality?

> The evidence must be this: that a certain point of teaching has been proposed by bishops repeatedly, in different times, in different places, in response to different challenges, that the bishops have articulated and defended this point of teaching in different intellectual frameworks, perhaps reinforcing it with

varying disciplinary measures. Moreover, there must be no evidence that the point of teaching has ever been questioned or denied by any bishop or by anyone else authorized to participate in the Church's teaching mission without eliciting an admonition and a reaffirmation of what had been universally taught. Obviously, one cannot expect or demand positive evidence that every bishop has proposed the same teaching; available historical sources always will fall short of establishing so extensive a set of factual conclusions. To demand such evidence would be to set up an arbitrary barrier against every appeal to tradition.[49]

This set of criteria for unanimity in episcopal teaching requires two responses: the first concerning the formal criteria proposed here and the second concerning whether the church's teaching on contraception has met these criteria.

Much like the first condition, this third condition concerns the bond of communion which exists among the bishops (and including the bishop of Rome). We examined earlier the compelling case made by Rahner and Pissarek-Hudelist that the exercise of the ordinary universal magisterium constituted a "strictly collegial act." Regardless of the concerns expressed in the *Nota Explicativa Praevia,* the exercise of the infallible teaching of bishops must be a *truly* collegial act. In other words, it cannot be the mere aggregate of the teachings of individual bishops but must be an exercise of the bishops teaching as a college. Yet Grisez and Ford do not appear to have adequately grappled with the question of what constitutes a true exercise of the episcopal college.

The true ecclesiological consequences of a silent or passive assent on the part of many bishops is given short shrift in Grisez and Ford's study. Yet here lies the heart of the difficulties: the problem of adequately identifying the character of a collegial act. For example, Francis Sullivan has remarked that "it is possible that some ordinary papal teaching, while not openly contradicted, might be given a rather passive reception or might even be qualified by a significant number of bishops."[50] In fact, we might identify at least four different kinds of episcopal responses which could all seriously qualify the nature of the reception to be attributed to the bishops. The first response would involve a qualified or conditioned reception due to a lack of interest or experience on the part of the bishops. One might think of numerous instances in history where a significant number of bishops have lacked the requisite experience to give a teaching anything more than a passive reception. One obvious example would be the response of many European bishops to the Roman treatment of the seventeenth and eighteenth century Chinese rites controversy. Few bishops possessed the requisite knowledge and experience to adequately respond to the papal teaching. A second form of qualified reception would be the result of a bishop's lack of education. By the nineteenth century the papacy was becoming increasingly involved in complex theological debates previously reserved to scholarly discussion. The result was a series of papal pronouncements on philosophical issues the complexity of which might easily have eluded many bishops. One might recall here the condemnations of Günther and Hermes in the first half of the nineteenth century and the later condemnations of modernism in *Lamentabili* and *Pascendi* (1907). In such a situation, many a bishop's response to these papal teachings would have been little more than a "passive reception."

A third qualified episcopal reception could be attributed to Roman repression of theological discussion regarding a particular issue. This repression might prevent bishops from being sufficiently informed of the historical or theological dimensions of a particular issue. The repression of new forms of biblical scholarship in the early twentieth century, for example, might have prevented bishops from responding adequately to the Pontifical Biblical Commission's numerous decisions between 1905 and 1915 on questions regarding biblical authorship and interpretation. While no bishops publicly dissented from these teachings, their reception would have to be seriously qualified, in light of the suppression of essential information provided by the tools of historical criticism. Finally, one might identify as a fourth species of qualified reception by bishops the response given under the subtle and sometimes not so subtle coercion of Rome. A cursory review of church history will provide numerous examples of a not infrequent coercion exercised by the Holy See and the Roman curia. Leo Cardinal Suenens, the Belgian cardinal who was among the most influential figures at Vatican II, offered the most succinct statement regarding this kind of coercion:

> We have heard arguments based on "what the bishops all taught for decades." Well, the bishops did defend the classical position. But it was one imposed on them by authority. The bishops didn't study the pros and cons. They received directives, they bowed to them, and they tried to explain them to their congregations.[51]

The dangers of this coercion cannot be exaggerated. As André Naud has pointed out in his discussion of the necessity of episcopal freedom to disagree with the papacy:

> The very serious problem which this vision of the relations between the magisterium of the bishops and that of Rome poses is that the magisterium of bishops is finding itself eclipsed and even completely erased. . . . That which disappears, in one blow, is the collegial dimension of magisterial teaching inasmuch as it implies a true co-responsibility concerning the contents of teaching. When the bishops are considered as nothing more than the faithful with respect to papal teaching, they are no longer true participants in the magisterial function of the church.[52]

All four of these forms of qualified reception would seriously compromise the import of a unanimous witness to a particular teaching. All would have to be considered in any attempt to assess episcopal unanimity.

The second response to Ford and Grisez's interpretation of this condition demonstrates the difficulties raised in the first response. Ford and Grisez claim that the requirement for unanimity of church teaching has been fulfilled in the case of the church's teaching on contraception. Yet four years after the publication of the Grisez/Ford essay, Garth Hallett offered a critical response to their thesis, focusing on their claim to a sufficient unanimity in tradition.[53] Hallett did not dispute matters of morals being a suitable object of magisterial teaching, but he did contend that the concrete determination of the content of moral norms has been oversimplified due to the assumption that moral statements function like historical or scientific statements and are primarily stable in their descriptive content.

Those who stress the unanimity in the tradition regarding the church's teaching on contraception often draw support from the historical study of John Noonan.[54] Noonan has offered an impressive case for the consistency of church teaching on this topic throughout the church's history. Yet Hallett contends that this unanimity is in part illusory because it does not adequately distinguish between the descriptive and the prescriptive content of church teaching. There can be little question that the church has consistently prohibited the use of contraception—the prescriptive element of the teaching has remained relatively stable. Yet the descriptive element has been quite variant, Hallett contends. Noonan's own study has indirectly corroborated Hallett's judgment, for Noonan has noted that in the early church the prohibition of contraception was oriented toward the principal purpose of marriage, namely procreation. Thus intercourse for the pregnant and sterile was condemned as it lacked the justifying end of procreation. Yet later in the tradition, and most notably in *Casti connubii,* sexual relations were to be permitted in such situations because they did not contravene the "nature of the act." Hallett has suggested that with neo-scholasticism a subtle shift occurred in the treatment of contraception, a shift from the purpose to the manner of the act. While the neo-scholastics couched their analyses in teleological language, it was in fact a carefully circumscribed teleology strictly bounded by a physicalist analysis of what constituted a "natural act." Noonan himself noted the irony in the fact that, because of their more consistent teleological perspective, the early church fathers were compelled to condemn the one method of contraception (periodic abstinence) which the neo-scholastic theologians approved.[55] Hallett claimed then that in church tradition, the precise character of the immorality of a contraceptive marital act differed significantly. For some it contravened the primary end of marriage, whereas for others it violated the physical nature of the sexual act. "Thus for the critic, at least within this discussion, 'moral' and 'immoral' now say something different descriptively; they may still condemn or condone, but beneath the common expressions we discern no common descriptive content present from the start."[56] Hallett further contended that the kind of episcopal unanimity required for the exercise of the ordinary universal magisterium seemed to require a unanimity throughout tradition in the descriptive rather than the prescriptive content of the moral norm.[57]

Another argument which placed a good deal of weight on the unanimity of the tradition on contraception contended that the Holy Spirit would not have permitted the church to err so consistently in its divine mission. This argument was employed by the minority report of the papal commission on birth regulation and before that it was offered by John Ford and Gerald Kelly in their much used text on marriage questions:

> [W]e can show the binding force, the finality, of the tradition simply by showing that during the last century and a half—a truly crucial period as regards marital morality—the church has constantly and emphatically taught that contraception is a grave violation of the law of God. For, if the teaching of the Catholic Church on a point so profoundly and intimately connected with the salvation of millions of souls has been the same over such a long period of time, the inevitable conclusion must be that that teaching is true and unchangeable. Otherwise the Church which God has established to interpret the moral law and to guide souls on the way of salvation would be failing substantially in its divine mission.[58]

This argument raises the question of how much error the Holy Spirit is willing to permit in the church. Michael Dummett cautions,

> [b]ut I should maintain that, precisely because no one has carried out a sufficiently careful and honest investigation of the limits beyond which we cannot, consistent with our faith, suppose the church to have gone astray, no one really knows at present whether this argument of the minority [minority report of the papal commission on birth regulation] is correct or not. . . .[59]

Church history teaches us that any assessment of the limits beyond which the Spirit would protect the church from harm must be undertaken with the utmost caution.

In summary, the task of ascertaining unanimity in episcopal teaching is a much more difficult matter than Grisez and Ford admit. This already difficult task becomes even more onerous when one seriously considers the actual application of the fourth condition as outlined in *Lumen gentium* #25.

The Fourth Condition: That a Teaching Be Proposed as a Matter "to Be Held Definitively"

The fourth condition holds that the bishops teach infallibly when they unanimously teach with the intention that the matter taught be "held definitively." We have already examined the understanding of several commentators regarding this key phrase. Grisez and Ford, however, offer a different reading.

> A point of teaching surely is proposed as one to be held definitively if a bishop proposes it in the following way: not at his option but as part of his duty to hand on the teaching he has received; not as doubtful or even as very probable but as certainly true; and not as one which the faithful are free to accept or to reject but as one which every Catholic must accept.[60]

This interpretation of *tamquam definitive tenendam* would effectively subsume almost all of the church's authoritative but non-infallible teaching under the infallible ordinary universal magisterium. If one examines official articulations of authoritative non-infallible church teaching (in other words, the vast majority of church teaching), it is seldom if ever proposed as something which the faithful is "free to accept or reject." It is the character of such authoritative teaching that the believer is always to give to it a presumption of truth with confidence in the assistance of the Holy Spirit. Virtually all authoritative teaching is taught as "certainly true"; the believer may confidently act on the general presumption of truth.[61] But this theological note has never denoted infallible teaching; rather, it has been attached to teaching upon which the believer may rely in confidence but which does not absolutely exclude the remote possibility of error. As Sullivan has observed: "if the argument proposed by Ford, Grisez and Küng were valid, it would mean that the Church could not declare any mode of conduct gravely wrong unless it were prepared to make an irreversible judgment on the matter."[62]

It is this "all or nothing" approach to church teaching which was the occasion for Congar's observation (already cited in chapter 5) regarding a growing tendency to inflate the category of infallible teaching, expanding it to such a degree as to exclude the "immense domain of partial truth, of probable certitude, of research and approximations, or even of the very precious truth not protected from the risks of human finitude."[63] Church teaching is proclaimed with varying degrees of authority and certitude. It is a serious misunderstanding of the nature of church authority to assume that the church possesses no authority aside from its power to teach infallibly.

This view of church teaching reflected in the writing of Ford, Grisez and others,[64] appears to have overlooked the obvious, namely, that an infallible dogma is not necessarily truer than a doctrine taught authoritatively. That the church has yet to irrevocably commit itself to a doctrine does not necessarily make it any less true, it simply reflects the church's relative commitment to the doctrine at that point in time. Ladislas Örsy has made a similar point:

> An infallible "determination" (ancient councils preferred that term to "definition") means that a point of belief has been marked, specially authenticated; but there are other points which have not been so singled out yet are no less true than those so "determined."[65]

Confusions regarding the distinction between the infallible and the fallible, and between truth and falsity seem to be lurking behind the theology of the magisterium found in the writings of Ford and Grisez.

The Ordinary Universal Magisterium in the New Code of Canon Law

This book explores the theologies of the ordinary universal magisterium which have appeared since its first ecclesiastical articulation in the mid-nineteenth century. It is not an exhaustive exegetical study of ecclesiastical texts. Nevertheless, some consideration must be given to the 1983 Code of Canon Law precisely because its formulations possess a certain normative status.

The new Code of Canon Law appeared in 1983, ending a process of revision begun when Pope John XXIII announced in 1959 both the impending convocation of a new ecumenical council and the creation of a pontifical commission whose task it would be to revise the 1917 Code of Canon Law. As it turned out, even without Pope John's decision, so far-reaching were the changes brought about by the council, that the establishment of a new code would have been necessary in any event in order to implement and give juridical form to the fruits of the council. At the opening session of the pontifical commission for the development of the new code Pope Paul VI formally linked the new code with the fruits of the council:

> Now, however, with changing conditions—for life seems to evolve more rapidly—canon law must be prudently reformed; specifically, it must be accommodated to a new way of thinking proper to the Second Ecumenical Council of the Vatican, in which the pastoral care and new needs of the people of God are met.[66]

This close relationship between the council and the code is clear throughout the new canons, many of which are taken verbatim from conciliar statements. Among the contributions of the council to find their way into the revised code was the re-contextualizing of the magisterium.

The new code is comprised of seven books, the third of which is devoted completely to the teaching office of the church. This book must be read, however, in the context of Book II on the People of God. In that book the second section is devoted to the hierarchical constitution of the church. It first considers the supreme authority in the church, and assumes a conception of the relationship between the papacy and the episcopal college which is drawn from the *Nota Explicativa Praevia*. The revised code employs the *Nota's* theory of two inadequately distinct subjects of the one supreme authority. At the same time, in canons 331–34, it stresses the independent prerogatives of the pope over against the episcopal college. In the context of this clear delineation of the powers and prerogatives of the pope, the bishop's role is clearly muted. Canon 334 proposes that the bishops only "assist" the pope in his primacy:

> In exercising his office the Roman Pontiff is assisted by the bishops who aid him in various ways and among these is the synod of bishops; moreover the cardinals assist him as do other persons and other institutes according to the needs of the times; all these persons and institutes, in his name and by his authority, carry out the task committed to them for the good of all the churches, according to the norms defined by law.[67]

The dangers of the theory of two inadequately distinct subjects are evident in this passage, where all too often this theory degenerates into a view which subordinates the episcopacy to the papacy. In this canon, the bishops, for example, are grouped together with a variety of other persons and institutes; their unique status as sharers in the supreme authority of the church is completely overlooked.[68]

In canons 336–37 the code turns directly to a consideration of the episcopal college. In particular, canon 337 outlines the college's exercise of its supreme authority, drawing its language substantially from *Lumen gentium* #22. The canon reads as follows:

> 1. The college of bishops exercises power over the universal Church in a solemn manner in an ecumenical council.
> 2. The college exercises the same power through the united action of the bishops dispersed in the world, which action as such has been inaugurated or has been freely accepted by the Roman Pontiff so that a truly collegial act results.
> 3. It is for the Roman Pontiff, in keeping with the needs of the church, to select and promote the ways by which the college of bishops is to exercise collegially its function regarding the universal Church.

A preeminent role is given to the papacy in the exercise of the ordinary universal magisterium of the bishops. It presumes the leadership of the pope, not just in inaugurating or accepting a collegial activity, but also in actually determining the various modes by which the college will exercise its proper authority. Canon 341.2 further restricts the ordinary exercise of the episcopal college:

> For decrees which the college of bishops issues to have obliga-
> tory force this same confirmation and promulgation [as that
> required for decrees of an ecumenical council] is needed, when
> the college takes collegial action in another manner, initiated or
> freely accepted by the Roman Pontiff.

At this point the code has clearly gone beyond *Lumen gentium*
#22. The council bishops stated in the dogmatic constitution that
papal acceptance, even without formal approbation, would be sufficient for an action to be deemed truly collegial. Canon 341 seems
to require a much more formal approbation in the phrase *confir-
matione et promulgatione*. It apparently assumes that the kind of
approbation required for conciliar decrees will be applied to the
collegial action of the bishops outside of a council. That the looser
requirement of a simple papal acceptance of an action, found in
earlier versions of canon 341, was explicitly dropped further
strengthens the impression that the commission fully intended this
more restrictive reading of the exercise of the supreme authority of
the episcopal college outside of council.[69]

Finally we must make a more architectonic observation regarding Book II. The order of topics considered suggests a continuation of the regrettable tendency of Vatican II to give priority to the
universal church over the local church. Book II began with a consideration of the faithful followed by a treatment of the supreme authority in the church exercised, first by the pope alone, and then by
the episcopal college. Only after these treatments is the place of the
local church given consideration. Hervé Legrand has commented
on the difficulties which this structure suggests.

> . . . [H]ow can one establish institutionally and even at the
> same time theologically, what the laity and the clerics, a pope, a
> bishop and the college of bishops are, before knowing what the
> local Church is and what the communion of the Churches
> represent?[70]

The consequence of this priority of the universal church over the
local church is a view of the episcopal college and the papacy as
quasi-independent governing organs which possess an authority
exercised *over* rather than *within* the communion of churches. We
shall return to this problem in chapter 7.

The teaching authority of the bishops is taken up in much greater detail in the third book of the revised code. The explicit consideration of the ordinary universal magisterium is located in canon 749, one of nine prefatory canons for this book which outlines the rights and responsibilities of the church's teaching authority. There, in the second paragraph, the code reads:

> The college of bishops also possesses infallible teaching author- ity when the bishops exercise their teaching office gathered to- gether in an ecumenical council when, as teachers and judges of faith and morals, they declare that for the universal Church a doctrine of faith or morals must be definitively held; they also exercise it scattered throughout the world but united in a bond of communion among themselves and with the successor of Peter when together with that same Roman Pontiff in their capacity as authentic teachers of faith and morals they agree on an opinion to be held as definitive.[71]

There is little in this canon which is new; it was drawn explic- itly from the old canon 1323.1, the pertinent passages in *Lumen gentium* #25 and the third chapter of *Dei Filius*. The *Lex Ecclesiae Fundamentalis* (a general canonical constitution originally in- tended for the whole church but eventually subsumed into the revised code) had included in this canon an additional subsection on the infallibility of the whole people of God in believing. The subsection was deleted in favor of an increased emphasis on the teaching role of the magisterium.[72] Canon 750, however, contains a significant reference to the role of the faithful:

> All that is contained in the written word of God or in tradition, that is, in the one deposit of faith entrusted to the Church and also proposed as divinely revealed either by the solemn magis- terium of the Church or by its ordinary and universal magiste- rium, must be believed with divine and catholic faith; it is man- ifested by the common adherence of the Christian faithful under the leadership of the sacred magisterium; therefore, all are bound to avoid any doctrines whatever which are contrary to these truths.

While most references to the infallibility of the *sensus fidelium* were deleted in the final text of the new code, this canon retains a veiled reference to a notion of "reception." The infallibility of the church teaching, either in its ordinary or extraordinary mode, will be "manifested in the adherence of the faithful."[73] This clause recalls the allusion to the "reception" of theologians in *Tuas libenter.* Vacant, too, had contended that the faith of the people might serve as a sign of infallible teaching. Of course the Latin *adhaesione* in this text does not have quite the active meaning of the word *sensus,* nevertheless, this canon appears to have made a significant advance over the formulations found in *Lumen gentium* #25 where, in connection with the ordinary universal magisterium, no explicit mention is made of that teachings' manifestation in the faithful.

The 1983 code's consideration of the ordinary universal magisterium reflects a certain internal tension. While canon 750 does propose the adherence of the faithful as a possible criterion for discerning the teaching of the ordinary universal magisterium, in the main, the intent of the code seems to be to restrict the ordinary exercise of the episcopal college by stressing the active role of the papacy in any collegial activity. This is in keeping with a neo-scholastic view of the nature and role of the episcopal college which subordinates the bishops to the pope. Furthermore, by attenuating the role of the local church in favor of the universal church, the code perpetuates one of the most serious ecclesiological difficulties of Vatican II and risks conceptualizing the episcopal college as an independent organ of the church divorced from the communion of the churches.

Conclusion

Hermann Pottmeyer has written perceptively of the transitional character of the Second Vatican Council.[74] At each step, tentative forays toward an ecclesiology of communion were juxtaposed, often side by side, with reaffirmations of a pre-conciliar ecclesiology which bore the stamp of Roman centralization and a fundamentally hierarchial conception of the nature and mission of the church. This methodology of juxtaposition would inevitably give rise to problems of internal coherence with respect to some of the council's formulations. The debates generated by the attempt to apply *Lumen gentium* #25 to the church's teaching on artificial contraception suggest that contemporary ecclesiology has yet to completely extricate itself from the peculiar problematic which the teaching on the ordinary universal magisterium poses: how to recognize a teaching proposed "definitively" which is not solemnly defined. The controversy surrounding *Humanae vitae* provided the most significant test case to date regarding Vatican II's formulation of this teaching.[75] The ecclesiological debates spawned by that encyclical highlighted a number of fundamental issues.

Clearly more attention needs to be given to the character of a "collegial act." Must it be defined juridically, as in the *Nota,* or does it admit more fluidity of expression? What role must the pope play in a true collegial act? Canon 341.2 of the 1983 Code assigns a much more formal role for the pope than seems to be demanded by *Lumen gentium.* How does one reconcile the permanent existence of the episcopal college with only a periodic exercise of collegiality? While the council made significant advances in its teaching on episcopal collegiality and on the universal church as a communion of churches, it was unable to connect these two notions in any systematic fashion.[76] An adequate conceptualization of the relationship between episcopal collegiality and the communion of the churches is necessary for understanding the nature of the college's teaching authority and its possible modes of exercise outside of council.

The contraception case has also highlighted the need for a more thorough consideration of the significance of the qualifying phrase *tamquam definitive tenendam* in the conciliar bishops' articulation of the ordinary universal magisterium. Rahner, Sullivan, et al., have succeeded in demonstrating the intent of the council bishops to utilize this phrase as a means of distinguishing teaching proposed *irrevocabiliter* from that only taught authoritatively. Yet while these theologians have exposed the inadequacy of Grisez and Ford's criteriological use of *Lumen gentium* #25, they have failed to provide their own criteriology for ascertaining the difference between teachings taught by the bishops irrevocably and those only taught authoritatively.

In the past six chapters we have traced the development in the understanding of the ordinary universal magisterium as a distinct mode of church teaching since its first ecclesiastical formulation. We have highlighted key questions which have not been adequately resolved and have suggested that many of these problematic aspects of the church's teaching on the matter are derived from an inadequately developed theology of the episcopacy. In the next chapter we will consider possibilities for a more fully developed ecclesiology which might provide a more helpful context for evaluating the function and status of the ordinary universal magisterium in the teaching ministry of the church.

The Church as a
Communio Ecclesiarum

One of the themes of this book has been the need for an adequate theology of the episcopacy as the necessary foundation for constructing a theology of the ordinary universal magisterium. We have suggested earlier that an ecclesiology of communion might provide a helpful foundation for a treatment of the episcopacy. This chapter will offer as at least a first step in this direction a consideration of the bishops' relationship to both the episcopal college and the local churches, followed by a treatment of the papacy's role within the episcopal college.

Membership in the Episcopal College and the College's Relationship to the Communion of Churches

The study of the neo-scholastic manual tradition in chapter 3 revealed a theology of the episcopacy dominated by the juridical issues of apostolic succession and episcopal jurisdiction. The treatment of the episcopacy in Franzelin's *Theses De Ecclesia Christi* was typical; the authority of the bishops and of the episcopal college was deduced from the assumption that the episcopal college was itself the successor to the apostolic college.[1] It was not the individual bishops who were successors to the individual apostles, rather it was the college of bishops as a whole which succeeded the college of apostles. This conception of apostolic succession reflected the primacy of the universal church over the local church in the ecclesiology of the manuals.

A Theology of the Episcopal College Founded on the Priority of the Universal Church

It would be a mistake, however, to assume that this view of the episcopacy was limited to the manualists. More recently, Karl

Rahner has offered much the same theology. The German theologian adopted an approach not unlike Franzelin in holding that since the episcopal college is the successor of the apostolic college, and since the Twelve derived their apostolicity not from their individual call but from their membership in the college of apostles, it follows that the bishops are first members of the episcopal college before they are heads of local churches.[2]

> The college of bishops, as successor of the apostolic college, takes priority over the individual bishops, their rights and responsibilities. . . . This follows first of all from the truth that the Church (even as visibly constituted) is primarily *one* (although, while one, she contains a basic pluralism in the differentiation of her members). And she is one, not merely through the activity of the individual faithful or individual churches (to which the nature of the Church is prior), as though these had created her unity by forming themselves into an association, but because she was originally founded as one and always so exists.[3]

Elsewhere he outlined several of the implications which follow from this schematization. Given the college's relationship to the universal church, its leadership takes on the character of an independent instrument of church governance:

> As a college it is not simply the union of *local* bishops as such, but a collegial governing board in the Church which cannot as such derive its authority from the locally limited authority of its members as local bishops.[4]

Rahner's ecclesiology weakened a bishop's relationship to the local church. He admitted that episcopal consecretion entails a pastoral charge, but insisted that this pastoral charge need not be territorial. While a bishop's pastoral charge normally takes the form of an assignment to a local church, it might legitimately be realized in a pastoral charge to some other body: he considered it quite legitimate that the rector of the Catholic University of Louvain or heads of religious orders might be consecrated into the episcopal *ordo*. Titular bishops also possessed the essential pastoral charge because, by reason of membership in the episcopal college, they already had a share in the pastoral responsibility of the whole church.[5] This weakening of the bishop's relationship to the local church leads to the question of the Roman pontiff's own status. Rahner posed the question rhetorically:

> Is the pope supreme pastor of the Church simply and solely because he is Bishop of Rome . . . or is he, at least from a really absolute point of view, logically "simultaneously" or even logically "first" head of the whole church and elected as *such,* so that *together* with this or through it he is also Bishop of Rome?[6]

By stressing the priority of the bishop's relationship to the college over his relationship to the local church, Rahner buttressed an ecclesiology which suggested that the pope's leadership of the whole church has priority over his leadership of the local church of Rome.

At other times Rahner seemed to reverse the priority given to the universal church over the local church. According to Rahner, for example, the local church was the event of the universal church. He wrote: ". . . we can also say that the Church as a whole, where she becomes 'event' in the full sense of the term, is necessarily a local Church. In the local Church the whole Church becomes tangible."[7] This view was further developed in his consideration of the eucharist as the paradigmatic event of the universal church's realization in the local:

> Therefore the Eucharist as an event in a place not only occurs in the Church; the Church herself becomes in the fullest sense an event only in the local celebration of the Eucharist. . . . It is not only true that the Eucharist exists because the Church exists; it is also true, if rightly understood, that the Church exists because the Eucharist exists. The Church is and remains, even as a whole, only because she is actualized again and again in the one all-embracing "event" of herself, that is, in the Eucharist. . . . Therefore a local Church is not brought about by an atomizing division of the world-territory of the universal Church, but by the concentration of the church into her own nature, as "event."[8]

Rahner's theology then, does represent an advance over neo-scholastic ecclesiologies inasmuch as his ecclesiology conceives of the local church not as a part (*pars*) of the universal church but as a realization or manifestation of it. Yet at the same time Rahner continued to view the episcopal college as an instrument of leadership for the universal church *over* the local churches. The bishops are first leaders over the universal church and only secondarily leaders of the local churches. Consequently, the bishops' collegial teaching can too easily be conceived (even if this did not occur in Rahner's own work) as the imposition of doctrine from an external authority. His ecclesiology ultimately failed in its treatment of the episcopal college because it did not employ the category of communion, and explicitly the communion of the churches, as the starting point for ecclesiological reflection.

An Ecclesiology of Communion: The Individual Bishop and the Local Church

For the early church the notion of *communio* was a basic ecclesiological category.[9] In baptism the believer was initiated into a twofold communion: it was at the same time an entrance into the triune life of God and a communion with other believers. The serious disputes over early trinitarian doctrine which transpired over the first six centuries of the church reflected the doctrine of the trinity's central place in Christian life and worship. Faith in the triune God whose very being was personal and relational called for a human participation in that same relational existence. An ecclesiology of communion was grounded in the fundamentally personal and relational character of human existence. Christian community was more than the free gathering of individual believers, it was the necessary realization of the existence to which all Christians were called.

The French Dominican J.M.R. Tillard has explored this theology of communion as realized in a number of contexts, which he calls "registers." These registers include: (1) the immediate human community where diversity is recognized and promoted without leading to division, (2) the historical communion throughout the ages, (3) the coincidence of the one and the many in the celebration of the eucharist, (4) the synodal expressions of the one in the many in the communion of churches, and (5) the participation in the triune divine life of God offered in grace to humankind.[10]

For most of the first millennium a bishop was ordained for a particular community; absolute ordinations would have been unintelligible. The bishop, called and elected by the community as head of the local church, was the servant of ecclesial communion.[11] Within this ecclesiology of communion, each local church, gathered around the eucharistic table under the presidency of the bishop, possessed a full catholicity—understood not as "universality" but as the possession of the fullness of faith. The universal church was manifested in the catholicity of each church, and the communion which they maintained with one another. For the first four centuries, according to Joseph Ratzinger, episcopal collegiality was considered only within the context of this communion among the local churches.[12] Indeed, the early foundations of the episcopacy were grounded not primarily in sacerdotal ministry or in the apostolic succession of the bishops but in pastoral leadership and in the eucharistic presidency of the local community.[13] The ministry of the bishop was manifested in different ways. First, the bishop exercised the ministry of apostolic witness. As pastoral and liturgical leader of the local church, he was called to discern that which was and was not in conformity with the apostolic tradition in the life of the community. Second, the bishop presided at the community's eucharistic celebration, the principal sacrament of communion. Third, the bishop exercised a ministry of representation. In his eucharistic presidency he stood as an icon of Christ surrounded by a *presbyterium* representing the apostolic college. The episcopal *cathedra* was an icon of ecclesial communion. Fourth, this ministry of representation was also realized in the local church's communion with the other churches. The community recognized itself in the bishop and saw itself being borne in the fraternal communion of the bishop with other bishops. Just as around the bishop's altar the many became one in the celebration of the eucharist so, too, the local bishop's interaction with other bishops manifested the communion of the many churches in the one church of Christ.

Much of the ecclesiological work which immediately preceded the Second Vatican Council and has continued to develop since the council has drawn upon the patristic theology of communion in order to develop a fuller theology of the episcopacy. A *communio* ecclesiology yields a theology of the episcopacy in which the bishops have a special responsibility for the authoritative attestation of the apostolic tradition, for teaching God's revelation in Christ. They do this as leaders of churches which are themselves the bearers of apostolicity. From their communities the bishops receive insight into the gospel to which they bear witness. In an ecclesiology of communion, in which the universal is realized in the local, the fundamental locus for this mutual listening is the local church. This dialectic of witness and verification, what Newman described as the *conspiratio fidelium et pastorum*,[14] flourishes within the community with the bishop as the community's *centrum unitatis*. The gospel to which the bishop gives authoritative witness cannot be separated from the community in which it is enfleshed. Francis Sullivan contended that only residential bishops participate in the authoritative magisterium: to support this he appealed to witnesses in the early church.[15] A bishop's authority to teach depended on the possession of a local flock precisely because it was in communion with that community that a bishop was nourished in the apostolic tradition. This does not mean that a bishop exercises an authority delegated by the people, but it does mean that a bishop's authority is grounded in his relationship to the flock. The authority of the bishop remains an authority which arises out of and is exercised in service to the local church. It is manifested not only in the bishop's coordination and direction of the ministries of the local church, but in his listening to and learning from the faithful. Tillard describes the manner in which a bishop exercises his teaching authority within the community according to this *communio* ecclesiology:

> The ordained hierarchical magisterium has as its ordinary organ the bishop of the local church, in *communion* with the bishops of other churches but also in close solidarity with that which the ancient Tradition called its *presbyterium*. This last constitutes the capillary network by which, on the one hand, the questions, the difficulties, the *praxis,* but also the convictions of the *sensus* of the community reach the bishop, and on the other hand, the decisions of the latter (both his own and those of the gathering of the episcopal body of which he is a member) are not only communicated but explained, and if it is required, translated to the community. In a sound ecclesiology of communion the vital osmosis of the faith is effected there, especially at the time of the eucharistic gathering where the

proclamation and explication of the word occupies an important place. . . . The weight of their magisterial word comes of
course undeniably from their proper mission for which they are
responsible, accomplished with a special assistance of the Holy
Spirit; but it comes also from that with which its contents are in
harmony, with that which their churches sense from instinct, in
their *sensus fidei*.[16]

Tillard's theology sets aside the ecclesiology, dominant for a century and a half, which looked to the bishops, and particularly to the
pope, independent of their communities, as the proximate rule of
faith. This neo-scholastic ecclesiology gave little attention to objective tradition and conceived of the exercise of the magisterium as a
determinatio fidei exercised in relative independence from the
practice and reflection of the ministers and all the faithful of the
local churches.

The primacy of the category of communion dictates that the
bishop's teaching authority be exercised as a *testificatio fidei*. The
bishop gives witness to the apostolic tradition preserved in the life
of his church. If his office brings with it the power to teach authoritatively, that which he teaches is, at least in part, received from his
community. The faith which he professes is not his own product,
not an inspired "new addition" to revelation, but is the received,
lived faith of the church.

An Ecclesiology of Communion: The College of Bishops and the Communion of Churches

Thus far we have considered a theology of the teaching authority of the individual bishop within an ecclesiology of communion,
but what of the teaching of the bishops as a college? For the early
church collegiality was fundamentally an expression of the communion of the churches and was manifested in the mutual exchanges
between the churches, particularly with regard to questions pertaining to the extension of eucharistic table fellowship to members
of other communities.[17] By the third century regional synods increasingly offered a forum for the resolution of doctrinal disputes.
The transition from regional synods to ecumenical councils cannot
be easily identified. There did not emerge in the early fourth century some new theology for ecumenical councils. Rather, what had

worked regionally was simply transposed to a larger stage with the emergence of improved communications and a growing recognition of the universality of the church.[18] Often the difference between a regional synod and an ecumenical council has more to do with the subsequent reception of the gathering by the churches than it does with the character of the gathering itself. The subsequent reception was important because the early councils flowed out of a synodal principle in which the council was understood not as an independent organ exercising authority over the churches but as an expression of the ontological unity of the church in its communion.[19] If the bishops exercised authority as a college, this ministry was not conceived as an authority over the local churches, but as a ministry grounded in the churches and oriented toward the united testimony of the apostolic tradition preserved in the faith of each community. Yves Congar has called attention to this synodal principle, which he calls "conciliarity":

> Councils, while creations of the Church, are an expression of the conciliarity which derives from the very nature of the Church, which is to be a communion, *koinonia*. . . . *The underlying meaning of koinonia,* communion, is very close to *metoché,* participation. It is because a number of people share in the same, totally identical realities, that a bond of unity exists between them. . . . A council seeks to express the community of views, the unanimity of the Church on the basis of the local or particular churches . . . whether this unanimity exists implicitly and has to be elicited and made explicit, or has to be sought in order to be expressed.[20]

Theologians from the Orthodox tradition have insisted that the ancient synodal principle rejected any opposition between the local and the universal church. Like the celebration of the eucharist, the ancient synod manifested the coinherence of the one and the many, the universal and the local. To divorce the bishops' magisterial authority from their relationship to their churches would be to set their episcopal authority as an authority over the churches. Early councils were not mandated by juridical processes to insure the proper governance of the church, but were occasional events by which the agreement in faith of the churches was given a concentrated expression.[21] They were not the normal means by which the churches expressed their communion, but were the occasions of its extraordinary expression in the face of threats to the church. Neither were these councils viewed as expressions of papal authority—the first time a pope explicitly ratified a council resolution occurred in the pontificate of Leo I in the fifth century. It would not be until the eleventh century that papal approbation would come to play a major role in ascertaining the ecumenicity of a council.[22] The ecumenical council does not have its origin in the creation of a new form of church governance, rather it emerged gradually as an expression of a more fundamental principle of conciliarity which expressed the communion of the many churches in the one faith. The superimposition of an external authority, as suggested in Rahner's theological understanding of the episcopal college as an independent governing body, represents a separation of episcopal collegiality from the communion of churches. A collegial act, whatever its concrete form and whatever the juridical conditions necessary for its formal realization, must be a manifestation of the communion of the churches.

Theologians who follow the ancient model drawn from this patristic ecclesiology of communion and ground episcopal collegiality in the communion of churches offer a distinct theology of teaching authority. In the fourth and fifth chapters we saw the beginnings of such an approach in the theologies of Newman, Schell and Congar.[23] They sought to overcome the dominant model of the church as a *societas perfecta* in favor of the church as a *congregatio fidelium,* one of the expressions for the church employed by Thomas Aquinas.[24] Newman, for example, understood an ecclesiology of communion to demand a mutual listening between the various organs of the church: the episcopate and papacy, the *schola theologorum* and the *sensus fidelium.* These theologians recognized that it was the whole church which was the bearer of God's word, not just the pope and bishops. This ecclesiology of communion can be employed as a foundation for a theology of teaching authority by firmly grounding that authority within the community. It demands that all church authority be exercised in service to the church. It does not abrogate the role of the pope and bishops but rejects a reduction of the tradition-bearing activity of the church to the pope and bishops alone.

The Understanding of Papal Headship

Vatican I's *Pastor aeternus* asserted the primacy and infallibility of one bishop, the bishop of Rome, and attributed to the papacy supreme authority in the church. Vatican II affirmed the teachings of Vatican I but also clearly affirmed that the college of bishops possessed supreme authority in the church. Since then, one of the fundamental questions in ecclesiology has concerned the relationship of the Roman pontiff to the episcopal college: is one or both the subject of supreme authority in the church?

This study has encountered three views of the relationship between the pope and the bishops with respect to the supreme authority of the church.[25] The first, evident in the manuals of figures like Domenico Palmieri and Bernard Tepe, and in the opinions of some of the bishops at Vatican II initially unwilling to support episcopal collegiality, held that the pope was the one true and proper subject of supreme authority in the church. The authority of the college, since it depended completely on the papacy for its legitimacy, was considered subordinate to the papacy. The claim of *Pastor aeternus* that the pope possessed a jurisdiction which was episcopal, immediate, ordinary and universal over the whole church provided a warrant for many after Vatican I to advocate an exaggerated papalism which went beyond the intent of the fathers at Vatican I in viewing the universal church in the manner of a universal diocese with the pope as its bishop and the bishops themselves reduced to vicars apostolic. The second view, found among most of the manualists, suggested in *Pastor aeternus* and given expression in the *Nota Praevia Explicativa,* saw the relationship between the papacy and the episcopal college as that between two inadequately distinct subjects of supreme authority in the church.[26] In accord with this view, the pope could either exercise his supreme power alone or in conjunction with the bishops. By acknowledging the possibility of the pope's independent action even as it insisted on the college's dependence on the pope, this view could easily collapse into the first in which the college is subordinated to the papacy. If the pope can truly act independent of the council in this second schema, then in what way is this view different from the first in which the pope alone possesses supreme authority? A third alternative would hold that even when the pope acts "alone" his action constitutes a kind of collegial act since he always acts as head of the college. This view can be found in certain passages of *Lumen gentium* and has been advocated by Rahner and Congar, among others.[27] According to these theologians, the subject of supreme authority resides in the college of bishops with the bishop of Rome as its head.

In the first two models there are certain situations in which the pope may exercise, independent of the college, the church's supreme authority in his office as teacher. This view was apparently sanctioned by *Pastor aeternus* and the claim that the *ex cathedra* teachings of the pope were irreformable by themselves and not by virtue of the church's consent.[28] But recent studies on the history of papal infallibility have stressed the need to place the two definitions of Vatican I (on papal infallibility and primacy) in the context of the contentious church-state relations of the late nineteenth century, and the proximate fear of a resurgence of Gallicanism.[29] *Pastor aeternus* clearly reflects a papalist ecclesiology, but it is also true that this constitution, subsequent to the council, was subject to ultramontanist readings which went far beyond the claims of the document itself. While the bishops were anxious to avoid the slightest taint of Gallicanism, the conciliar debates provide clear evidence that the papal definitions were not intended to abrogate the proper authority of the bishops which they possessed by divine right. Even within *Pastor aeternus* itself one can find evidence of attempts to preserve the legitimate authority of the bishops.[30] One often overlooked passage in *Pastor aeternus* clearly asserted that the prerogatives of the papacy were not in any way to be construed as an obstacle to legitimate episcopal authority.

> This power of the sovereign pontiff in no way obstructs the ordinary and immediate power of episcopal jurisdiction, by which the bishops, established by the Holy Spirit (Acts 20:28) as successors to the Apostles, feed and govern as true pastors the flock committed to each one. On the contrary, this power is asserted, strengthened and vindicated by the supreme and universal pastor, as Gregory the Great says: "My honor is the honor of the universal church. My honor is the solid strength of my brothers (the bishops). Then am I truly honored when honor is not denied to each one to whom it is due" (DS 3061).

Whatever the prerogatives acceded to the papacy, they must not be so interpreted as to replace, obstruct or diminish the legitimate authority of the bishops throughout the world.

Scholars have also questioned the reading which the *ex sese autem non ex consensu* passage from *Pastor aeternus* has been given. The theology which has stressed papal independence seems to have come more from the fears, in 1870, of Gallicanism. This qualification is best read as a repudiation of an absolute requirement for a *subsequent* approval of the whole church; this approval had been demanded in the Gallican "Four Articles" of 1682. Vatican I was rejecting a juridical restriction. Bishop Gasser's *relatio* indicates that the proper exercise of papal authority demanded a real relationship between pope and bishops and that frequent consultation with the bishops and faithful could hardly be set aside.[31] Gustave Thils's study of the council debates has led him to conclude that it was only the consent of the church as a *sine qua non* for the validity of a solemn papal definition which was being rejected.

> Moreover, that which is rejected by the Catholic conciliar declarations [of Vatican I and II] is the *absolute* necessity of a formal approbation of the church as a *sine qua non* condition of the value and validity of an infallible definition. . . . A theologian can perfectly defend the idea of the relative necessity (but not absolute) of the assent of the church, as a habitual condition (but not a *sine qua non*) of the value of infallibility.[32]

If Vatican I did not undermine the legitimate role of the episcopacy, still it did not provide an adequate conceptualization of the relationship between the episcopacy and the papacy. How can one posit that both pope and episcopal college possess supreme authority within the church? What are the implications of the pope being both head and member of the college? Can the pope ever truly act *alone* in the exercise of supreme authority? When the pope does act as head of the college, does this action demand any participation by the rest of the college? Tillard suggests that it was not until the Second Vatican Council that we find the necessary components for an adequate response to these questions. One contribution was the council's teaching on the sacramentality of the episcopacy.

> For it is clear that whatever is founded upon a sacrament must
> have priority within the Church of God: the Church comes
> about by faith and sacraments and all its essential marks are to
> be found within the osmosis of faith and sacraments.[33]

The election of the pope has never been regarded as sacramental. Should a pope resign he would cease to be pope. Tradition has
consistently held that the new pope must be ordained bishop of
Rome. Vatican II's teaching on the sacramentality of the episcopacy suggests that it is the episcopacy which provides the clue for
understanding the papacy, and not the other way around. Against
Rahner's position, Tillard contends that within an ecclesiology of
communion the authority which the pope possesses is derived from
his episcopal leadership of the church of Rome, the church which,
since ancient times, possessed, in Irenaeus's phrase, the *potentior
principalitas* among the churches. In other words, papal primacy
derives from the primacy of the church of Rome. This means that
papal authority is, at root, an episcopal authority. But does this not
reduce the pope to simply the "first among equals?" No, for each
bishop must receive, through episcopal consecration, that power
which is necessary for the achievement of his pastoral charge.

> For the bishop of Rome, as for all the bishops, everything de-
> rives from one and the same sacrament (episcopacy), from one
> and the same mission to build and to keep the Church in com-
> munion, from one and the same power given for the sake of this
> mission. But this power operates in different ways according to
> the office which each member receives within the college. In the
> case of the bishop of Rome, the dimension of *solicitudo univer-
> salis* is extended to a special degree, though always remaining
> within the sacramental grace of the episcopate.[34]

The peculiar demands placed, since ancient times, on the see
(*sedes*) of Rome, requires that the episcopal authority of the one
who possesses the see (*sedens*) take a peculiar form. The basic principle operative here is that the power (*potestas*) associated with
episcopal authority only exists in relation to the particular pastoral
charge (*officium*). Thus the *officium* of the bishop of Rome demands a *potestas* which, while not duplicated by the *potestas* of
other bishops, is nevertheless episcopal in form.

Vatican I taught that the pope possessed ordinary, immediate and universal jurisdiction over the whole church. Does this ecclesiology vitiate the proper authority of the bishops? Gustave Thils insists that it was not the intent of the conciliar bishops to place papal jurisdiction in competition with the jurisdiction of the local bishop.[35] Rather, this jurisdiction must be understood in a manner which supports rather than abrogates episcopal jurisdiction. It seems plausible to conclude with Tillard that the jurisdiction of the pope in the church of Rome must therefore differ from the "ordinary, immediate and universal jurisdiction" of the pope over the universal church. Even *Pastor aeternus* states that the power of the papacy must serve and strengthen the episcopal authority of the bishops (DS 3061). In his jurisdiction over the whole church the bishop of Rome acts as a vigilant sentinel seeing to it that, as Tillard puts it, the "memory of the apostolic faith" is kept alive in the other bishops.

> This is a bishop among other bishops who is commissioned, on the basis of the shared grace of episcopacy, to gather his brother bishops into a college of which he is the *centrum unitatis*. He is a bishop within the college who must by the Lord's expressed will extend the *sollicitudo* of all the churches which is shared throughout the body of bishops to the point where it becomes a personal "watch" over whatever in these churches affects the apostolic faith and the communion in the *catholica*.[36]

But how is the bishop of Rome to be understood as head of the episcopal college? Since early in the nineteenth century two models of papal headship have dominated. The first emerged out of a Franciscan ecclesiology of the Middle Ages inspired by Pseudo-Dionysius, an essentially Neoplatonic schema which understood the church on earth as a mirror of the heavenly church, an angelic universe structured according to descending hierarchies. This theology gained enormous import due to the broader influence of Neoplatonism, the structure of medieval society and the conviction that Dionysius was a disciple of St. Paul. In this context "hierarchy" named a fundamental metaphysical interpretation of reality. The hierarchy of the church corresponded to the celestial hierarchy. Christ, the head of the celestial hierarchy was represented by the pope, head of the terrestrial hierarchy, who was the means and source of all power on earth, spiritual and temporal. Thus the authority of all the lower hierarchies of the church were thought to be subsumed under the power of the papacy.[37] Moreover, the lower orders contributed nothing to the higher orders; the higher contained within it all the powers of the lower levels. This conceptualization made it difficult to maintain the legitimate authority of the episcopacy.

The second view of papal headship corresponded to the model of the baroque secular monarch. Appropriated by French traditionalists like Joseph de Maistre and Louis de Bonald, this view of the papacy attributed to the pope the unilateral powers of a monarch whose authority is received by divine right. The power of the monarch's ministers is strictly delegated and contingent. Like the secular monarch, the pope receives his power as vicar of Christ on earth, surrounded by bishops whose principal responsibility was to disseminate the decrees of the pope. Neither the Pseudo-Dionysian model nor the monarchical model attributed an integral role to the episcopacy, and certainly neither supported the claim of Vatican II that the episcopal college possesses supreme ecclesiastical authority.

In order to propose an alternative notion of headship, Tillard has turned to patristic theology and a model more consonant with an ecclesiology of communion. One of the ancient notions which aptly expressed the relationship of head and college was that of the "corporate personality." The phenomenon of the "corporate personality" occurs when the values and convictions of a community become so concentrated in one individual that the community actually "recognizes" itself in the individual and receives the actions of the individual as its own.[38] This notion of headship, when applied to the papacy and the episcopal college, may be distinguished from the Pseudo-Dionysian and monarchical models in several respects. First, the bishop of Rome, as head of the college, is clearly situated within the college and not above it. Second, the pope's authority as head of the college is derived not solely by juridical fiat, but by virtue of the convictions and values of the college which are concentrated in the head. Third, the bishop of Rome's ministry as head of the college requires the maintenance of a dynamic relationship of mutual learning and listening. Without the dynamic interaction of the bishop of Rome and the other bishops, the college would be unable to recognize itself in the actions of its head. According to this model, it is impossible to conceive of the pope, even in the *ex cathedra* pronouncement of solemn definitions, apart from the college. When the pope speaks "alone," his position demands that as head of the college he be in true communion with his fellow bishops. This "bond of communion" requires more than doctrinal orthodoxy, the recognition that no bishop is in a state of formal schism. It implies, on the part of the bishop of Rome, a real solicitude for his fellow bishops and their churches. It is this "bond of communion" that effects the concentration of the "mind of the college" in the head of the college.

We have discussed in this chapter two aspects of an ecclesiology of communion which have relevance to the ordinary universal magisterium. First we explored the basic outlines of a theology of the episcopacy. This theology viewed the pastoral charge of a bishop to a local church as integral to membership in the episcopal college. The episcopal college, in turn, was situated within the communion of the churches. Second, we proposed the biblical model of the "corporate personality" as an alternative to the Pseudo-Dionysian and monarchical models for conceiving the pope's relationship to the bishops. In the final chapter we will consider the effects which these elements of an ecclesiology of communion might have on a contemporary understanding of the ordinary universal magisterium.

8

An Alternative Theology

One of the principal difficulties in pursuing a mature theology of the ordinary universal magisterium is that this mode of teaching was first explicitly articulated as part of a concerted ultramontane agenda bent on consolidating authority in the papacy. Theologians like Joseph Kleutgen, curial officials like Cardinal August von Reisach, and popes like Pius IX were intent upon blocking theologians who sought alternative paths to the timeless, fixed thought forms of neo-scholasticism. In this climate, without an adequate theology of episcopal collegiality, the ordinary universal magisterium of bishops would remain theologically undeveloped.

Beginning in the theology of Vacant at the end of the nineteenth century, and continuing in the writings of Louis Billot, Joseph Salaverri, Paul Nau and Joseph Clifford Fenton, the ordinary universal magisterium became accepted by many as, at times, a legitimate expression of the ordinary papal magisterium. The influential view that the episcopal college could be considered apart from the communion of the bishops' churches contributed to this development. Rahner, for example, in seeking to overcome the separation of the pope from the episcopal college, suggested that all papal activity was already collegial activity because the pope always acted as head of the college. In order to emphasize this point he contended that even when the pope taught by solemn definition he taught collegially insofar as he summed up the college in his actions. Still (as we saw above), because Rahner's consideration of the episcopal college was not grounded in the communion of churches, he further suggested that the college's ordinary teaching might also "assume concrete form in a special act of the pope. . . ."[1] Rahner seemed to leave the door open for identifying, at least in some situations, the ordinary universal magisterium with the ordinary papal magisterium.

The Ordinary Universal Magisterium within an Ecclesiology of Communion

The situation of the ordinary teaching of the bishops dispersed throughout the world within an ecclesiology of communion yields a different perspective. First, according to an ecclesiology of communion, the authority of the bishops flows from their leadership of local communities. This point of departure leads to an emphasis on the witnessing function of the bishops. The bishops teach, preach and express variously a *testificatio fidei,* a testimony to the faith of the local church. The bishops do not so much teach something "new" which was hitherto unknown to the faithful, as they affirm publicly that which the faithful already believe, and give to that belief a clarity and explicitness which it previously lacked. As the college of bishops is a manifestation of the communion of churches, the teaching of the college is a corporate testimony to the faith of the churches. Consequently, the dynamism of the ordinary universal magisterium shifts; the movement is no longer one from Rome out to the local churches. Rather, the ordinary universal magisterium gives expression to what is in fact believed by the local churches. The starting point is the local community; the unity which the faith of the churches possesses is then reflected in the universal teaching of the episcopate. It follows, as Sullivan contended, that only residential bishops participate in the exercise of the ordinary universal magisterium. A titular bishop lacks the necessary relationship to a local community.

By shifting the ecclesiological starting point from the papacy to the communion of churches, the ordinary universal magisterium is transformed from a means for extending papal influence to the ordinary means by which the fundamental truths of our faith are in fact communicated authoritatively. As such, this mode of teaching will generally not be exercised by the pope alone. The exercise of the ordinary universal magisterium will be, as even the manuals recognized, *quotidian,* a daily testimony to and reflection of the faith of the churches by the communities themselves and their leaders. This *communio* ecclesiology has placed, then, a new accent on the theological significance of the most distinctive characteristic of this mode of teaching: its exercise by the bishops *dispersed throughout the world.* The relocation of the locus of this teaching from the papacy to the local church has enabled us to highlight the primacy of the witnessing function of the bishop in his ministry as teacher.

A second way in which a *communio* ecclesiology contributes to a theology of the ordinary universal magisterium concerns the bishop of Rome's relationship to the other bishops. This *communio* ecclesiology circumvents the ultramontane tendency to collapse the ordinary universal magisterium of bishops into the ordinary papal magisterium. Within an ecclesiology of communion the papacy can never replace the indispensable task of the bishops to witness to the faith of their communities. The bishop of Rome exercises his ministry in service of the authentic ministries of the local bishops. His role in the ordinary universal magisterium will include developing and supporting communication and dialogue between the churches and their bishops. This might entail the creation and support of ecclesiastical structures which facilitate a spirit of mutual listening and learning among the bishops.

This was the clear intent of Vatican II in its enthusiastic support of episcopal conferences[2] in both *Lumen gentium* #23 and *Christus Dominus* #36–38. This was also the intent of Pope Paul VI in his creation of the universal episcopal synod. These structures were not to serve merely as a forum for either deliberation over matters of church governance or for instruction by curial officials. Rather, the bishop of Rome, as a servant of episcopal communion, must see to it that these provide opportunities for the bishops to be enriched by their encounters with other bishops. It is a mistake to limit the activity of the ordinary universal magisterium to the promulgation of summary documents by such episcopal gatherings. These formal statements may express the universal teaching of the bishops, but the actual interaction of the bishops is as much a part of the exercise of their teaching as is the promulgation of any formal documents. These gatherings then, would not constitute the exercise of the ordinary universal magisterium as much as they would facilitate its exercise by encouraging episcopal interaction.

One consequence of this theology of the ordinary universal magisterium is that the teaching of the universal episcopate dispersed throughout the world will not be easily distinguished from the broader and more complex processes by which the church preserves and develops its doctrinal tradition. In fact, the origins of the ordinary universal magisterium, prior to its explicit formulation in the nineteenth century, lie in this more fundamental notion: it was in the common, ordinary teaching of the bishops that the truths of Christianity were preserved and passed on. Understood in this way, the universal teaching of the bishops seems to resist easy verification. How is it possible to identify those teachings which have been taught infallibly by the ordinary universal magisterium? What criteria are to be employed for the verification of the ordinary universal magisterium's exercise? It is to these questions that we turn in the next section.

The Problem of Verification

Curiously, since the formal expression of the ordinary universal magisterium almost 125 years ago, little attention has been given to the problem of verification. How do we recognize those teachings which have been taught infallibly by the universal episcopate? Since Vatican II some theologians have sought to identify a kind of criteriology in *Lumen gentium* #25. They have seen in the council's articulation of the ordinary universal magisterium a set of conditions by which one could ascertain those teachings which had been taught infallibly by the bishops dispersed throughout the world. Theologians as diverse as Küng and Rahner, Congar, Ford and Grisez all assume that *Lumen gentium* #25 does yield a set of conditions which may be applied to particular teachings. But there is disagreement over the interpretation of these conditions. What is the precise meaning of *tamquam definitive tenendam?* What is the character of a "strictly collegial action"? But the more fundamental question is whether it is even possible to identify and then employ a distinct set of conditions or criteria for verifying when a teaching has been taught by the ordinary universal magisterium. The answer to this question depends largely on the model employed for understanding this mode of episcopal teaching.

What Is the Proper Model for Identifying the Function and Character of the Ordinary Universal Magisterium?

The church possesses a plurality of means for the preservation and transmission of the apostolic tradition. While ascribing an authoritative role to the teaching of the pope and bishops, Roman Catholicism has recognized, with more or less enthusiasm, that all the faithful participate in the transmission of the faith. We can identify a number of different and complementary means by which this faith is transmitted. The first, and the most common, means involves the whole faithful in the proclamation of the gospel, the celebration of the liturgy and the witness of Christian living. This mode, in its diverse manner of expression, is called the *sensus fidelium.* The insight and convictions of the faithful, enfleshed in their daily Christian living, are a fundamental means by which the faith of the church is recognized, preserved and proclaimed. A second means is the community of theologians, Newman's *schola theologorum,* who through the canons of scholarly inquiry seek to elucidate the faith of the church. A third means can be attributed to most daily teaching of the pope and bishops; while benefiting from the assistance of the Holy Spirit, this teaching is not absolutely protected from error, it is non-infallible. The vast majority of church teaching is proclaimed in this mode. Finally, we can identify a fourth means by which the faith of the church is transmitted, the exercise of the extraordinary magisterium by pope or ecumenical council, a relatively infrequent response of the church to a serious threat to the faith.

This plurality of means by which the faith is preserved and transmitted was muted in the neo-scholastic and papalist theologies which held sway between 1860 and 1960. In spite of theologians like Scheeben, Newman and even Franzelin, who attempted to preserve a role for the laity in the tradition-bearing task of the church, this dominant ultramontanist ecclesiology generally stressed the authoritative teaching of the pope and the bishops at the expense of the contributions of the whole faithful. The magisterial exercise of the pope and bishops was not understood in the context of preaching, the proclamation of the gospel. Rather, it was exercised in the style and atmosphere of canon law and abstract metaphysics. The influence of canon law meant that authoritative pronouncements were proposed according to the model of command and obedience. The priority of metaphysics over history meant that these teachings were conceived as absolute unassailable claims to truth. However, this kind of authoritative pronouncement in doctrinal matters had, prior to the nineteenth century, been relatively rare. Its exercise in previous centuries corresponded to what we speak of now as the extraordinary magisterium, the solemn teaching of either pope or council in response to a proximate threat to the faith of the church. In the nineteenth century the extraordinary magisterium became the model for virtually all church teaching.

The Ordinary Universal Magisterium according to the Model of the Extraordinary Magisterium

We outlined above four different ways in which the church is able to preserve and transmit its apostolic tradition. But how does the role of the ordinary universal magisterium of bishops contribute to this tradition-bearing function of the church? Since the formal articulation of the teaching on the ordinary universal magisterium in Pius IX's *Tuas libenter,* the model for understanding the teaching of the universal episcopate has been the extraordinary magisterium, that is, the solemn definition of either an ecumenical council or the pope when he teaches *ex cathedra.* The second chapter's consideration of the origins of the ordinary universal magisterium revealed the explicit intent of Pius IX, to reassert the ancient belief regarding the authenticating value of the consensus of the universal episcopate against those who would minimalize the dogmatic content of the faith. At the same time, however, Pope Pius' articulation of the infallibility of the ordinary magisterium could be used to forestall theological dissent by extending infallibility to teachings with which scholars had voiced disagreement. Like the extraordinary magisterium, the formulation of the teaching on the ordinary universal magisterium was originally intended as a response to a perceived doctrinal threat. This application of the model of the extraordinary magisterium to the universal teaching of the bishops outside of council continued for over a century up to and including the 1983 Code of Canon Law which required for the exercise of the ordinary universal magisterium a formal papal approbation modelled on that given to conciliar decrees.

What factors contributed to the application of this model to the ordinary universal magisterium? Certainly the perduring influence of Vatican I's treatment of papal infallibility must be considered. There, for the first time, conditions for the infallible exercise of the extraordinary magisterium (at least as exercised by the pope *ex cathedra*) were explicitly articulated. This criteriology was proposed not simply in order to describe the conditions in which the pope taught infallibly. These conditions were also intended as a means for verifying the exercise of the infallible papal magisterium. This criteriology left its mark on the consciousness of the church. For instance, we saw in chapter 4 that J. Robert Dionne found Vatican II's delineation of conditions for the exercise of the ordinary universal magisterium wanting. His solution, however, was simply to offer a further specification intended to make these conditions more explicit. He, too, seemed to imagine that one could look to the tradition and identify particular teachings which met a specified set of conditions and therefore could be verified as having been infallibly taught by the universal episcopate.

A second factor which contributed to this interpretation of the ordinary universal magisterium was the recognition that the episcopal college existed permanently, not just when gathered in council. In chapter 2 we saw that most of the manualists began their considerations of the teaching of the episcopal college with the bishops' exercise of their teaching apostolate in an ecumenical council. Herman Dieckmann alone was the exception insofar as he began his treatment of the episcopal college by considering the relationship of the bishops dispersed throughout the world. After describing the bond of communion which the bishops already possessed, he then moved to the expression of that bond in an ecumenical council. For most of the manualists, however, the ecumenical council was the norm for considering the teaching of the college of bishops.

We might summarize then a set of presumptions operative in the most common treatments of the ordinary universal magisterium from *Tuas libenter* to Vatican II as follows. (1) The episcopal college exists permanently; that which holds for the college in council must hold for the college outside of council. (2) The true nature of the episcopal college is most fundamentally expressed in an ecumenical council—it must then serve as a model for the activity of the college outside of council. (3) When the bishops teach infallibly in ecumenical council, this teaching is proposed in response to some particular doctrinal threat. (4) Therefore, the infallible teaching of the ordinary universal magisterium is exercised (a) in response to some particular doctrinal threat which demands (b) a clearly identified set of conditions by which its exercise may be verified. The neo-scholastic theology of the ordinary universal magisterium was consequently incapable of conceiving of the universal teaching of the bishops according to other models.

We saw in chapter 6 the difficulties inherent in any attempt to employ a set of conditions for the purpose of verifying the exercise of the ordinary universal magisterium. This is particularly the case with respect to disputed individual teachings. The teachings of the ordinary universal magisterium do not, in and of themselves, appear to possess the clarity necessary for this task. Having granted the historically conditioned character of its nineteenth century formulation and its subsequent interpretations within a broadly neo-scholastic framework, one might ask, however, whether the ordinary universal magisterium, as a particular mode of episcopal teaching, might be considered according to an alternative model.

The Ordinary Universal Magisterium according to the Model of the Sensus Fidelium

Is it not more plausible to view the ordinary universal magisterium according to the model of the *sensus fidelium* which possesses its own proper infallibility? *Lumen gentium* #12 claimed that when the people of God as a whole are in agreement on a matter of faith they cannot err.

> The holy people of God shares also in Christ's prophetic office. It spreads abroad a living witness to Him, especially by means of a life of faith and charity and by offering to God a sacrifice of praise, the tribute of lips which give honor to His name. . . . The body of the faithful as a whole, anointed as they are by the Holy One . . . cannot err in matters of belief. Thanks to a supernatural sense of the faith which characterizes the People as a whole, it manifests this unerring quality when, "from the bishops down to the last member of the laity," it shows universal agreement in matters of faith and morals. For by this sense of faith which is aroused and sustained by the Spirit of truth, God's People accepts not the word of men [and women] but the very word of God. . . . It clings without fail (*indefectibiliter adhaeret*) to the faith once delivered to the saints . . . , penetrates

it more deeply by accurate insights, and applies it more thor-
oughly to life. All this it does under the lead of a sacred teaching
authority (*magisterii*) to which it loyally defers (*obsequens*).[3]

It is significant that the council did not attempt to articulate specific conditions by which we may know when the faithful have
exercised this infallibility in believing, for this freedom from error
in matters of belief resists easy verification.[4] We may trust that the
assistance of the Holy Spirit preserves the whole faithful from error
in matters of belief. The sure location and expression of beliefs
which have been so held is another matter altogether.

An analysis of the teaching of the bishops dispersed throughout the world suggests that it, too, resists easy verification. Scheeben, Vacant, Zapelena and others understood that the teaching of
the ordinary universal magisterium would find expression in a plurality of forms: in the liturgy, preaching, regional synods, in the
catechetical ministry of the laity, in the teaching of priests and
theologians. The vast majority of the bishops' teaching "when dispersed throughout the world" is addressed to their particular communities, and so the teaching of the common faith will often be
expressed in response to the particular questions and concerns of a
local church. The expressions of the faith bear the marks of the
local church's peculiar culture and are a result of the philosophical
and theological constructs appropriate to that culture. The bishop
does not simply translate some abstract universal notion into the
appropriate cultural form. The bishop himself will be formed and
influenced by the particularity of the community to which he
ministers.

Peter Chirico has viewed the teaching ministry of the bishop as
primarily prophetic rather than dogmatic in character. The local
bishop seeks to apply the dogmas of the church to the concrete
situations of his local community.[5] For that reason, he compares
the ordinary universal magisterium to the *sensus fidelium:*

> In the present context we can say that the teaching of the univer-
> sal episcopate can be compared to a concentrated *sensus fide-
> lium.* It contains in an implicit fashion the universal ecclesial
> meanings that ground infallible recognition. . . . It is this im-
> plicit nature of the universal teaching of the Church as it ap-

pears in the teachings of the scattered bishops that has made the theological attempts to call any given teaching of the Church *de fide* by the ordinary and universal magisterium of the bishops such a hazardous venture. We simply do not have the techniques to uncover the universal intentionality that exists in an implicit way in the multifaceted teachings of bishops in the various parts of the world and over the many centuries of the Church's life.[6]

Chirico has properly identified the problem of ascertaining the intent of the bishops which has been noted throughout this book. This is not simply a matter of identifying what the bishops actually teach. One must further identify the stance of each bishop toward the given teaching: is it proposed as a theological opinion, as a teaching held authoritatively, or as a teaching "to be held definitively"?

Some theologians would identify the intent of the bishops by focusing the exercise of the ordinary universal magisterium in a distinct, explicit collegial act. This has been suggested in various forms by Salaverri,[7] Rahner,[8] Michael Schmaus[9] and Gérard Philips.[10] Here an action of the college would produce some formula explicitly identifying the appropriate theological note (in this case, *de fide catholica*) to be attached to a given teaching. As an exercise of the ordinary universal magisterium rather than the extraordinary magisterium, this collegial act would have to be an extra-conciliar event.[11]

Such an extra-conciliar collegial act can be understood in two different ways. First, there might be something like an extra-conciliar solemn definition. This could be the product of either written correspondence with the entire episcopate, or even some kind of international teleconference involving all the bishops. As Sullivan has noted, the theological commission at Vatican II implicitly acknowledged this possibility.[12] The commission accepted a proposed emendation of the *De Ecclesia* schema, changing the text in *Lumen gentium* #25 from "when either a Roman Pontiff or a Council defines a doctrine . . ." to "but when either the Roman Pontiff or the body of bishops together with him defines a doctrine. . . ."[13] The commission acknowledged that a solemn definition of the pope and bishops (distinct from the pope teaching *ex cathedra*) need not be limited to ecumenical councils. They did not, however, offer any examples regarding the concrete form of such extra-conciliar definitions of the whole college. As a solemn definition, however, this would no longer be an expression of the *ordinary* universal magisterium but rather an expression of a new extra-conciliar mode of the extraordinary magisterium.

The second possibility for understanding the exercise of the ordinary universal magisterium in an explicit collegial act involves a gathering of some but not all of the bishops, the teaching of which would then be received by the whole episcopate. Rahner mentions, for example, a universal synod conducted by residential bishops. One might imagine the production and approbation of a universal catechism as another example. The promulgation of a doctrinal formula at a universal synod or in a universal catechism could not be, *a priori,* an expression of the ordinary universal magisterium. For the product of a gathering of a limited number of bishops, the reception of all the bishops would be required. This, however, returns us to the problem of verifying that reception.

The ordinary universal magisterium involves several thousand bishops. What do they intend to teach in their daily ministry? What do they intend to teach as a college? Like the *sensus fidelium,* the infallible teaching activity of the bishops worldwide is not easy to summarize. It resists the application of any set of criteria by which its exercise may be readily verified. The aim of this mode of episcopal teaching is not, as with the extraordinary magisterium, the clarification of disputed doctrinal questions, but rather the transmission of the faith of the church in the daily ministry of the bishops exercised in their local churches.

The Distinction between a Defined Dogma and a Non-Defined Dogma Taught Definitively

The difficulty in verifying the exercise of the ordinary universal magisterium, while seldom explicitly acknowledged, has been indirectly admitted in a longstanding distinction in tradition between defined and non-defined dogma. In chapter 4 attention was drawn to Matthias Scheeben's recognition that generally the "law of faith" is proclaimed in the church as a "law of custom," that is, through the ordinary teaching of the church. In the face of obstinate doctrinal conflict, however, Scheeben maintained that the church must turn to more explicit formulations of the faith, namely, to the solemn judgments of the extraordinary magisterium. The German theologian contended that both forms of the magisterium carried the same authority, expressing the one law of faith. The second form, however, that of solemn definitions, was better suited to address doctrinal controversies because its form of expression was more explicit and tangible.

A decade later, Vacant proposed that the teachings of the ordinary universal magisterium, although taught infallibly, could not be considered as dogmas of Catholic faith. He based this claim, in part, upon an analysis of tradition. He could find no evidence of the negative theological note of "heresy" being attached to the rejection of a teaching of the ordinary universal magisterium. The French seminary professor had in mind the dogma of the immaculate conception. He concluded that the denial of the immaculate conception, prior to its solemn definition, had never been deemed a heresy. Some seventy years later, Rahner and Karl Lehmann, in their consideration of "dogma" as a fundamental theological category, would make a similar observation:

> But in ordinary reception and interpretation this concept has been up till now almost exclusively evaluated on the model of a "definition"; that the "subject matter" through the ordinary and universal magisterium would receive the name "dogma" in an explicit determination is here hardly consciously affirmed and is little developed, conceptually and objectively by theologians.[14]

Rahner and Lehmann identified a tendency in tradition to consider only solemn definitions as dogmas. This narrower application of the term "dogma" gave recognition to the higher degree of certitude (*Gewissheitsgrad*) which defined dogmas possessed. The authors, while admitting that Vatican I considered the teachings of the ordinary universal magisterium to be dogma, did not consider the designation helpful in the practical order.

The issue which Scheeben, Vacant, and now Rahner and Lehmann have raised is whether to apply the term "dogma" to any infallible teaching, or only to those teachings whose infallibility has been formally declared. The application of the term "dogma" illustrates a peculiar problematic inherent in the nature of the ordinary universal magisterium. The infallible teaching of the bishops dispersed throughout the world is not "defined," but it is to be held "definitively." But if a teaching has not been defined, how are the faithful to know that the teaching is to be held definitively? This question appeared earlier in this study with the consistent inability of most accounts of the ordinary universal magisterium to explain how the faithful were to discern episcopal consensus and to verify the exercise of the ordinary universal magisterium.

One concrete example taken from contemporary biblical theology may serve to elucidate this problem. Raymond Brown in his book *The Virginal Conception and Bodily Resurrection of Jesus* claimed that, as best as he could determine, the conditions for a teaching to have been taught infallibly by the ordinary universal magisterium had been met by the doctrine of the virginal conception. He also admitted that not all theologians agreed with him on the infallible status of this teaching.[15] In a later book, Brown responded to criticism for writing "I think that it is infallibly taught" and not "it is infallibly taught."[16] The biblical scholar contended that only the pope and bishops have the authority to say whether a teaching has or has not been taught infallibly. Thus, while Brown was personally convinced that this teaching had been taught by the ordinary universal magisterium, he was willing to grant that others might disagree with this assessment. Only the pope and bishops could authoritatively decide the matter. In contending that only the pope and bishops could settle the matter Brown was apparently referring to an exercise of the extraordinary magisterium, a solemn definition on the virgin birth which would clarify the teaching's theological note. This example suggests that in the face of controversy, the determination of the authoritative status of any teaching not solemnly defined can only be pursued tentatively. In other words, short of a solemn definition, the attachment of a theological note to a given teaching is not itself an infallible judgment, and is subject to legitimate disagreement on the part of theologians and, at times, the faithful.

The discernment and verification of the teachings of the ordinary universal magisterium is not always so fraught with difficulty. A second example of the teaching of the ordinary universal magisterium presented by Francis Sullivan is the relatively non-controversial teaching that "Jesus is Lord, and that God has raised him from the dead."[17] There are several articles of the baptismal creed, he asserts, which have been taught infallibly by the ordinary universal magisterium but which have never been solemnly defined because they have never been seriously questioned. For such teachings, no rigorous set of criteria are demanded.

Our contention in this section has been that the teaching of the universal episcopate outside of council is not well suited for bringing clarity to disputed doctrinal questions. Magnus Löhrer, concurs, observing that the ordinary universal magisterium does not best function "criteriologically."

> All these considerations demonstrate that the question of an obligation, out of faith, on the basis of the universal and ordinary teaching office must be examined, in an individual instance, very cautiously. The actual import of this mode of the church teaching office does not seem to lie so much in its criteriological function. Rather it constitutes the ordinary manner of presentation of the Catholic faith. This is clearly expressed in the liturgy which is properly designated as the most important aspect of the ordinary teaching office.[18]

The exercise of the ordinary universal magisterium cannot be verified in particular instances by the application of a set of concrete criteria. Where serious questions are levelled against a particular teaching of the church, appeals to the ordinary universal magisterium cannot be expected to resolve the matter. Rather, the ordinary universal magisterium is that mode of teaching operative in the ordinary transmission of the faith by the bishops in the local churches throughout the world.

The Ordinary Universal Magisterium: Teaching Infallibility and the Assistance of the Holy Spirit

Given the vast literature on the many theological, philosophical and historical issues pertaining to infallibility, it is impossible to do more than suggest some of the general implications to be drawn from this study for a theology of infallibility. What follows is a brief history of the development of infallibility and an attempt to clarify two different applications of the term infallibility operative in Vatican II's *Lumen gentium.* This will lead to a theological consideration of the Holy Spirit's assistance in the teaching of the church.

A Brief Excursus on Infallibility

The most basic meaning of the term "infallibility" is immunity from error. This immunity from error is not predicated of a teaching or a proposition but of a judgment. It is more accurate to speak of the truth or falsehood of propositions and to refer to the church's judgment regarding these propositions as being either fallible or infallible. As Henri Gouhier has observed:

> The adjective "infallible" signifies a certain power to never take the false for the true and, since such a power could only be recognized in the world of discourse, the exact formula would be: never to speak the false in taking it for the true. "Infallible" qualifies therefore the one who speaks: it is not at all the spoken word which is infallible—that is either true or false—but the one who offers it.[19]

In chapter 6 we alluded to the problems which can result from a failure to distinguish adequately between the question of the truth/falsehood of a proposition and the fallibility/infallibility of a teaching judgment. A fallible magisterial judgment regarding a doctrinal question may nevertheless yield a true doctrine. What infallibility adds to a proposition or doctrine is a guarantee, an assurance that a given doctrine is true. If we conceive of infallibility as applied to particular doctrinal judgments we must admit soberly that this notion and application of infallibility did not appear in Christian theological writings until the ninth century with respect to ecumenical councils[20] and the late thirteenth century with respect to the papacy.[21] What does possess a more ancient provenance is what the tradition has come to speak of as indefectibility. In the common statement of the Roman Catholic-Lutheran dialogue on teaching authority and infallibility, indefectibility is defined as ". . . the continued existence of the Church in all its essential aspects, including its faith. Such fidelity is not an automatic quality of everything that the Church's leaders may say or endorse, but is the result of divine grace."[22] However, this notion of indefectibility, if it is to mean more than that the church will simply continue to exist, demands, it would appear, some notion of infallibility.

> If the Church is understood as being essentially a community of Christian faith and proclamation, its indefectibility would seem to involve a certain infallibility in belief and in preaching, at least in the sense that God will see to it that the gospel is preached and believed in its purity somewhere.[23]

This infallibility in belief and in preaching need not have been applied to particular, juridically qualified judgments of the church. If the church, in its early centuries, did not explicitly speak of an infallibility in proposing specific Christian teachings, it certainly believed that the rule of faith, the fundamental profession of Christian belief, was preserved from error through the assistance of the Spirit. This assistance was not primarily applied to individual doctrinal judgments but rather to the whole apostolic *paradosis,* the transmission of the apostolic *kerygma.*

Infallibility, conceived as a protection of the church from error in specific doctrinal determinations, may have been implicit in the fundamental trust which the church maintained in the Spirit's assistance in the transmission of the faith. As an explicitly articulated concept, it appears to have emerged out of a gradual ecclesial reflection on the success of the early councils in staving off heretical attacks on the core of the Christian faith. Thus infallibility rose to explicit consciousness in the church inductively as the determinations of the ancient councils (e.g., Nicea, Chalcedon) bore fruit in protecting the church from error. Put simply, the infallibility of these councils was acknowledged only after their teachings had been received by the church.[24]

If the idea of papal infallibility first significantly entered theological discourse in the thirteenth century (largely by the Franciscans as an attempt to restrict papal authority by binding it to the teaching of prior popes), at the beginning of the nineteenth century papal infallibility could still be considered a "new idea"[25] in the sense that up till that time there had been no universal consensus among theologians. Before long, however, ultramontane theologians would view papal infallibility as one of the principal tools for preserving the sovereignty of the papacy and with it, the authority of the church. The ultramontane ecclesiology which ensued made infallibility the linchpin for its theology of the Spirit's assistance to the teaching office of the church.

Nevertheless, as was noted earlier in chapter 7, the pronounced papalism expressed in Vatican I's *Pastor aeternus* was not as extreme as the infallibilist camp at the council would have liked and as later commentators on the council often pretended. According to Sullivan, the careful limitations and conditions inserted in the council's definition on papal infallibility reflect the definition's foundation in two fundamental principles:

> 1. That the Roman Catholic church is indefectible in faith and therefore can never be led into contradiction with the truth of the Gospel by those whose definitive judgments on matters of faith Catholics are ready to accept as binding on their faith;
> 2. That while such definitive judgments are normally the fruit of the deliberation of the whole episcopate with the pope, the "Petrine ministry" on behalf of the faith and communion of the whole People of God includes the function, when circumstances warrant it, of pronouncing definitive judgments on matters of faith, which are equally as binding as the decisions of ecumenical councils.[26]

Sullivan's "when circumstances warrant it" is of the utmost significance. Prior to the nineteenth century, while there endured a firm conviction that the general assistance of the Spirit preserved the church from error in its transmission of the faith, there was not the tendency to ascribe infallibility to virtually every teaching act of the church.

By the end of the nineteenth century, however, many ecclesiological tracts of the period viewed the interrelation of the human and divine within the church according to the model of the hypostatic union and attributed to the church's teaching office the very authority of Christ. The gift of infallibility ceased to be an extraordinary charism employed in order to preserve the church's indefectibility and increasingly came to be viewed as an ordinary means by which the Spirit assisted the church in its proclamation of the gospel. *Tuas libenter*'s teaching that revealed truth was not limited to those teachings proposed by solemn definition must be read in light of this nineteenth century tendency to view infallibility as the primary way in which the Spirit assisted the church in its teaching.

At the Second Vatican Council the majority of the council bishops, along with their *periti,* were convinced that the ultramontane ecclesiology of Vatican I required a certain moderation; the pronounced papalism which it espoused had to be balanced with a fuller consideration of the episcopacy. A similar moderation was required with respect to the church's teaching on infallibility. The response of the council was to follow the lead of Newman and broaden the base of infallibility by recognizing that it was a gift given, in the first instance, not to the hierarchy but to the whole church. This development of the council's consideration of infallibility did not involve the presentation of any "new" teaching as much as it involved placing the received teaching in a broader context, that of the whole people of God. In this respect the development did represent a distinct advance over the nineteenth century understanding of papal infallibility. For example, again following Newman, the distinction between the passive infallibility of the *Ecclesia discens* and the active infallibility of the *Ecclesia docens* was implicitly rejected.[27] The council, at least haltingly, recognized that such distinctions were not representative of the fundamental constitution of the church as the one people of God. If infallibility was exercised by particular organs within the church, it was the church as a whole which was the proper subject of infallibility. The whole people of God was, at the same time, a teaching and learning church. This approach represented at least a tentative ecumenical advance. It responded to both Protestant and Orthodox concerns that infallibility, as treated in *Pastor aeternus,* described a juridical authority exercised by a select few to arbitrarily determine the contents of revelation. By grounding infallibility in the whole church, the council demonstrated that the infallible teaching office of the church was at the service of the gospel and was to give witness to the faith of the whole people of God.

The Differing Roles of the Conditions for the Exercise of Infallibility

In the documents of Vatican II, a distinction was made between an infallibility in teaching (*in docendo*) and in believing (*in credendo*). This was not, as it might initially appear, a return to the distinction between the teaching and the learning church, nor between a passive and an active infallibility, both of which functionally separated the laity from the clergy. Rather, Vatican II considered the infallibility in believing to be a dynamic and active process which is predicated not only of the laity, but of the whole people of God. However, this utilization of the term "infallibility" with regard to Christian belief can be confused with the infallibility ascribed to the church in its solemn definitions. The distinction lies in the role of the conditions outlined for the exercise of infallibility. For example, according to *Lumen gentium* #12, the charism of infallibility is assumed to be present in the *sensus fidelium* when the whole people of God are in agreement on a matter of faith or morals. In the case of an *ex cathedra* papal pronouncement, *Pastor aeternus* identified four conditions: (1) The pope must be speaking in his capacity as supreme pastor of the church. (2) He must appeal to his supreme apostolic authority which belongs to him as Peter's successor. (3) The object of his teaching must pertain to faith or morals. (4) He must explicitly propose the teaching as one having universal obligatory force.[28] In any exercise, then, of the charism of infallibility, it is understood that certain conditions must be fulfilled. But these conditions may be understood in two different ways. In the case of the *sensus fidelium* the conditions appear to function descriptively. We know that in the life of the church there are instances when these conditions are fulfilled, and in those instances we believe the charism of infallibility to be operative. But we cannot use these conditions to *identify* the particular instances in which the charism of infallibility has been operative. This belief in the infallibility of the *sensus fidelium* flows from the faith of the community that the *congregatio fidelium* as a whole cannot be led astray in the essential matters of Christian belief. The use of the term "infallibility" in this sense recalls Dulles' contention that indefectibility demands at least an infallibility "in belief and preaching."

On the other hand, the conditions for the exercise of infallibility in the extraordinary doctrinal judgments of the church seem to function differently. Here the conditions do not only describe objectively what must be the case whenever the charism of infallibility is operative, they also function criteriologically. That is, these conditions can and must serve as a means by which the church as a whole can *verify* that the charism of infallibility is operative in a doctrinal judgment. This follows from the character of the church's authoritative teaching ministry. "Infallibility" in these instances names the guarantee given to the church that in certain modes of exercise of the church's teaching office, the faithful may be assured that what is taught truly pertains to the faith of the church. In this second case, the setting forth of an adequate set of criteria or conditions does not just describe what must be the case for the charism of infallibility to be operative, it provides the necessary means for the verification of an infallible judgment. This was the importance (stressed by Bishop Gasser in his *relatio* at Vatican I) of the qualifying conditions which *Pastor aeternus* ascribed to papal infallibility. A doctrinal judgment is only considered infallible in clearly specified circumstances. The 1983 Code of Canon Law similarly declared that "[n]o doctrine is understood to be infallibly defined unless it is clearly established as such."[29] We may profess belief in the infallibility of the *sensus fidelium* without having to clearly establish when it is operative. This is not the case with the exercise of the extraordinary magisterium.

A solemn doctrinal judgment made in response to a crisis threatening the faith of the church represents a serious ecclesial enterprise. In such instances the necessity of a criteriology by which the faithful may ascertain when an infallible judgment is being exercised is crucial. This has created difficulties with respect to the solemn pronouncements of ecumenical councils. This exercise of the extraordinary magisterium of ecumenical councils is intended to provide a clear response to proximate threats to the faith of the church, but no conditions for its exercise have ever been articulated and there exists no definitive list of the infallible definitions of ecumenical councils.[30] Sullivan has pointed out that one must distinguish between the actual fulfillment of conditions for an infallible teaching (what we have called the descriptive use of such conditions) and the verification on the part of the faithful that those conditions have been fulfilled (what we have called the criteriological use of such conditions). He admits that even with the extraordinary magisterium (the solemn judgments of pope and council) it is not always easy to discern when these conditions have been met.[31] But given the criteriological function of the extraordinary magisterium, the articulation of a clear set of conditions for its exercise by both pope and council is essential. In the case of ecumenical councils, this could easily be rectified. At Vatican II, for example, the theological commission, in the announcement which accompanied the *Nota Explicativa Praevia,* explicitly enunciated the authoritative status which the dogmatic constitution possessed. While this clarification was not formally approved by the bishops at Vatican II, it would not be difficult to incorporate clarifications of this kind in future conciliar documents.

The different usages of the conditions for infallibility follow from the different nature of the *sensus fidelium* and the extraordinary magisterium. The infallibility of the former expresses what we trust must be the case for the continued existence of the church in fidelity to the gospel. The continuing existence of the church itself would be in jeopardy if the whole faithful could be misled in belief on matters pertaining to faith or morals. But while we believe that on these central matters, the charism of infallibility must be operative, these conditions need not be subject to easy verification. The guarantee of infallibility is offered in a more general manner, assuring us of the continued fidelity of the church. In the case of the exercise of the extraordinary magisterium, the conditions must admit of a criteriological function; we must be able to verify their fulfillment.

The Infallibility of the Ordinary Universal Magisterium: A Descriptive or Criteriological Application?

The paucity of theological reflection on the ordinary universal magisterium is particularly evident in the discussion of the kind of infallibility attributed to this mode of episcopal teaching. *Tuas libenter* assumed that the conditions for the infallible exercise of the ordinary universal magisterium functioned criteriologically. That papal brief was clearly a response to theologians who recognized as dogmas only teachings which had been solemnly defined (e.g., Jacob Frohschammer, I. von Döllinger). The pope assumed that one might clearly enumerate teachings of the ordinary universal magisterium just as one might enumerate solemn papal judgments.

Since the publication of that papal brief the conditions for the exercise of the ordinary universal magisterium have consistently been employed criteriologically as a means for identifying the infallibility of individual teachings. In chapter 6 we reviewed the attempt to apply criteriologically these conditions for infallibility to the church's teaching on artificial contraception. A more recent example is evident in the correspondence between Cardinal Ratzinger, Prefect for the CDF, and Charles Curran, in which Ratzinger rejected the legitimacy of Curran's dissent from certain moral teachings on the grounds that they had been taught infallibly by the ordinary universal magisterium.[32] However, the criteriological use of a set of conditions for infallibility demands that the faithful be able to verify when these conditions have been met. Yet, as was demonstrated above, the universal teaching of the bishops throughout the world resists this verification. That is, there are instances, as with the teaching on artificial contraception, when it is not possible to know, with absolute certitude, whether the conditions outlined in *Lumen gentium* #25 have, in fact, been fulfilled. The conditions for the exercise of the ordinary universal magisterium must therefore be employed descriptively, as is the case with the *sensus fidelium,* rather than criteriologically.

Theology of the Assistance of the Holy Spirit

A theology of the ordinary universal magisterium demands a much clearer distinction between the descriptive and the criteriological applications of the conditions for the exercise of the charism of infallibility. This task requires, in turn, a consideration of a theology of the assistance of the Holy Spirit which goes beyond the underdeveloped, monochromatic treatments of many of the neoscholastic ecclesiologies.

In the ultramontane ecclesiologies which dominated from 1850 to 1960, the theology of the Spirit's assistance to the church was both forcefully and meagerly stated. One finds a consideration of the Spirit's assistance to the church as a distinct force activated apart from basic human processes. Charles Journet's theology of teaching authority was not atypical. The human processes and historical limitations of the church were generally overlooked. The hierarchy, and the hierarchy alone, functioned as a conduit for the Holy Spirit. Some neo-Thomist theologies, including that of Journet, reduced the human element to an instrumental causality. The proper contributions of the laity, theological history and the liturgy were all largely absent. The mode of the Holy Spirit's activity in individuals and groups was not explained. These theologies failed to imagine the gradations by which the Spirit might act in and through the human members of the church in order to preserve it in the truth.

This theology of the Spirit's assistance followed from an ecclesiology which tended toward Christo-monism. The church, instituted by Christ was bestowed with all that was necessary for its survival and flourishing. Where the assistance of the Spirit was required, the offices of the church were assumed to function as conduits for the Spirit's guidance. Lacking was an adequate consideration of the animating presence of the Holy Spirit in the life of the church. Yet an adequate consideration of the pneumatologically conditioned character of the church is essential for considering the Spirit's activity in the teaching of the church. This pneumatological ecclesiology will recognize that the Spirit's presence is not actualized only intermittently through the exercise of certain juridically constituted offices. Rather, the Spirit's assistance is effective not only in doctrinal teaching but in preaching, theological reflection, catechesis in all its many forms, worship and the praxis of daily Christian living. The operation of the Spirit is much more subtle and diverse than the neo-scholastic theologies recognized. Its effectiveness varies as it is enhanced or inhibited by human freedom. This assistance does not preclude but rather works within not only the inevitable limitations of history and human finitude, but even within the weakness and frailty of the church itself.[33]

That the church is preserved by the Spirit in truth does not mean that the gospel will not suffer from an inadequate and at times even misguided presentation, nor does it deny that at any given moment in the church some individual members may fundamentally depart from the gospel. Indefectibility means only that at least some of the church's members will always live in substantial fidelity to the gospel. This more modest evaluation of the assistance of the Spirit is consonant with the insight of Schell, and later Congar, that the human element of the church is not related to the divine according to the neo-scholastic model of the hypostatic union of the Logos and the human nature of Christ but according to the model of the covenantal union reflected in the people of

Israel's covenant with their God. This silent but varied activity of the Spirit, operative in and through the real freedom of human lives, is resistant to easy verification. Nevertheless, this more modest conceptualization of the Spirit's influence must be recognized as the normal manner in which the Spirit animates the church and preserves it in truth. If we are to acknowledge the Spirit's steadfast presence and activity in the life of the church, we must also accept the extent to which the effectiveness of the Spirit is both enhanced and inhibited by human freedom. It is precisely this plurality of modes and gradations of the activity of the Spirit which makes the distinction between the infallible and the fallible expressions of the ordinary teaching of the bishops so difficult. These infallible and fallible expressions are often intertwined in the bishops' complex teaching activity. And yet the proper distinction between the two is absolutely essential.

What of the extraordinary magisterium and its criteriological use of the conditions for infallibility? Tillard suggests that "[i]nfallible judgment represents the extreme limit of the 'point of reference for the faith' function."[34] If all of the authoritative teaching of the pope and bishops functions as a reference for the faith, the criteriological employment of the conditions for an infallible exercise finds its intelligibility as the identification of one particular manner in which the Spirit assists the church. It is a special and extraordinary assistance of the Spirit in which, in the face of a proximate threat to the fundamental integrity of the church's gospel proclamation, exercised under clearly discernible conditions, the faithful may rest secure in the knowledge that, in this particular instance, the church's proclamation is preserved from error. Within this theology of the assistance of the Holy Spirit the extraordinary magisterium will not be the normal mode by which the Holy Spirit assists the church in its proclamation of the gospel. Rather, the extraordinary magisterium represents in its solemn doctrinal judgments an intensified assistance of the Spirit necessary for the resolution of a disputed matter crucial to the faith of the church.

A theology of teaching authority which grounds itself in the broader notion of indefectibility and a richer, more developed theology of the assistance of the Holy Spirit will not preclude the notion of infallibility but will want to highlight the distinction between the descriptive and the criteriological uses of the conditions for the exercise of this special charism. It will recognize that the criteriological employment of the conditions for an infallible judgment will occur only infrequently. It will further acknowledge that there are many situations where, in spite of the church's trust that it will be preserved by the Spirit in truth, it cannot always be certain precisely when, how and to what extent the Spirit's assistance will be manifested.

Conclusion

In the eight chapters which have comprised this book we have reviewed ecclesiological works representing a number of different genres, theological schools and historical periods. The theologies of the ordinary universal magisterium have been articulated in ecclesiastical documents, neo-scholastic manuals, elaborate ecclesiological systems, and specific theological debates. Given the importance which questions of teaching authority have played in ecclesiology from the pontificate of Gregory XVI to that of John Paul II, one of the surprising discoveries has been the paucity of theological reflection on the universal teaching of the bishops dispersed throughout the world. Multivolume ecclesiological tracts, like Christian Pesch's manual of nine volumes, devoted no more than twenty and often as few as two or three pages to this topic. Amid this scarcity of theological reflection, J.M.A. Vacant's late nineteenth century monograph on the topic stands out. Even after Vatican II, Francis Sullivan's 1983 work on the magisterium was the only monograph to give this mode of church teaching more than a cursory nod. In usually brief theological treatments of this topic the most problematic aspect of the teaching, the verification of the exercise of the ordinary universal magisterium, was rarely considered. The conditions for the exercise of this mode of church teaching were articulated with little thought as to their suitability for discerning which particular teachings have been proposed by the ordinary universal magisterium. Related ecclesiological themes like covenant, pneumatology, the people of God, and charism were largely absent.

There were, however, elements in the ecclesiological contributions of Newman, Schell, Congar, Legrand and Tillard, which could provide a new foundation for a theological consideration of the ordinary universal magisterium. The work of these and other contemporary theologians suggests one possibility for reconceiving the church's teaching on the ordinary universal magisterium. This possibility rests in the integration of an ecclesiology of communion with a theology of teaching authority. This integration, tentatively explored here, requires much more development.

There are at least four important issues closely related to our topic which have been largely bracketed from this work but which deserve a fuller treatment than could be provided here: (1) the ancient role of the ordinary teaching of the episcopate as an expression of the *regula fidei*, (2) the proper response owed on the part of the faithful to the teachings of the ordinary universal magisterium, (3) the nature of a "strictly collegial act," and (4) a theology of the assistance of the Holy Spirit.

1. We have been concerned with the ordinary infallible teaching of the episcopal college. Its historical focus has been directed toward the nineteenth and twentieth centuries when the church's understanding of this ordinary infallible teaching shifted demonstrably and came to be understood according to the model of the extraordinary magisterium and was invoked explicitly by Pius IX in order to quell theological dissent among a number of German theologians. The universal teaching of the bishops which was prominent in the early church as the normative expression of the *regula fidei* gradually became bound to the doctrinal formulations of the papacy. This ancient understanding of the ordinary teaching of the bishops, reflected in Augustine's famous "*securus judicat orbis terrarum*" and Vincent of Lerins' "*quodsemper, quod ubique, quod ab omnibus creditum est*" requires a much more ambitious exploration than was possible here.

2. The proper response which a believer owes to a particular church teaching must be commensurate with the commitment which the church itself has made to that particular teaching. If the church has yet to bind itself irrevocably to a teaching then it cannot demand an irrevocable assent from the faithful. Over the last two decades numerous studies

have appeared on the important question of the response owed to teachings of the ordinary non-universal (non-infallible) magisterium. The tentative conclusions offered in chapter 8 regarding the ascription of infallibility to the teachings of the ordinary universal magisterium suggest that more work needs to be done concerning the response owed to the teachings of the universal episcopate outside of council. The contention of many scholars that one cannot attach the negative note of heresy to the rejection of a teaching of the ordinary universal magisterium suggests that the response owed to such teachings cannot be collapsed without qualification into the response of faith owed to defined dogma. Similarly, the difficulties in employing the conditions for the exercise of the ordinary universal magisterium criteriologically suggests a reconsideration of the status of the theologian who dissents from teachings purportedly taught infallibly by the ordinary universal magisterium.[35] While the dissent of a theologian in this situation must be distinguished from that of the theologian offering legitimate dissent to an authoritative non-infallible teaching, such dissent need not be interpreted as separating the theologian from the Roman Catholic communion.

3. It has been asserted throughout this study that an adequate theology of the ordinary universal magisterium requires a coherent theology of the episcopacy. It is not an exaggeration to say that the movement toward a rich, fully developed theology of the episcopacy which attempts to incorporate the many advances made at the Second Vatican Council is still in its infancy. For example, one of the more perplexing questions raised by the council concerns the nature of a "strictly collegial act." This matter has ramifications not only for an adequate understanding of the ordinary universal magisterium but for another contemporary debate of at least equal importance—the collegial status of episcopal conferences. The term "strictly collegial act" may represent what Ladislas Örsy has called a "seminal locution," ". . . an expression which conveys an insight into the truth but without defining it with precision; it needs to be developed further. It is a broad and intuitive

approach to a mystery that leaves plenty of room for future discoveries."[36] As a seminal locution, however, future work is needed in order to flesh out the true nature of collegial activity. It may be necessary to bring the overly juridical understanding of "strict collegial acts" into harmony with a recognition of the fundamentally collegial character of all episcopal ministry.

4. One of the striking features of Eastern theology is its pronounced pneumatological vision of the church. The Western church's Christo-monist tendencies have left little room for a consideration of the Holy Spirit's animating presence in the church. One consequence has been the West's sparsely developed theology of the assistance of the Holy Spirit. While the modest outlines for such a theology were offered in chapter 8, the topic demands much more attention than it has received to date. The sad consequence of this impoverished theology has been a tendency in many church quarters toward a Catholic fundamentalism too eager to attribute the hand of God to every doctrinal formulation.

A theology of the ordinary universal magisterium of bishops demands a consideration not only of the magisterium and the episcopacy, but also the papacy, collegiality, infallibility, the local church and pneumatology. The basic conclusions of this book confirm the close relationship which exists between questions of authority and questions of community. The subject matter of this book, the ordinary universal magisterium, reveals more about the current state of ecclesiology in general then it does about any one theology of teaching authority. Indeed, our study of this mode of church teaching suggests a church in the midst of an ecclesiological paradigm shift. What was true of Vatican II is true of the Roman Catholic church itself twenty-five years after the council: this is a church in transition. Whether one uses as an indicator the development of the third world churches, the more active role of episcopal conferences or the multiplication of lay ministries, there is ample evidence for the gradual but real emergence of the Roman Catholic communion as what Rahner called a *Weltkirche.*

The fundamental dynamism of the church has shifted; if for a century and a half, beginning with the pontificate of Gregory XVI, the dynamic movement of the church was consistently centripetal, the fundamental dynamism of the church now appears to be centrifugal. But the transformation of large-scale institutions and social structures seldom takes place at a uniform rate; if signs of a broad ecclesiological transformation are apparent, evidence of a transformation in the theology of teaching authority is less pronounced. Most of the theologies of the ordinary universal magisterium examined here are at odds with many of the more promising trajectories sanctioned by Vatican II. The identification of the ordinary universal magisterium with the ordinary papal magisterium, the attempt to use the ordinary universal magisterium as a means of stifling theological dissent, the attenuation of the witness of the local communities by an episcopal college almost half of whose membership possess no pastoral charge to a true local church—all reflect a general tension between a more centrifugal, relational and communal vision of the church and a view of teaching authority too often dominated by a rigid hierarchical juridicism cautious of the principles of collegiality and subsidiarity articulated in the documents of Vatican II.

Yves Congar once suggested that at least fifty years were required for the full effects of an ecumenical council to be internalized by the church. It should not be surprising then that the *aggiornamento* which Vatican II represented has not yet been fully realized. Our attempt has been to resituate the ordinary universal magisterium within an ecclesiology of communion and represents, one would hope, at least a modest contribution toward a fuller implementation of the vision of the Second Vatican Council and a greater integration of the teaching authority of the church into that vision.

Notes

Introduction

[1] Floyd Anderson, ed., *Council Daybook,* Sessions 1 & 2 (Washington, D.C.: NCWC, 1965), 27.

[2] Hans Küng, *Infallible? An Inquiry* (Garden City, N.Y.: Doubleday, 1971).

[3] John C. Ford and Germain Grisez, "Contraception and the Infallibility of the Ordinary Magisterium," *Theological Studies* 39 (1978): 258–312.

[4] See the July 25th, 1986 letter from Cardinal Ratzinger to Fr. Curran in Charles E. Curran, *Faithful Dissent* (Kansas City: Sheed & Ward, 1986), 268–69. This volume contains the complete documentation of the correspondence between Curran and the CDF.

Chapter 1

[1] For the history of teaching authority in the church see: John P. Mackey, *The Modern Theology of Tradition* (New York: Herder and Herder, 1963); Hans von Campenhausen, *Ecclesiastical Authority and Spiritual Power in the Church of the First Three Centuries* (Stanford: Stanford University Press, 1969); Yves Congar, "Theologians and the Magisterium in the West: From the Gregorian Reform to the Council of Trent," *Chicago Studies* 17 (Summer 1978): 210–24; John E. Lynch, "The Magistery and Theologians from the Apostolic Fathers to the Gregorian Reform," *Chicago Studies* 17 (Summer 1978): 188–209; Michael D. Place, "From Solicitude to Magisterium: Theologians and Magisterium from the Council of Trent to the First Vatican Council," *Chicago Studies* 17 (Summer 1978): 225–241; Avery Dulles, "The Magisterium in History: Theological

191

Considerations," chapter in *A Church to Believe In* (New York: Cross-road, 1982), 103–117.

Many of the patristic references cited here have been drawn from three seminal essays by Yves Congar: "The Historical Development of Authority in the Church," in *Problems of Authority,* ed. John M. Todd (Baltimore: Helicon Press, 1962), 119–156; *"Bref historique des formes du terme 'magisterium',"* Revue des sciences philosophiques et théologiques 60 (1976): 99–112; *"Pour une histoire sémantique du terme 'magisterium',"* Revue des sciences philosophiques et théologiques 60 (1976): 85–97; [References will be made to the English translations of the last two articles found in *Readings in Moral Theology No. 3,* ed. Charles E. Curran and Richard A. McCormick (New York: Paulist, 1982), 297–331].

[2] Yves Congar, "A Semantic History of the Term 'Magisterium'," in *Readings in Moral Theology No. 3, 297.*

[3] Ibid., 297f. This application of *magisterium* to God rather than the church is common in patristic writings. Congar cites as further examples, Tertullian, *Cod. Theod.* 16, 5,5; Lactantius, *Epitome* 39; Augustine, *Sermo* 298, 5. Later it will still be found in the writings of Thomas Aquinas, *Contra impugnantes,* c.2, and in Bonaventure, *Sermo* IV n. 20.

[4] Congar, "A Semantic History . . . ," 302ff.

[5] Congar justifies his decision to treat the first ten centuries of the church as one period: "I wondered at first whether it was not necessary, from our present standpoint, to distinguish as two separate periods the Church of the Martyrs and the Church from the fourth to the tenth century. In spite of certain slight reservations I shall indicate, I do not think this advisable. As regards the idea of authority, they both belong to the same ecclesiological world." Yves Congar, "The Historical Development of Authority in the Church," 124–25.

[6] *Epist.* 14.4.

[7] *Magnesians* 4 and 7; *Smyrnaeans* 8.

[8] Yves Congar, *Tradition and Traditions* (New York: Macmillan, 1967), 279.

[9] Irenaeus of Lyons, *Adversus haereses,* lib. 3, c. 3.

[10] Congar, *Tradition and Traditions,* 177–78. See also "The Historical Development of Authority in the Church," 126ff.

[11] John E. Lynch, "The Magistery and Theologians from the Apostolic Fathers to the Gregorian Reform," 194ff. See also W. Telfer, *The Office of a Bishop* (London: Darton, Longman & Todd, 1962), 148; John Zizioulas, "The Development of Conciliar Structures to the Time of the First Ecumencial Council," in *Councils and the Ecumenical Movement* (Geneva: World Council of Churches, 1968), 34–51.

[12] *De Synodis* 5, as quoted in Congar, "A Brief History of the Forms of the Magisterium . . . ," in *Readings in Moral Theology No. 3,* 316.

[13] Congar, "The Historical Development of Authority in the Church," 130. Congar finds many references in early ordination rites to the demand that the bishop focus not on his *dominium* or *potestas* but on his *ministerium.* For the bishop the *prodesse* was always to be an integral part of the *praeesse.*

[14] Ibid., 127.

[15] Josef Pieper, *Guide to Thomas Aquinas* (New York: Pantheon, 1962), 60.

[16] M.-D. Chenu, *Toward Understanding Saint Thomas* (Chicago: Regnery, 1964), 20. Pieper also has commented on the unique status of the *magistri,* a status which was foreign to the Eastern church: "The Christian East, the Eastern Orthodox Church, knows no such phenomenon. In the East it was inconceivable that a corporate body should exist, like the *magistri* of the theological faculty taken as a whole, who possessed firm authority in matters of Christian doctrine (though in a way difficult to comprehend and to describe) without being clearly integrated into the ecclesiastical hierarchy." Pieper, 59–60.

[17] For these distinctions in Thomas see IV *Sent.* d. 19, q. 2, a. 2, q^a 2 ad 4 and *Quodlibet* III, 9 ad 3.

[18] Yves Congar, "Theologians and the Magisterium in the West: From the Gregorian Reform to the Council of Trent," 214ff.; Avery Dulles, "The Magisterium in History: Theological Considerations," 109ff.

[19] Yves Congar, *L'Église de Saint Augustin à l'époque moderne* (Paris: Cerf, 1970), 153–55.

[20] Thomas Aquinas, for example will continue to speak of the church as the *congregatio fidelium.*

[21] Michael D. Place, "From Solicitude to Magisterium . . . ," 226.

[22] Congar, *L'Église de Saint Augustin à l'époque moderne,* 371–89.

[23] For more developed treatments of this shift from a bipartite to a tripartite ecclesiology see Joseph Fuchs, *"Origines d'une trilogie ecclésiologique a l'époque rationaliste de la théologie," Revue des sciences philosophiques et théologiques* 53 (1969): 186–211; Hermann Josef Pottmeyer, *Unfehlbarkeit und Souveränität: Die päpstliche Unfehlbarkeit im System der ultramontanen Ekklesiologie des 19. Jahrhunderts* (Mainz: Matthias-Grünewald, 1975), 145–72.

[24] As quoted in Congar, "A Semantic History of the Term 'Magisterium'," in *Readings in Moral Theology No. 3,* 307.

[25] For Franzelin's use of the tripartite schema see *"Thesis V: Declaratur distinctio triplicis potestatis in Ecclesia."* Johann Baptist Franzelin, *Theses de Ecclesia Christi* (Rome: Cong. for the Prop. of the Faith, 1887), 43ff.

[26] *Acta Apostolicae Sedes* (hereafter rendered as *AAS*) 28 (1896): 721–23.

[27] Louis Billot, *De Immutabilitate Traditionis Contra Modernam Haeresim Evolutionismi* (Rome: Gregorian University, 1922), 20n.1.

[28] See Roger Aubert, Johannes Beckmann, Patrick J. Corish and Rudolf Lill, *The Church in the Age of Liberalism,* vol. 8 of *History of the Church* (New York: Crossroad, 1981), 304–18; Yves Congar, *"L'Ecclésiologie de la révolution française au concile du Vatican, sous le signe de l'affirmation de l'autorité," Revue des sciences religieuses* 34 (1960): 77–114.

[29] For evidence of this movement in pontifical documents see *Humani Generis* [*AAS* 42 (1950): 561–78]; *Si Diligis* [*AAS*, 46 (1954): 313–17]; *Magnificate Dominum mecum* [*AAS* 46 (1954): 667–77]. In these documents Pius XII effectively subsumed all teaching authority under the formal teaching authority of the papacy. On this point see also Max Seckler, "*Die Theologie als kirchliche Wissenschaft nach Pius XII. und Paul VI*," *Theologische Quartalschrift* 149 (1969): 212–14; Georg Rheinbay, *Das ordentliche Lehramt in der Kirche: Die Konzeption Papst Pius XII und das Modell Karl Rahners im Vergleich* (Trier: Paulinus, 1988), 25–65.

Chapter 2

[1] Congar, "*L'Ecclésiologie de la révolution française . . . ,*" 90.

[2] Gerald McCool, *Catholic Theology in the Nineteenth Century: The Quest for a Unitary Method* (New York: Seabury, 1977), 24–25.

[3] For more on ultramontanism see Roger Aubert, *Le Pontificat de Pie IX,* volume 21 of *Histoire de l'Eglise,* ed. A. Fliche and V. Martin (Paris: Bloud & Gay, 1952), 262–310, 537–41; Roger Aubert, "*La géographie ecclésiologique au XIXe siècle,*" in *L'Ecclesiologie au XIXe Siècle,* ed. M. Nédoncelle, R. Aubert, et al. (Paris: Cerf, 1960), 11–55; Congar, "L'Ecclésiologie de la révolution française . . . ," 97–106.

[4] Prior to the 1960s it was common for studies of nineteenth century German Catholic theology to briefly note the heretical excesses of Hermes and Günther and the dead end street of the Tübingen school before turning to the German neo-scholastics. Recent work in Germany and the United States on nineteenth century German Catholic theology has done much to correct this distortion. See Heinrich Fries and Georg Schweiger, eds., *Katholische Theologen Deutschlands im 19. Jahrhundert,* 3 volumes (Munich: Kosel, 1975); Thomas F. O'Meara, *Romantic Idealism and Roman Catholicism: Schelling and the Theologians* (Notre Dame: University of Notre Dame Press, 1982); *Culture and Church: German Catholic Theology, 1860–1914* (Notre Dame: University of Notre Dame Press, 1991); Heinrich Schmidinger and Bernhard Braun, eds., *Christliche Philosophie im katholischen Denken des 19. und 20. Jahrhunderts,* 3 volumes (Graz: Styria, 1987).

[5] O'Meara, *Romantic Idealism and Roman Catholicism,* 94ff. For more on the Catholic Tübingen school see J.R. Geiselmann, *Die katholische Tübinger Schule: Ihre theologische Eigenart* (Freiburg: Herder, 1964).

[6] In *Mirari Vos* (1832) Gregory condemned the French *L'Avenir* movement and warned of the consequences of rationalism; in 1835 the work of Bautain and Hermes were condemned (the latter posthumously).

[7] On the revolution of 1848 and the impact of these events on the church see Aubert, Beckmann, et al., 83–330; L. Salvatorelli, *La rivoluzione europea* (Milan: Rizzoli, 1949); H. Hermelink, *Das Christentum in der Menschheitsgeschichte von der Französischen Revolution bis zur Gegenwart,* vol. 2 (Stuttgart: Metzler and Wunderlich, 1951–55), 40–95; E. Hales, *Pius IX. A Study in European Politics and Religion in the 19th Century* (New York: Kenedy, 1954); *The Catholic Church in the Modern World: A Survey from the French Revolution to the Present* (Garden City: Hanover House, 1958), 17–133; J. Schmidlin, *Papstgeschichte der neuesten Zeit,* vol. 2 (Munich: Kosel-Pustet, 1833–39), 1–330; Roger Aubert, *Le Pontificat de Pie IX.*

[8] Joseph Kleutgen, *Die Philosophie der Vorzeit* (Münster: Theissing, 1863); *Die Theologie der Vorzeit* (Münster: Theissing, 1853, 2nd edition, 1867).

[9] Döllinger used this expression in his opening speech at the 1863 Munich Congress. Ignaz von Döllinger, *"Die Vergangenheit und Gegenwart der katholischen Theologie,"* in *Kleinere Schriften,* ed. F.A. Reusch (Stuttgart: Cotta, 1890), 161–81.

[10] McCool, 137.

[11] Aubert, Beckmann, et al., 308.

[12] Thomas O'Meara, *Culture and Church: German Catholic Theology, 1860–1914,* chapter 2.

[13] Aubert, Beckmann, et al., 239. Much of the material in this section is drawn from the work done by John P. Boyle on the historical and theological background to the Munich Congress and *Tuas libenter* in "The Ordinary Magisterium: Towards a History of the Concept," *Heythrop Journal* 20 (1979): 380–98; 21 (1980): 14–29.

[14] For a study of the influence of the papal nuncios in Munich during this time period, see Rudolph Lill, *"Die deutschen Theologieprofessoren im*

Urteil des Münchener Nuntius," in *Reformata Reformanda (Festgabe* for Hubert Jedin), vol. 2, ed. Erwin Iserloh and Konrad Repgen (Münster: Aschendorff, 1965), 483–507.

[15] Frohschammer, in response to the Congregation of the Index's placement of an earlier work on the Index, had published *Über der Freiheit der Wissenschaft* (1861), in which he asserted the independence of the sciences in relation to the dogmatic authority of the church. This work elicited from Rome a letter (*Gravissimas inter,* 1862), addressed to Archbishop von Scherr, condemning Frohschammer's views. Boyle, "The Ordinary Magisterium: Towards a History of the Concept (1)," 382.

[16] Letter from Gonella to Antonelli, August 21, 1863, as quoted in Boyle, 384–85.

[17] Boyle, 387. Reisach knew as well of Johann Evangelist Kuhn's disagreement with Franz Jakob Clemens, a lay neo-scholastic who had chided theologians and philosophers for not taking sufficient account of ecclesiastical directives in their writings. See Aubert, Beckmann, et al., 243–44.

[18] Boyle, "The Ordinary Magisterium: Towards a History of the Concept (1)," 390.

[19] Pius Gams, ed., *Die Verhandlungen der Versammlung katholischen Gelehrter in München* (Regensburg: Manz, 1863), 5–8.

[20] The key section reads in the Latin text: "... *Namque etiamsi ageretur de illa subiectione, quae fidei divinae actu est praestanda, limitanda tamen non esset ad ea, quae expressis oecumenicorum Conciliorum aut Romanorum Pontificum huiusque Sedis decretis definita sunt, sed ad ea quoque extendenda, quae ordinario totius Ecclesiae per orbem dispersae magisterio tamquam divinitus revelata traduntur ideoque universali et constanti consensu a catholicis theologis ad fidem pertinere retinentur.*" DS 2879. I have used John Boyle's English translation of this passage. Boyle, "The Ordinary Magisterium: Towards a History of the Concept (1)," 397.

[21] The term *ordinarium* did appear in other ecclesiastical contexts. In the writings of canonists it was used to distinguish that power which was *adnexum officio,* a power exercised by a bishop in his own diocese or a pastor in his own parish. This was a *potestas ordinaria* as opposed to a *potestas delegata.*

It was also used in the late eighteenth century by Gallican writers in reference to papal primacy; they distinguished the exercise of ordinary power from an extraordinary exercise of power and held that the pope could intervene in the affairs of the local church only in extraordinary situations. Vatican I's declaration that the pope's jurisdiction over the local churches was full, ordinary, immediate and episcopal was a reaction to this Gallican distinction. See Gustave Thils, *"Potestas Ordinaria,"* in *L'Episcopat et l'Eglise Universelle,* ed. Yves Congar and B.-D. Dupuy (Paris: Cerf, 1962), 693.

[22] Kleutgen was born in Munich. He was ordained in 1837 for the Society of Jesus under another name because of difficulties with the Prussian government over the question of military service. He taught at Fribourg and Brig, Switzerland from 1838 to 1843. He was called to Rome in 1843 and resided at the German College. In 1851 he was appointed Consultor to the Congregation of the Index and was an influential *peritus* at Vatican I. He died at Kaltern in 1883. John P. Boyle, "The Ordinary Magisterium: Towards a History of the Concept (2)," 14–29; Konrad Deufel, *Kirche und Tradition: Ein Beitrag zur Geschichte der theologischen Wende im 19. Jahrhundert am Beispiel des kirchlich-theologischen Kampfprograms, P. Joseph Kleutgens, S.J.* (Munich: Schöningh, 1976).

[23] Deufel, 118. For the theology of tradition in the Roman school see Walter Kasper, *Die Lehre und Die Tradition in Der Römischen Schule,* 392–401.

[24] Joseph Kleutgen, *Die Theologie der Vorzeit* (1st ed.), 35–63.

[25] Kleutgen, *Die Theologie der Vorzeit,* 46–47.

[26] Ibid., 41–42.

[27] Ibid., 47.

[28] While *Tuas libenter* actually does not specifically mention the bishops but speaks of that teaching maintained by the *"ordinario totius Ecclesiae per orbem dispersae magisterio . . ."* Kleutgen's own writing makes it clear that the college of bishops is to be understood by *ecclesia:* *"Wir verstehen hier unter Kirche den Lehrkörper, dem alle Gläubigen unterworfen sind, also die Bischöfe in Vereinigung mit ihrem Haupte, dem Papste."* Ibid., 42.

[29] Ibid., 50–52.

[30] John P. Boyle, "The Ordinary Magisterium: Towards a History of the Concept (2)," 25–26.

[31] Ibid., 21.

[32] This reading of the text was first suggested to me by Prof. Francis Sullivan during a conversation in Rome on May 13, 1990.

[33] For the history and analysis of *Dei Filius* see J.M.A. Vacant, *Etudes théologiques sur les Constitutions du Concile du Vatican d'après les Actes du Concile*, 2 volumes (Paris: Delhomme et Briguet, 1895); Roger Aubert, *"La Constitution Dei Filius du Concile du Vatican*," chapter 4 in *Le Problème de l'Acte de Foi* (Louvain: Wainy, 1945), 131–91; J. P. Torrell, *La théologie de l'épiscopat au premier concile du Vatican*, (Paris: Cerf, 1961); Hermann J. Pottmeyer, *Der Glaube vor dem Anspruch der Wissenschaft: Die Konstitution über den katholischen Glauben "Dei Filius" des 1. Vatikanschen Konzils und die unveröffentlichten theologischen Voten der vorbereitenden Kommission* (Freiburg: Herder, 1968).

[34] Marc Caudron, *"Magistère ordinaire et infaillibilité pontificale d'après la constitution Dei Filius,"* *Ephemerides Theologicae Lovanienses* 36 (1960): 398. This section on Vatican I draws on Caudron's study of the treatment of the ordinary magisterium in *Dei Filius*.

[35] *"Porro fide divina et catholica ea omnia credenda sunt, quae in Verbo Dei scripto vel tradito continentur, et ab Ecclesia, sive solemni iudicio sive ordinario magisterio credenda proponuntur."* *Sacrorum Conciliorum Nova, et Amplissima Collectio,* vol. 1, ed. Giovanni Domenico Mansi (Paris: Welter, 1901–27), 51, 35a.

[36] Ibid., 51, 47c.

[37] Ibid., 51, 215d–216a.

[38] Ibid., 51, 224c–d.

[39] Ibid., 51, 322.

[40] Caudron, 426–28.

[41] *AAS* 42 (1950), 757.

[42] For a study of the development of the papal encyclical as a distinct mode of magisterial teaching, see Arthur Peiffer, *Die Enzykliken und Ihr formaler Wert für die dogmatische Methode* (Freiburg: Universitätsverlag, 1968).

[43] In *Humani Generis* Pius XII wrote: "*Neque putandum est, ea quae in Encyclicis Litteris proponuntur, assensum per se non postulare, cum in iis Pontifices supremam sui Magisterii potestatem non exerceant. Magisterio enim ordinario haec docentur, de quo illud etiam valet: 'Qui vos audit, me audit'.*" *AAS* 42 (1950): 568 (DS 3885). Along with Caudron's refutation of this interpretation of the ordinary universal magisterium, see Gustave Thils' fine analysis of the documents of Vatican I and his subsequent rejection of the attribution of infallibility to the ordinary papal magisterium based on the important *relatio* of Bishop Gasser. Gustave Thils, *Primauté et infaillibilité du Pontife Romain à Vatican I* (Leuven: Leuven University Press, 1989), 305–14.

[44] Deufel, 93.

[45] Aubert, Beckmann, et al., 85.

[46] Joseph Hoffman has suggested the inseparability of the debate regarding the role and nature of theological inquiry and the broader church/state debate. Joseph Hoffman, "*Théologie, magistère et opinion publique,*" *Recherches de science religieuse* 71 (1983): 245–58.

[47] Giuseppe Alberigo, "The Authority of the Church in the Documents of Vatican I and II," in *Authority in the Church,* ed. Piet Fransen (Leuven: Leuven University Press, 1983), 124.

[48] Congar, "*L'Ecclésiologie de la révolution française . . . ,*" 105; see also Giuseppe Ruggieri, " *'Magistère Ordinaire.' La Lettre 'Tuas Libenter' de Pie IX du 21 Decembre 1863,*" *Recherches de science religieuse* 71 (1983): 266.

[49] For this shift from the *testificatio fidei* to the *determinatio fidei* see Hermann J. Pottmeyer, "*Die Bedingungen des bedingungslosen Unfehlbarkeitsanspruchs,*" *Theologische Quartalschrift* 159 (1979): 92–109; "*Das Lehramt der Hirten und seine Ausübung,*" *Theologisch-praktische Quartalschrift* 128 (1980): 336–48; Ruggieri, 261–62.

[50] Alberigo, 126.

Chapter 3

[1] Joseph A. Komonchak, "The Ordinary Papal Magisterium and Religious Assent," in *Readings in Moral Theology No. 3,* ed. Charles E. Curran and Richard A. McCormick (New York: Paulist, 1982), 70–71.

[2] John A. Gallagher, *Time Past, Time Future: An Historical Study of Catholic Moral Theology* (New York: Paulist Press, 1990), 31, 51.

[3] McCool, 32.

[4] For the foundational influence of Giovanni Perrone, Carlo Passaglia and Clemens Schrader see Walter Kasper, *Die Lehre von der Tradition in der Römischen Schule* (Freiburg: Herder, 1962); Catalino Arévalo, *The Ecclesiology of Giovanni Perrone, Carlo Passaglia and Clemens Schrader* (Rome: Gregorian, 1959); Heribert Schauf, *Carl Passaglia und Clemens Schrader, Beitrag zur Theologiegeschichte des neunzehnten Jahrhunderts* (Rome: Gregorian, 1938).

[5] McCool, 32, 82–84.

[6] Karl Neufeld notes the positive contributions to ecclesiology made by this "school" and forcefully rejects the scholarly tendency to speak of the "Roman school" pejoratively as having been negative and anti-historical. Karl Neufeld, " *'Römische Schule,' Beobachtungen und Überlegungen zur genauren Bestimmung,"* *Gregorianum* 63 (1982): 677–99.

[7] Born in Turin, Perrone entered the Jesuits in 1815, and taught theology first at Orvieto (1817–1824), and then at the Roman College for most of his career. His *Praelectiones* would eventually go through 34 editions.

[8] Kasper, 53; T. Howland Sanks, *Authority in the Church: A Study in Changing Paradigms* (Missoula, Montana: Scholars' Press, 1974), 23.

[9] Giovanni Perrone, *Praelectiones Theologicae,* vol. 4 (Rome: Cong. for the Prop. of the Faith, 1844), 141.

[10] Ibid., 169–72.

[11] Ibid., 18–19.

[12] Kasper, 77–79.

[13] Perrone, 398–426.

[14] Ibid., 527.

[15] Ibid., 792–93.

[16] Carlo Passaglia was born in Lucca, Italy and became a Jesuit in 1827. From 1840 to 1844 he was a prefect of studies at the German College and

in 1844 he became a professor of dogmatic theology at the Roman College. In 1859 he left the Jesuits and was later involved in several controversies, including the placement of one of his works on the Index, forcing
his departure from Rome. He accepted a professorship in moral philosophy at the state University of Turin and edited a number of Italian
journals. From 1868 on he sought reconciliation with the church, finally
achieving it weeks before his death in Turin in 1887.

Clemens Schrader was born in Hanover, Germany, studied at the
German College in Rome and was ordained in 1846. He became a Jesuit
in 1848 and two years later was prefect of studies at the German College.
One year later he was given a faculty position at the Roman College.
Schrader and Passaglia collaborated on a number of works, undertaking
joint studies on both the early fathers of the church and the dogma of the
immaculate conception. Schrader was involved in the planning of the
First Vatican Council and became noted for his increasingly extreme
pro-papalist positions.

[17] Carlo Passaglia, *De Ecclesia Christi* (Ratisbone: Manz, 1853), 35.

[18] Sanks, 39.

[19] Kasper, 56–59.

[20] Franzelin, born in Tyrol, entered the Jesuits in 1834, and after complet-
ing his theological studies in Rome and Louvain, returned in 1850 to
teach theology at the Gregorian University in Rome. He was an important consultant to various Roman congregations and was the probable
author of the first draft of Vatican I's *Dei Filius*. His theological work
exemplified the more positive direction of the theology of the Roman
School. In 1876 he was made cardinal by Pius IX.

[21] Michael Place, "From Solicitude to Magisterium: Theologians and
Magisterium from the Council of Trent to the First Vatican Council,"
Chicago Studies 17 (Summer, 1978): 234.

[22] Johann Baptist Franzelin, *De Divina Traditione et Scriptura* (4th ed.,
Rome: Cong. for the Prop. of the Faith, 1896), 11–21. On Franzelin's
theology of tradition see Sanks, 41–61. There is some debate regarding
whether the complete identification of tradition with the magisterium
occurred with Franzelin or only later with Billot. If Franzelin did not
explicitly make this identification, his theological stance made that con-

clusion a natural one, and one quickly developed by those who followed after him. For the various positions on this debate see Walter Burghardt, "The Catholic Concept of Tradition in the Light of Modern Theological Thought." *CTSA Proceedings* 6 (1951): 42–77; J. P. Mackey, *The Modern Theology of Tradition* (New York: Herder and Herder, 1963), 3ff.

[23] Franzelin, *De Divina Traditione,* 104ff.

[24] Sanks, 55.

[25] Franzelin, *De Divina Traditione,* 111.

[26] Johann Baptist Franzelin, *Theses De Ecclesia Christi* (Rome: Cong. for the Prop. of the Faith, 1887), 261.

[27] Sanks, 60–61.

[28] Franzelin, *De Divina Traditione et Scriptura,* 122–23.

[29] Ibid., 281.

[30] Domenico Palmieri, *Tractatus de Romano Pontifice cum Prolegomena de Ecclesia* (2nd ed., Prati: Officina Libraria Giachetti, 1891). Born in Piacenza, Italy, Palmieri entered the Jesuits in 1852 and taught at the Gregorian University in Rome from 1861 to 1878. Palmieri maintained some distance from the theology of the neo-Thomists. Because of some philosophical problems regarding the neo-Thomist movement he eventually fell out of favor in Rome. He was replaced by Camillo Mazella and in 1878 left for Maastricht, Holland, not returning to Rome until 1894 where he remained until his death in 1909.

Mazella was the better known figure of the two and eventually became an influential cardinal. However, as Sanks has noted, his theology of the magisterium differed little from that of Palmieri on the key points and was less developed. Sanks, 64.

[31] Sanks, 71; Kasper, 349.

[32] Palmieri, 637.

[33] Ibid., 206.

[34] Bernard Tepe, *Institutiones Theologicae in Usum Scholarum* (Paris: Lethielleux, 1894–96). Bernhard Tepe was born in Lindern, entered the

Jesuits in 1861, and taught in England for 32 years. He died in Valkenburg, Holland in 1904, where he taught for the last two years of his life.

[35] Ibid., 498.

[36] Ibid.

[37] Ibid., 294. Francis Sullivan makes a persuasive case for not translating the Latin *authenticum* and *authentice* as *authentic* which in modern English carries the sense of *genuine*. Sullivan generally translates it as *authoritative*. Francis A. Sullivan, *Magisterium: Teaching Authority in the Catholic Church* (New York: Paulist Press, 1983), 26ff.

[38] Pesch, 293.

[39] Ibid., 310.

[40] Ibid., 311.

[41] Michael, D'Herbigny, *Theologia de Ecclesia* (2nd ed., Paris: Beauchesne, 1921), 309–11. Michael D'Herbigny was born in Lille, France and entered the Jesuits in 1897. In 1912 he became a professor of Sacred Scripture and theology at the Jesuit scholasticate in Enghien, Belgium. In 1921 he was appointed director of graduate studies at the Gregorian University in Rome and in 1926 the rector of the Pontifical Oriental Institute. Although most of his life was spent in Oriental studies, his *Theologia de Ecclesia,* published in 1921, was acclaimed for its erudition.

[42] Hermann Dieckmann, *De Ecclesia* (Freiburg in Breisgau: Herder, 1925). Dieckmann taught at the Jesuit theologate in Valkenburg, Holland, from 1915 to 1928.

[43] Ibid., 65.

[44] Cf. D'Herbigny, 311, cited above, who began with the extraordinary magisterium of the bishops in council and then considered the ordinary universal magisterium according to the model of an ecumenical council.

⁴⁵ Dieckmann, 72.

⁴⁶ Ibid., 74.

⁴⁷ Sullivan, *Magisterium,* 125. Salaverri taught at the Gregorian University from 1933 to 1940, and then went to teach at Comillas, Spain until his retirement. While teaching in Spain he wrote the *De Ecclesia* of the *Sacrae Theologiae Summa.* Nicolau contributed to the later edition of the work used in this study.

⁴⁸ Michael Nicolau and Joseph Salaverri, *Sacrae Theologiae Summa* (5th ed., Madrid: Biblioteca de Autores Cristianos, 1962), 665.

⁴⁹ Ibid., 666. Once again there is a return to Pesch's contention that an implicit or tacit concord of the bishops is sufficient for the ordinary universal magisterium.

⁵⁰ Sullivan has cited Salaverri's use of the word *irrevocabilem* as evidence for a more restrictive reading of the conditions for infallibility outlined in the conciliar text. J. Robert Dionne, however, rejected Sullivan's citation of a manual text as a means for interpreting a conciliar text and suggests that the conditions in article 25 could be given a broader reading. See Sullivan, *Magisterium,* 125–27; J. Robert Dionne, *The Papacy and the Church* (New York: Philosophical Library, 1987), 351 n.18.

⁵¹ Salaverri, 671.

⁵² Timothy Zapelena was born in Navarre, Spain in 1883. He entered the Society of Jesus, studying at Pamplona and at the University of Salamanca, and completed those studies in 1903. Ordained in 1917, he received his STD at the Gregorian University in 1921. He then taught at the Jesuit faculty in Oña, Spain from 1922 to 1928. In 1929 he began teaching at the Gregorian University and first published his *De Ecclesia Christi* in 1930. He continued teaching at the Gregorian until 1960.

⁵³ Timothy Zapelena, *De Ecclesia Christi,* vol. 2 (6th ed., Rome: Gregorian, 1954–55), 158.

[54] Ibid., 171.

[55] Ibid., 184.

[56] Ibid.

[57] Ibid., 185.

[58] Ibid., 185–86.

[59] Ibid., 187.

[60] Quoted from correspondence between Francis Sullivan and the author, September 9, 1989.

[61] Francis A. Sullivan, *De Ecclesia I: Quaestiones Theologiae Fundamentalis* (Rome: Gregorian, 1963). 281.

[62] Ibid., 283.

[63] Ibid., 304.

[64] Thomas Kuhn, *The Structure of Scientific Revolutions* (Chicago: The University of Chicago Press, 1962). See Sanks 109ff. Sanks's own study was limited to the manuals of Jesuit professors at the Roman College and the Gregoriana, beginning with Perrone and ending with Zapelena.

[65] Sanks, 113.

[66] For an historical treatment of the distinction between proposing the truth versus the safety of certain propositions, see John P. Boyle, "Theologians and Bishops: Freedom and Assent," *CTSA Proceedings* 44 (1989): 91–102.

[67] A theological note is a judgment by theologians, and occasionally the magisterium, regarding the truth or falsehood of doctrinal propositions. Positive theological notes are attached to true or safe propositions (e.g., *de fide divina et catholica, de fide definita, fidei proximum, theologice certum*). Negative notes are attached to false or at least dangerous propositions (e.g., *haeresi proxima, haeresim sapiens, errori proxima, errori sa-*

piens, temeraria, scandalosa, injuriosa). "The ultimate purpose of theological notes is both to safeguard the faith and to prevent any confusion between real divine revelation and theological opinion." Karl Rahner and Herbert Vorgrimler, eds., *Dictionary of Theology* (2nd ed., New York: Crossroad, 1981), s.v. "Theological notes."

Chapter 4

[1] Newman was familiar with the works of Giovanni Perrone and Carlo Passaglia and frequently cited Perrone, but that seems to have been the extent of his contact with the manual tradition.

[2] *AAS* 55 (1963): 1025.

[3] Miller, *John Henry Newman on the Idea of the Church* (Shepherdstown, W. Virginia: The Patmos Press, 1987), 3. Newman was born in 1801 and graduated from Trinity College, Oxford, in 1817 and in 1822 received a fellowship to Oriel College where he came under the influence of the high church Anglican tradition. Ordained an Anglican priest in 1825, he soon became one of the intellectual leaders of the Tractarian or Oxford movement. He was received into the Roman Catholic communion in 1845 and was ordained a Roman Catholic priest. He established the Oratory of St. Philip Neri in Birmingham, England where he lived the rest of his life. Created a cardinal in 1879, Newman died in 1890.

[4] Newman further wrote of the illative sense: ". . . in coming to its conclusion, it proceeds always the same way, by a method of reasoning, which, as I have observed above, is the elementary principle of mathematical calculus of modern times, which has so wonderfully extended the limits of abstract science." John Henry Newman, *An Essay in Aid of a Grammar of Assent*, 281.

[5] Miller, 34.

[6] John Henry Newman, *The Arians of the Fourth Century* (London: Longmans, Green and Co., 1908, originally published, 1833), 148.

[7] Avery Dulles, "Newman on Infallibility," *Theological Studies* 51 (1990): 442.

[8] S. Femiano, "A Sound Theology of the Laity," *Catholic Mind* 64 (October, 1966): 46; see also S. Femiano, *Infallibility of the Laity: The Legacy of Newman* (New York: Herder & Herder, 1967).

[9] John Henry Newman, *On Consulting the Faithful in Matters of Doctrine,* ed. John Coulson (Kansas City: Sheed & Ward, 1961, originally published, 1859), 63.

[10] Ibid., 73. This connection was made by Katherine Tillman in an unpublished paper, "*Phronesis:* The Economy of Reason," (1990).

[11] Newman is not always consistent in his differentiation between the terms *sensus fidelium* and *consensus fidelium.* They are often employed synonymously. However, I shall use *sensus fidelium* to refer generally to the sense of the faithful, that which they in fact believe. *Consensus fidelium* then will add the aspect of universal agreement to the notion of the *sensus fidelium.* See Francis A. Sullivan, *Magisterium: Teaching Authority in the Catholic Church* (New York: Paulist, 1983), 23.

[12] Newman, *On Consulting the Faithful,* 54–55.

[13] Miller, 151–52.

[14] Newman, *On Consulting the Faithful,* 64–71.

[15] For this contrast see Sanks, *Authority in the Church,* 148. Cf. T. Lynch, ed., "The Newman-Perrone Paper on Development," *Gregorianum* 16 (1935): 402–47; Allen Brent, "Newman and Perrone: Unreconcilable Theses on Development," *Downside Review* 102 (1984): 276–89; Owen Chadwick, *From Bossuet to Newman. The Idea of Doctrinal Development* (Cambridge: The University Press, 1957), 182–83.

[16] Quoted in Wilfrid Ward, *The Life of John Henry Cardinal Newman,* vol. 2 (London: Longmans, Green, and Co., 1912), 374. Avery Dulles has suggested that Newman may have gone too far in his resurrection of the medieval *schola theologorum.* While Newman used the analogy of courts of law interpreting acts of Parliament, Dulles notes that the courts are official governmental institutions whereas theologians in the modern world belong to the private sphere. Avery Dulles, "Newman on Infallibility," 447–48.

[17] Gary Lease, *Witness to the Faith: Cardinal Newman on the Teaching Authority of the Church* (Pittsburgh: Duquesne University, 1971), 114.

[18] Newman describes dogmas as ". . . supernatural truths irrevocably committed to human language, imperfect because it is human, but definitive and necessary because given from above." John Henry Newman, *An Essay on the Development of Christian Doctrine* (revised 1878 edition, Notre Dame: University of Notre Dame Press, 1989), 325. For more on Newman's principle of sacramentality as it applied to dogma see Miller, 17ff.

[19] Letter to Isy Froude, July 28, 1875, in *The Letters and Diaries of John Henry Newman,* vol. 27, ed. C.S. Dessain and Thomas Gornall (Oxford: Clarendon, 1975), 337–38.

[20] Letter to Henry Oxenham, November 9, 1865, in *The Letters and Diaries of John Henry Newman,* vol. 22, ed. C.S. Dessain (London: Nelson, 1972), 99.

[21] Though Newman was largely ignorant of the influence of romanticism on continental theologians, he likely came across several of the fundamental motifs of romanticism through the writing of Coleridge.

[22] For more on the episcopacy see A.J. Boekraad, "Newman's Vision of Episcopacy," in *Episcopale Munus (Festschrift* for J. Gijsen), ed. P. Delhaye and L. Elders (Assen: Van Gorcum, 1982), 329–49.

[23] Dulles, 448.

[24] Scheeben was born near Bonn in 1835. In 1852 he attended seminary in Rome and in 1858 was ordained a priest. He pursued graduate work at the Roman College where among his teachers were great figures from the Jesuit Roman school like Passaglia, Schrader, Franzelin and R. Cercia. Scheeben received doctorates in philosophy (1855) and theology (1859) and at the age of twenty-six he became a professor of dogmatic theology at the Cologne Seminary where he remained until his death in 1888.

[25] Eugen Paul, *Matthias Joseph Scheeben* (Graz: Styria, 1976), 10. Paul also offers an extensive bibliography on Scheeben in his *Denkweg und*

Denkform der Theologie von Matthias Joseph Scheeben (Munich: Huebner, 1970), X–XXI.

[26] Paul, *Denkweg,* 315ff.

[27] On Scheeben and Aquinas see G. Fritz, "Scheeben, M.J.," *Dictionnaire de théologie catholique* 14, 1272.

[28] Heribert Schauf and A. Eross, eds., *M.J. Scheeben, Briefe nach Rom* (Paderborn: Schöningh, 1940), 132; Paul, *Denkweg,* 32f.

[29] Yves Congar, *L'Église de Saint Augustin à L'époque moderne* (Paris: Cerf, 1970), 429–35.

[30] Nevertheless, Scheeben has been criticized for continuing in his ecclesiology that dualism so prominent in his theology of grace. See M.D. Koster, *Ekklesiologie im Werden* (Paderborn: Verlag der Bonifacius-Druckerei, 1940).

[31] Matthias Scheeben, *Handbuch der Katholischen Dogmatik,* vol. 3 [Volume 5 of *Gesammelte Schriften*] (Freiburg: Herder, 1959), 276.

[32] Thomas Aquinas, *De Veritate,* q.29, a. 4c; *Summa Theologiae,* III, q.8, a. 1, 5 and 6; III *Sentences,* dist. 13, q.2, a.2, sol.2.

[33] Paul, *Matthias Joseph Scheeben,* 25. See also L. Scheffczyk, "*Die Lehranschauungen M.J. Scheebens über das ökumenische Konzil,*" *Theologische Quartalschrift* 141 (1961): 129–73.

[34] Scheeben, *Dogmatik,* vol. 1, 86 (#145a).

[35] Ibid.

[36] Ibid., 87 (#148).

[37] Ibid., 88 (#150).

[38] Ibid., 89 (#154).

[39] W. Bartz, "*Le magistère de l'Église d'après Scheeben,*" in *L'Ecclésiologie au XIXe Siècle,* ed. M. Nédoncelle, R. Aubert, et al. (Paris: Cerf, 1960), 318.

[40] Ibid., 188 (#399).

[41] Ibid., 190 (#402).

[42] Scheeben, *Dogmatik,* vol. 1, 190 (403).

[43] Congar, *L'Église de Saint Augustin à l'époque moderne,* 435.

[44] Schell was born in Freiburg in Breisgau in 1850. He was ordained in 1873, after which he spent several years working in a parish. From 1879 to 1881 he studied at Rome and in 1884 began teaching at the University of Würzburg.

[45] Bernard Welte, *Auf der Spur des Ewigen* (Freiburg: Herder, 1965), 405.

[46] Herman Schell, *Der Katholizismus als Princip des Fortschritts* (Würzburg: Göbel, 1897), 88ff.

[47] Cited in O'Meara, *Culture and Church,* chapter 6.

[48] Herman Schell, *Christus* (Mainz: Kirchheim, 1906), 120.

[49] Herman Schell, "*Lehrende und lernende Kirche. Wissenschaft und Autorität,*" in *Kleinere Schriften,* ed. Karl Hennemann, (Paderborn: Schöningh, 1907), 485.

[50] Herman Schell, *Katholische Dogmatik,* vol. 3-1, (Paderborn: Schöningh, 1889–93), 397.

[51] Ibid., 408ff.

[52] Ibid., 420.

[53] Vacant was born in Morfontaine and in 1871 entered the Sulpician seminary at Metz. At Saint-Sulpice in Paris he came under the neo-scholastic influence of M. Brugère. In 1876 he was ordained for the diocese of Nancy, and after a brief period working in a parish, was appointed professor at the seminary in Nancy where he taught fundamental theology. While maintaining this teaching position, Vacant obtained degrees in theology and canon law from the seminary in Poitiers. From 1890 until his death he taught dogmatic theology. Vacant contributed in the editorship of numerous French journals, wrote a study on Vatican I and was the founder of the *Dictionnaire de théologie catholique.* Other works by Vacant include: *Histoire de la conception du sacrifice de la messe dans*

l'Église latine (Paris: Delhomme et Briguet, 1894); *Ètudes théologiques sur les constitutiones du Concile du Vatican d'après les actes du Concile,* 2 vols. (Paris, Lyon: Delhomme et Briguet, 1895).

[54] (Paris-Lyon: Delhomme et Briguet, 1887).

[55] Ibid., 18–19.

[56] Ibid., 22.

[57] Ibid., 25.

[58] Ibid., 29.

[59] Ibid., 35ff.

[60] Ibid., 38.

[61] Ibid., 39.

[62] Ibid., 41–42.

[63] Ibid., 44.

[64] Ibid., 48–49.

[65] Ibid., 56.

[66] Ibid., 63.

[67] Ibid., 67.

[68] Ibid., 80–81.

[69] Ibid., 84.

[70] Ibid., 87.

[71] Ibid., 94.

[72] Ibid., 98.

[73] Ibid., 104–05.

[74] Ibid., 107.

[75] Arthur Peiffer has reckoned Vacant the modern founder of the theological position opting for the infallibility of the ordinary papal magisterium. Arthur Peiffer, *Die Enzykliken und lhr formaler Wert für die dogmatische*

Methode (Freiburg: Universitätsverlag, 1968), 73. For a similar observation see also J. Robert Dionne, *The Papacy and the Church: A Study of Praxis and Reception in Ecumenical Perspective* (New York: Philosophical Library, 1987), 31ff. This claim for an infallible ordinary papal magisterium would be taken up by a number of writers in the twentieth century. Joseph Salaverri's position, early in his career, was that the ordinary papal magisterium was infallible whenever the pope made known his intention to bind the whole church to an absolute assent, as was the case, Salaverri claimed, with Pius IX's *Quanta cura* and the *Syllabus of Errors.* Joseph Salaverri, *"Valor de las Encíclicas a la luz de 'Humani Generis',"* *Miscelánea Comillas* 17 (1952): 135–72. Later he seemed to become more cautious and suggested only that the *ex cathedra* conditions could be fulfilled apart from a solemn pronouncement, as in an encyclical, when the pope's intent to teach *ex cathedra* is clearly manifest. Gustave Thils has expressed some sympathy for this more moderate reading as well. Joseph Salaverri, "Encyclicals," in *Sacramentum Mundi: An Encyclopedia of Theology,* vol. 2 (New York: Herder and Herder, 1968–70), 229–30; Gustave Thils, *Primauté et infaillibilité du Pontife romain à Vatican I* (Leuven: Leuven University Press, 1989), 305–14. Joseph Fenton maintained that the pope's putting an end to open discussion of a topic was sufficient for assuming that the charism of infallibility was operative. J. Clifford Fenton, "The Doctrinal Authority of Papal Encyclicals," *American Ecclesiastical Review* 121 (1949): 136–50, 210–20. Paul Nau proposed that when a series of popes can be established to have expounded in unanimity to the whole church on a matter of faith and morals that teaching may be assumed to be infallibly true. Paul Nau, *"Le Magistère pontifical ordinaire, lieu théologique,"* *Revue Thomiste* 56 (1956): 389–412. Later, Nau clarified his position, suggesting a distinction between an "infallible judgment," which pertained to solemn papal definitions, and "teaching faithful to revelation" which was similarly infallible but which pertained to any ordinary papal teaching which met his earlier criteria. Paul Nau, *"Le Magistère pontifical ordinaire au premier concile du Vatican,"* *Revue Thomiste* 62 (1962): 341–97. For other theologians holding variations of these positions, see J. Bellamy, *La théologie catholique au XIXe siècle* (Paris: Beauchesne, 1904), 239–41; Louis Billot, *Tractatus de Ecclesia Christi* (3rd, ed., Prati: Officina Libraria Giachetti, 1909–10), 640; Edmond Dublanchy, *"Infaillibilité du Pape,"* in *Dictionnaire de théologie catholique,* vol. 7, (Paris: Letouzey et Ané, 1927), 1638–1717; M. Labourdette, *"Les enseignements de l'Encyclique 'Humani Generis',"* *Revue Thomiste* 50 (1950): 32–55; Fidelis Gallati, *Wenn die Päpste sprechen: das ordentliche Lehramt des apostolischen Stuhles und die Zustimmung zu dessen Entscheidungen* (Vienna: Herder, 1960).

Chapter 5

[1] Journet was born in Geneva and attended the *Grand Seminaire* in Fribourg, Switzerland where he received advanced degrees and taught there from 1924 to 1970. In 1965 Pope Paul VI created him a cardinal.

[2] Congar, *L'Église de Saint Augustin à l'époque moderne,* 464.

[3] Jean-Pierre Torrell, "*Paul VI et le Cardinal Journet. Aux sources d'une ecclésiologie,*" *Nova et Vetera* 61 (1986), 161–74.

[4] Journet, *The Church of the Word Incarnate* {I. *The Apostolic Hierarchy* (New York: Sheed and Ward, 1954); II. *Sa Structure interne et son unité catholique* (Paris: Desclée de Brouwer, 1951); III. *Essai de théologie de l'histoire du salut* (Paris: Desclée de Brouwer, 1969)}.

[5] For a study of Journet's theology of the episcopal teaching office, see Thomas F. O'Meara, "The Teaching Office of Bishops in the Ecclesiology of Charles Journet," *The Jurist* 49 (1989): 23–47.

[6] O'Meara, "The Teaching Office of Bishops," 26.

[7] Journet, *The Apostolic Hierarchy,* 332.

[8] Ibid., 409.

[9] Ibid., 403.

[10] Ibid., 412. Emphasis found in text.

[11] Ibid., 415n[2].

[12] O'Meara, "The Teaching Office of Bishops," 34–47.

[13] Ibid., 36.

[14] Ibid., 40.

[15] Congar was born and raised in the Ardennes. After obligatory military service he entered the Dominican order in 1925 and was ordained in

1930. Congar committed his life to the ecumenical movement, primarily through a rigorous recovery of the rich ecclesiological tradition of the church often neglected since the Counter-Reformation. While studying at the Saulchoir, he came under the influence of the notable Thomistic scholar, M.-D. Chenu. Congar would spend most of the next 25 years teaching the *De Ecclesia* tract at the Saulchoir. In 1936 he began the ecclesiological collection *Unam Sanctam,* a gathering of important historical, theological and ecumenical studies which drew on the rich tradition of the church as a resource for contemporary theological reflection. Between the time of his first major publication in 1937 and his vindication at the Second Vatican Council, Congar would write under suspicion and with the imposition of severe limitations placed on him by Rome. He was a *peritus* and influential theologian at the council. Congar continued to write for two decades after the council before his fading health forced him to severely limit his scholarly output.

[16] David Louch, "The Contribution of Yves Congar to a Renewed Understanding of Teaching Authority in the Catholic Church" (Ph.D. diss., University of St. Michael's College, 1979), 53–56. See Yves Congar, *Sainte Église. Études et approches ecclésiologiques* (Paris: Cerf, 1963, 33ff).

[17] See Yves Congar, *Esquisses du Mystère de l'Église* (Paris: Cerf, 1941).

[18] Yves Congar, *Tradition and Traditions: An Historical and Theological Essay* (New York: Macmillan, 1967), 312–13; see also *Sainte Église,* 96–104.

[19] Congar has noted the important role in which the structure-life dialectic has played in his thought. "*Nous entendons par structure les principes qui, venant du Christ et à ce titre, représentant avec lui et de par lui les causes génératrices de l'Église, sont en celle-ci, comme sa pars formalis, ce qui constitue les hommes en Église de Jésus-Christ. Ce sont essentiellement le dépôt de la foi, le dépôt des sacrements de la foi et les pouvoirs apostoliques qui les transmettent l'un et l'autre. L'Église a, par là, son essence. Nous entendons par vie de l'Église l'activité que les hommes, formés en Église par les principes susdits, exercent pour que cette Église remplisse sa mission ou atteigne sa fin, qui est, à travers l'espace et le temps, de faire des hommes et d'un monde réconcilié le temple communionnel de Dieu.*" Yves Congar, *Jalons pour une théologie du laicat* (Paris: Cerf, 1953), 355–56. Timothy MacDonald employs this dialectic between structure and life

as a starting point for a consideration of Congar's ecclesiology. See Timothy I. MacDonald, *The Ecclesiology of Yves Congar: Foundational Themes* (Lanham, Md.: University of America Press, 1984), chapter 1.

[20] Yves Congar, "*Notes sur les mots 'confession', 'église', et 'communion',*" *Irenikon* 23 (1950): 3–36.

[21] Yves Congar, "*De la communion des Églises à une ecclésiologie de l'Église universelle,*" in *L'Épiscopat et l'Église universelle,* ed. Y. Congar and B.-D. Dupuy (Paris: Cerf, 1962), 227–60.

[22] Yves Congar, "*Pneumatologie ou 'Christomonisme' dans la tradition latine?*", in *Ecclesia a Spiritu Sancto edocta* [*Festschrift* for G. Philips] (Louvain: Ducolot, 1970), 41–63; *I Believe in the Holy Spirit,* vol. 3 (New York: Seabury, 1983).

[23] This is evident in the first edition of Congar's *Jalons pour une théologie du laicat.*

[24] Yves Congar, "*Mon cheminement dans la théologie du laicat et des ministères,*" in *Ministères et communion ecclésiale* (Paris: Cerf, 1971), 37ff. Congar criticized certain understandings of the hierarchy as an instrumental cause of the church, as in Journet's ecclesiology, for not properly situating the hierarchy within the church. See also Yves Congar, "*Insuffisance d'une certaine façon de concevoir les ministères comme 'cause instrumentale' faisant l'Église. Ministères et Communauté,*" in *Ministères et communion ecclésiale,* 34–40.

[25] Yves Congar, *Blessed is the Peace of My Church* (Denville, N.J.: Dimension Books, 1973), 75–78.

[26] J.-P. Jossua, *Le Père Congar. La théologie au service du peuple de Dieu* (Paris: Cerf, 1967), 93.

[27] Louch, 108–09.

[28] Yves Congar, "The Hierarchy as Service," in *Power and Poverty in the Church* (London: Geoffrey Chapman, 1964), 98.

[29] The following draws on the analysis of David Louch, 120–70.

[30] Congar, *Jalons,* 386–400.

[31] Louch suggests that Congar prefers the term "reception," perhaps because it avoids certain confusions attendant on the meaning of the word "consent." Louch, 199. For Congar's notion of "reception" see "*La 'réception' comme réalité ecclésiologique,*" *Revue des sciences philosophiques et théologiques* 56 (1972): 369–403; "*Quod omnes tangit ab omnibus tractari et approbari debet,*" *Revue historique du droit français et étranger* 36 (1958): 210–59.

[32] Congar, *Tradition and Traditions,* 327. Congar borrows this expression from Newman's *On Consulting the Faithful,* 65.

[33] Louch, 125.

[34] Yves Congar, "*La Consécration épiscopale et la succession apostolique constituent-elles chef d'une église locale ou membre du collège?*", in *Ministères et communion ecclésiale* (Paris: Cerf, 1971), 123–40. For Congar's study of the historical development of episcopal collegiality see "*La collégialité de l'épiscopat et la primauté de l'évêque de Rome dans l'histoire,*" in *Ministères et communion ecclésiale,* 95–122; "*Notes sur le destin de l'idée de collégialité épiscopale en occident au Moyen Age,*" in *La collégialité épiscopale,* ed. Yves Congar (Paris: Cerf, 1965), 99–129.

[35] Yves Congar, "*De la communion des églises à une ecclésiologie de l'église universelle,*" in *L'Épiscopat et l'Église universelle,* ed. Y. Congar and B.-D. Dupuy (Paris: Cerf, 1962), 227–60. More recently, Congar has cited approvingly the writing of Hervé Legrand on this subject. See, for example, Hervé Legrand, "*La réalization de l'église en un lieu,*" in *Initiation à la pratique de la théologie,* ed. Bernard Lauret and François Refoulé (Paris: Cerf, 1986), 143–345.

[36] Yves Congar, *Fifty Years of Catholic Theology: Conversations with Yves Congar,* ed. Bernard Lauret (Philadelphia: Fortress, 1988), 51.

[37] Congar, "Authority, Initiative, and Co-responsibility," in *Blessed is the Peace of My Church,* 88. Elsewhere, Congar writes: "[t]his role of the magisterium entails its giving the primary emphasis to the aspect of wit-

ness, rather than to that of 'definition' or exercise of authority." Congar, *Tradition and Traditions,* 334.

[38] Yves Congar, *La foi et la théologie* (Tournai: Desclée, 1962), 157–68.

[39] Ibid., 159.

[40] Ibid.

[41] Yves Congar, "*Indéfectibilité et infaillibilité du corps organique de l'Église,*" in *Ministères et communion ecclésiale,* 151.

[42] See Paul Nau, "*Le Magistère pontifical ordinaire, lieu théologique,*" *Revue Thomiste* 56 (1956): 389–412; "*Le Magistère pontifical ordinaire au premier concile du Vatican,*" *Revue Thomiste* 62 (1962): 341–97.

[43] Nau, "*Le Magistère pontifical ordinaire, lieu théologique,*" 396.

[44] Congar, "*Indéfectibilité et infaillibilité,*" 151. In opposition to the view of Vacant and Nau, Congar expresses sympathy with the criticism of their reading of Vatican I articulated by Marc Caudron. See chapter 2 above.

[45] Congar, "*De la communion des églises a une ecclésiologie de l'église universelle,*" 247; *L'Église du Saint Augustin à l'époque moderne,* 225–28.

Chapter 6

[1] John Henry Newman, *The Letters and Diaries of John Henry Newman,* vol. 27, ed. Charles Stephen Dessain and Thomas Gornall (Oxford: Clarendon Press, 1973), 310.

[2] Yves Congar, "*En guise de conclusion*" in *L'Église de Vatican II: Études autour de la constitution conciliare sur l'Église,* vol. 3, ed. Guilherme Baraúna and Yves Congar (Paris: Cerf, 1966), 1365; see also *L'Église de Saint Augustin à l'époque moderne,* 446–50.

[3] For commentary on this chapter see Umberto Betti, *La Dottrina sull'Episcopato del Concilio Vaticano II* (Rome: Pontificium Athenaeum

Antonianum, 1984); Heribert Schauf, *Das Leitungsamt der Bischöfe. Zur Textgeschichte der Konstitution "Lumen Gentium" des II. Vatikanischen Konzils* (Munich: Schöningh, 1975).

[4] See chapter 7 for a fuller development of this theology.

[5] See Jan Grootaers, *Primauté et Collégialité: Le dossier de Gérard Philips sur la Nota Explicativa Praevia* (Leuven: Leuven University Press, 1986); Joseph Ratzinger, "Announcements and Prefatory Notes of Explanation," in *Commentary on the Documents of Vatican II*, vol. 1, ed. Herbert Vorgrimler (2nd ed., New York: Crossroad, 1989), 297–306.

[6] *Nota Explicativa Praevia* #1.

[7] *Nota Explicativa Praevia* #4.

[8] *Lumen gentium* #22.

[9] English translation is the author's.

[10] *Acta Synodalia Sacrosancti Concilii Oecumenici Vaticani II*, vol. 3–1, (Vatican City: Typis Polyglottis, 1973), 250–51.

[11] Karl Rahner, "Dogmatic Constitution on the Church: The Hierarchical Structure of the Church, with Special Reference to the Episcopate, Articles 18–27," in *Commentary on the Documents of Vatican II*, vol. 1, ed. Herbert Vorgrimler (New York: Crossroad, 1989), 211. Herlinde Pissarek-Hudelist has come to much the same conclusion. See, *"Das ordentliche Lehramt als kollegialer Akt des Bischofscollegiums,"* in *Gott in Welt* (Festschrift for Karl Rahner), vol. 1, ed. Herbert Vorgrimler (Freiburg: Herder, 1964), 166–85.

[12] Francis A. Sullivan, "On the Infallibility of the Episcopal College in the Ordinary Exercise of its Teaching Office," in *Acta Congressus Internationalis de Theologia Concilii Vaticani II,* ed. Eduardo Dhanis and Adolph Schönmetzer (Vatican City: Typis Polyglottis, 1968), 194. Cf. Miguel Nicolau, *"El Magisterio universal "ordinario" y la colegialidad episcopal,"* in *El Colegio Episcopal,* vol. 2, ed. Jose Lopez Ortiz and Joaquin Blazquez (Madrid: Consejo Superior de Investigaciones Cientificas, 1964), 567–87; Teodoro I. Jiménez Urresti, *"La Colegialidad Episco-*

pal en el Magisterio Pontificio desde el Vaticano I al Vaticano II," in *El Colegio Episcopal,* vol. 2, 411–521.

[13] Antonio Acerbi, *Due Ecclesiologie: Ecclesiologia giuridica ed ecclesiologia di communione nella "Lumen Gentium,"* 243–45, 444–47.

[14] Karl Rahner, "The Hierarchical Structure of the Church . . . ," 215.

[15] Michael Schmaus, *The Church: Its Origin and Structure,* vol. 4 of *Dogma* (Kansas City and London: Sheed and Ward, 1972), 158. It is interesting to note the extent to which Schmaus, and indeed numerous theologians, models the activity of the ordinary universal magisterium on the collegial action of ecumenical councils.

[16] Ibid., 159.

[17] Joseph Komonchak, *"Humanae vitae* and Its Reception: Ecclesiological Reflections," *Theological Studies* 39 (1978): 243. Komonchak's position counters Vacant's assumption (Vacant, *Le Magistère ordinaire,* 87ff.) that submission to papal authority meant complete agreement with all papal teaching.

[18] Heinrich Fries, *Fundamentaltheologie* (Graz: Styria, 1985), 489.

[19] *Acta Synodalia Sacrosancti Concilii Oecumenici Vaticani II,* vol. 3–1, 251.

[20] Ibid. The author finds the literal translation of *definitive* to be more precise than Abbot's rendering of it as "conclusively."

[21] Karl Rahner, "The Hierarchical Structure of the Church . . . ," 210; *Sacramentum Mundi,* vol. 3, s.v. "Magisterium," 356; Francis A. Sullivan, *Magisterium: Teaching Authority in the Catholic Church* (New York: Paulist, 1983), 125–27; Yves Congar, *La foi et la théologie* (Tournai: Desclée, 1962), 159.

[22] Sullivan, *Magisterium,* 127. Komonchak also sees Salaverri's use of the phrase as an important interpretive clue to the conciliar text. Komonchak, *"Humanae vitae . . . ,"* 246.

[23] J. Robert Dionne, *The Papacy and the Church: A Study of Praxis and Reception in Ecumenical Perspective* (New York: Philosophical Library, 1987), 351.

[24] Ibid., 352. Dionne further points out that, without the clarification of the restrictive intent of the *tamquam definitive tenendam* phrase, the church's teaching on religious liberty, for example, held with consistency from the time of Pius IX up through Pius XII might meet the conditions for infallible teaching.

[25] Joseph Creusen, *"L'enseignement du Magistère ordinaire,"* *Nouvelle revue théologique* 559 (1932): 132–42; Marcellino Zalba, *Theologiae Moralis Summa,* vol. 3 (Madrid: Biblioteca de Autores Cristianos, 1958), n. 1518; Sixtus Cartechini, *De Valore Notarum Theologicarum et De Criteriis Adeas Dignoscendas* (Rome: Gregorian University, 1951), 29. For a summary of this line of thought see the discussion of the minority report of the Papal Commission on Birth Regulation below. Interestingly, one can also find authors who held that the teaching of *Casti connubii* on contraception had met the conditions for an *ex cathedra* papal teaching. See Francis Ter Haar, *Casus Conscientiae,* vol. 2 (2nd ed., Rome, Turin: Marietti, 1939), n. 136; A. Piscetta and A. Gennaro, *Elementa Theologiae Moralis,* vol. 7 (4th ed., Turin: Società Editrice Internazionale, 1944), n.215; Felix Capello, *De Matrimonio* (7th ed., Rome: Marietti, 1961), n. 816.

[26] Hans Küng, *Unfehlbar? Eine Anfrage* (Zurich: Benziger, 1970) [E.T.: *Infallible? An Inquiry* (Garden City: Doubleday, 1971)].

[27] The minority report is published in Daniel Callahan, *The Catholic Case for Contraception* (New York: Macmillan, 1969).

[28] Ibid., 202–03.

[29] Ibid., 188.

[30] Küng, *Infallible?,* 72ff.

[31] Karl Rahner, *"Kritik an Hans Küng,"* *Stimmen der Zeit* 186 (December, 1970): 361–77 [E.T.: "A Critique of Hans Küng," *Homiletic and Pastoral Review* 71 (May, 1971): 10–26].

[32] Rahner, "A Critique of Hans Küng," 14–15.

[33] Ibid., 16.

[34] Hans Küng, "To Get to the Heart of the Matter," *Homiletic and Pastoral Review* 71 (June, 1971): 21 [originally published in *Stimmen der Zeit* 187 (1971): 43–64, 105–22 as *"Im Interesse der Sache"*].

[35] Rahner, "A Critique of Hans Küng," 15.

[36] John C. Ford and Germain Grisez, "Contraception and the Infallibility of the Ordinary Universal Magisterium," *Theological Studies* 39 (1978): 258–312.

[37] *Gaudium et spes* #51.

[38] See Piet Fransen, "A Short History of the Meaning of the Formula *'Fides et Mores'*," in *Hermeneutics of Councils and Other Studies,* ed. H.E. Mertens and F. de Graeve (Leuven: Leuven University Press, 1985), 287–318; John Mahoney, *The Making of Moral Theology* (Oxford: Clarendon, 1987), 120–74; M. Bévenot, "Faith and Morals in Vatican I and in the Council of Trent," *Heythrop Journal* 3 (1962): 15–30.

[39] *Mansi* t.52, 1224. See also Gustave Thils' study of papal infallibility for a fine treatment of this question. *L'Infallibilité pontificale. source—conditions—limitations* (Gembloux: Duculot, 1969), 222–51.

[40] Mahoney, *The Making of Moral Theology,* 166.

[41] Sullivan, *Magisterium,* 140–41.

[42] See Francisco Suarez, *Tractatus de legibus,* lib. 10, cap. II, n. 3, in *Opera Omnia,* vol. 5 (Paris: Vives, 1856), 554.

[43] Joseph Kleutgen, *Die Theologie der Vorzeit,* vol. I (2nd ed., Innsbruck, 1978), 146. See also Johann Baptist Franzelin, *De Divina Traditione et Scriptura* (Rome: Propaganda Fide, 1870), 110, 547–51. For a more detailed study of this question see John Boyle, "The Natural Law and the Magisterium," *CTSA Proceedings* 34 (1979): 189–210.

[44] For variations on this view, see André Naud, *Le magistère incertain* (Montreal: Fides, 1987), 77–95; Francis A. Sullivan, *Magisterium,* 137ff.; Joseph Fuchs, "*Sittliche Wahrheiten—Heilswahrheiten?*" *Stimmen der Zeit* 200 (1982): 662–76; John Boyle, "The Natural Law and the Magisterium"; Joseph Komonchak, "*Humanae vitae* and Its Reception: Ecclesiological Reflections"; Jacob David, *Loi naturelle et autorité de l'église* (Paris: Cerf, 1968); Bruno Schüller, "*La théologie morale peut-elle se passer du droit naturel?*" *Nouvelle revue théologique* 88 (1966): 449–75; "*Zur theologischen Diskussion über die Lex Naturalis,*" *Theologisch-praktische Quartalschrift* 41 (1966): 481–503.

[45] Ford and Grisez, "Contraception and the Infallibility of the Ordinary Universal Magisterium," 286–87. In a commentary on the 1989 revised Profession of Faith, Umberto Betti maintained that while the whole of the natural law may not belong to revelation *per se,* all the precepts of the natural law could still be included among irreformable definitions as part of the secondary object of infallibility: "*Può rientrare nell'oggetto di definizioni irreformabili, anche se non di fede, tutto ciò che si riferisce all legge naturale, essa pure espressione della voluntà di Dio.*" *L'Osservatore Romano* (February 25, 1989), 6.

[46] This is confirmed by the explanation offered by the theological commission at Vatican II: "*Objectum infallibilitatis Ecclesiae, ita explicate, eandem habet extensionem ac depositum revelatum; ideoque extenditur ad ea omnia, et ad ea tantum, quae vel directe ad ipsum depositum revelatum spectant, vel quae ad idem depositum sancte custodiendum et fideliter exponendum requiruntur.*" *Acta Synodalia Sacrosancti Concilii Oecumenici Vaticani II,* vol. 3–1, 251. The verb *requiruntur* seems to justify restricting the secondary object only to those things strictly necessary for safeguarding revelation.

[47] The recent 1990 CDF instruction on the vocation of the theologian holds that revelation ". . . also contains moral teachings which per se could be known by natural reason. . . . It is a doctrine of faith that these moral norms can be infallibly taught by the magisterium." "Instruction on the Ecclesial Vocation of the Theologian," *Origins* 20 (July 5, 1990): 121 (#16). This does not mean, however, that all moral norms necessarily belong to revelation. For an analysis of this document, see Francis A. Sullivan, "The Theologian's Ecclesial Vocation and the 1990 CDF Instruction," *Theological Studies* 52 (1991): 51–68; Ladislas Örsy, "Magisterium and Theologians: A Vatican Document," *America* 163 (July 21,

1990): 30–2; Peter Knauer, *"Das kirchliche Lehramt und der Beistand des Heiligen Geistes,"* *Stimmen der Zeit* 208 (October, 1990): 661–75.

[48] Ford and Grisez, "Contraception . . . ," 274.

[49] Ibid.

[50] Sullivan, *Magisterium,* 127.

[51] Quoted by Robert Blair Kaiser, *The Politics of Sex and Religion* (Kansas City: Leaven Press, 1985), 170.

[52] André Naud, *Le Magistère incertain,* 127.

[53] Garth Hallett, "Contraception and Prescriptive Infallibility," *Theological Studies* 43 (1982): 629–50.

[54] John T. Noonan, *Contraception: A History of Its Treatment by the Catholic Theologians and Canonists* (New York: New American Library, 1967).

[55] Ibid., 152.

[56] Hallett, "Contraception and Prescriptive Infallibility," 640.

[57] After Hallett's essay, Germain Grisez published a response in which he contended that Hallett had been misled in assuming that he and Ford had interpreted the demands regarding the universality of a teaching as requiring unanimity throughout the entire Christian tradition. Rather, while he felt that such a broad unanimity could be found in tradition on the matter of contraception, it was not necessary to demonstrate this. "In the unified exercise of the ordinary magisterium there will be many distinct acts, which will extend over some stretch of time. For this reason, constancy in teaching over some stretch becomes a necessary condition for unity in teaching. However, the necessary stretch need not be the whole history of the Church. In a matter such as contraception, a more limited period easily accessible to study will do." Germain Grisez, "Infallibility and Contraception: A Reply to Garth Hallett," *Theological Studies* 47 (1986): 138. Hallett would later respond that verifying a descriptive constancy would be no easy task even over a significantly shorter span of church

history. Garth Hallett, "Infallibility and Contraception: The Debate Continues," *Theological Studies* 49 (1988): 526.

[58] John C. Ford and Gerald Kelly, *Contemporary Moral Theology,* vol. 2 (Westminster: Newman Press, 1963), 257–58.

[59] Michael Dummett, "The Documents of the Papal Commission on Birth Control," *New Blackfriars* 50 (1969): 246, quoted in Hallett, 649.

[60] Ford and Grisez, "Contraception . . . ," 276.

[61] John J. Reed writes: ". . . it is important to distinguish the notions of infallibility and certainty. In matters of conduct, a doctrine which is not taught with the plenitude of infallibility may still be taught with certainty, in the sense of moral, practical, certitude, so as to exclude any solidly probable opinion to the contrary here and now. . . . Infallibility excludes the absolute possibility of error. Certitude, in the sense of moral, or practical certitude, excludes the prudent, proximate fear of error." "Natural Law, Theology and the Church," *Theological Studies* 26 (1965): 56.

[62] Sullivan, *Magisterium,* 147.

[63] Congar, *"Indéfectibilité et infaillibilité,"* in *Ministères et communion ecclésiale,* 151.

[64] For a similar stance to that of Grisez and Ford, see Marcellino Zalba, *"Infallibilità del Magistero Ordinario e Contracezione,"* *Renovatio* (1979): 79–90.

[65] Ladislas Örsy, *The Church: Learning and Teaching* (Wilmington: Glazier, 1987), 58.

[66] *Communicationes* 1 (1969): 41, as quoted in *The Code of Canon Law: A Text and Commentary,* ed. James A. Coriden, Thomas J. Green and Donald E. Heintschel (New York: Paulist, 1985), 5.

[67] All references to the revised code are taken from the *Code of Canon Law: Latin-English Edition* (Washington: Canon Law Society of America, 1983).

[68] John P. Boyle, "Church Authority in the 1983 Code," in *Readings in Moral Theology, No. 6,* ed. Charles E. Curran and Richard A. McCormick (New York: Paulist, 1988), 195.

[69] *The Code of Canon Law: A Text and Commentary,* 278.

[70] Hervé Legrand, "Collegiality of the Bishops and Communion of the Churches in the Reception of Vatican II," (an unpublished paper delivered at the "Twenty-Five Years After Vatican II" Conference held at the University of Notre Dame, December, 1990), 4.

[71] For historical background and commentary see *The Code of Canon Law: A Text and Commentary,* 547.

[72] Boyle, "Church Authority in the 1983 Code," 202.

[73] Ibid., 203.

[74] Hermann J. Pottmeyer, "A New Phase in the Reception of Vatican II: Twenty Years of Interpretation of the Council," in *The Reception of Vatican II,* ed. Giuseppe Alberigo, Jean-Pierre Jossua and Joseph A. Komonchak (Washington: Catholic University of America Press, 1987), 27.

[75] While most attention has been drawn to moral questions like that regarding artificial contraception, Raymond Brown has suggested an example from the area of biblical studies, not without some controversy, namely the church teaching on the virginal conception of Jesus. See Raymond E. Brown, *The Virginal Conception and Bodily Resurrection of Jesus* (New York: Paulist, 1973), 35; *Biblical Exegesis and Church Doctrine* (New York: Paulist, 1985), 27.

[76] For more on this observation, see Hervé Legrand, "Collegiality of the Bishops and Communion of the Churches in the Reception of Vatican II."

Chapter 7

[1] Franzelin, *Theses De Ecclesia Christi,* 259ff.

[2] Karl Rahner, in *Das Amt der Einheit,* ed. Wilhelm Stahlen (Stuttgart: Schwabenverlag, 1964), 253–57.

[3] Karl Rahner, *The Episcopate and the Primacy* (New York: Herder, 1962), 84.

[4] Karl Rahner, "The Episcopal Office," in *Theological Investigations,* vol. 6 (New York: Crossroad, 1982), 323.

[5] Ibid., 328ff.

[6] Ibid., 322.

[7] Rahner, *The Episcopate and the Primacy,* 23.

[8] Ibid., 26–7.

[9] For contemporary considerations of an ecclesiology of communion see J.M.R. Tillard, *Église d'Églises: L'écclésiologie de communion* (Paris: Cerf, 1987); James H. Provost, ed., *The Church as Communion* (Wash., D.C.: Canon Law Society of America, 1984); Antonio Acerbi, *Due ecclesiologie. Ecclesiologia giuridica ed ecclesiologia di communione nella "Lumen Gentium"* (Bologna: Dehoniane, 1975); Ferdinand Klostermann, *Gemeinde—Kirche der Zukunft. Thesen, Dienste, Modelle,* 2 vols. (Freiburg: Herder, 1975); Ludwig Hertling, *Communio: Church and Papacy in Early Christianity* (Chicago: Loyola University Press, 1972); Jerome Hamer, *The Church Is a Communion* (New York: Sheed & Ward, 1964); Yves Congar, "*Notes sur les mots 'confession,' 'église,' et 'communion,'*" *Irenikon* 23 (1950): 3–36; "*De la communion des Églises à une ecclésiologie de l'Église universelle,*" in *L'Épiscopat et l'Église universelle,* ed. Y. Congar and B.-D. Dupuy (Paris: Cerf, 1962), 227–60.

[10] Tillard, *Église d'Églises,* 13–65.

[11] Ibid., 217–318.

[12] Joseph Ratzinger, "*La collégialité épiscopale. Développement théologique,*" in *L'Église de Vatican II,* vol. 3 (Paris: Cerf, 1966), 776.

[13] For a study of the bishop as president of the eucharist see Hervé Legrand, "The Presidency of the Eucharist according to the Ancient Tradition," *Worship* 53 (1979): 413–38.

[14] Newman, *On Consulting the Faithful*, 65ff. This phrase from Newman, who himself claimed to have found the notion in Perrone, is employed in Vatican II's Constitution on Divine Revelation, *Dei Verbum* #10.

[15] Sullivan, *De Ecclesia I: Quaestiones Theologiae Fundamentalis*, 283.

[16] Tillard, *Église d'Églises*, 150–51.

[17] For more on eucharistic table fellowship among the churches see Kenneth Hein, *Eucharist and Excommunication: A Study in Early Christian Doctrine and Discipline* (Frankfurt: P. Lang, 1975); Werner Elert, *Eucharist and Church Fellowship in the First Four Centuries* (St. Louis: Concordia, 1966); Yves Congar, *"De la communion des Églises à une ecclésiologie de l'Église universelle,"* In *L'Épiscopat et l'Église universelle*, ed. Yves Congar, and B.D. Dupuy (Paris: Cerf, 1962), 227–60.

[18] John E. Lynch, "The Magistery and Theologians from the Apostolic Fathers to the Gregorian Reform," *Chicago Studies* 17 (1978): 194–95.

[19] Hervé Legrand, *"Nature de l'Église particulière et rôle de l'évêque dans l'Église,"* in *La charge pastorale des évêques*, ed. W. Onclin, R. Bézac, et al. (Paris: Cerf, 1969), 118.

[20] Yves Congar, "The Conciliar Structure or Regime of the Church," in *The Ecumenical Council: Its Significance in the Constitution of the Church*, ed. Peter Huizing and Knut Walf (New York: Seabury, 1983), 3–4. See also *"Konzil als Versammlung und gründsätzliche Konziliarität der Kirche,"* in *Gott in Welt*, Vol. 2 (*Festchrift* for Karl Rahner). ed. Herbert Vorgrimler (Freiburg: Herder, 1964), 135–65. This synodal principle has been at the heart of the Orthodox criticism of Western conceptions of collegiality. See John D. Zizioulas, *Being as Communion* (Crestwood: St. Vladimir's Seminary Press, 1985), 123–42; "The Development of Conciliar Structure to the Time of the First Ecumenical Council," in *Councils and the Ecumenical Movement* (Geneva: World Council of Churches, 1968), 34–51; Nikos Nissiotis, "The Main Ecclesiological Problem of the Second Vatican Council and the Position of the non-Roman Churches Facing It," *Journal of Ecumenical Studies* 2 (Winter, 1965): 31–62; Alexander Schmemann, *"La notion de primauté dans l'ecclésiologie orthodoxe,"* in *La Primauté de Pierre*, ed. John Meyendorff, et al. (Neuchatel: Delachaux & Niestle, 1960), 136–37.

[21] Hermann Josef Sieben, *Die Konzilsidee der Alten Kirche* (Paderborn: Schöningh, 1979), 309. Sieben identifies the presence of a twofold manner in which the communion of the churches is given expression in councils, the horizontal expressing the church's catholicity, and the vertical expressing its apostolicity.

[22] Georg Denzler, "The Authority and the Reception of Conciliar Decisions in Christendom," in *The Ecumenical Council: Its Significance in the Constitution of the Church,* ed. Peter Huizing and Knut Walf (New York: Seabury, 1983), 13.

[23] We should note also the seminal influence of Johann Adam Möhler on both Schell and, later, Congar. For Möhler's influence on Congar see Thomas F. O'Meara, "Revelation and History: Schelling, Möhler, and Congar." *Irish Theological Quarterly* 53 (1987): 17–35.

[24] Yves Congar, "The Idea of the Church in St. Thomas Aquinas," *Thomist* 1 (1939): 331–59.

[25] See also Yves Congar, "*Le problème ecclésiologique de la papauté après Vatican II,*" in *Ministères et communion ecclésiale* (Paris: Cerf, 1971), 167–86.

[26] Karl Mörsdorf, *Sacramentum Mundi,* vol. 1, s.v. "Bishop: Canon Law," 231–32.

[27] Karl Rahner, "On the Relationship Between the Pope and the College of Bishops," in *Theological Investigations,* vol. 10 (New York: Herder, 1973), 50–70; *The Episcopate and the Primacy* (New York: Herder, 1962), 92ff; Yves Congar, "*Le problème ecclésiologique de la papauté après Vatican II*"; *Fifty Years of Catholic Theology: Conversations with Yves Congar,* 130–31; J.M.R. Tillard, *Bishop of Rome* (Wilmington: Glazier, 1983); *Église d'Églises: L'ecclésiologie de communion* (Paris: Cerf, 1987). Hervé M. Legrand, "*Collégialité et primauté à la suite de Vatican II,*" in *Initiation à la pratique de la théologie,* ed. Bernard Lauret and François Refoulé (Paris: Cerf, 1986), 300–27.

[28] DS 3074.

[29] See Gustave Thils, *Primauté et infaillibilité du pontife Romain à Vatican I* (Leuven: Leuven University Press, 1989); *La primauté pontificale.*

La doctrine de Vatican I (Gembloux: Duculot, 1972); *L'infaillibilité pontificale: source, conditions, limites* (Gembloux: Duculot, 1969); Hermann Pottmeyer, *Unfehlbarkeit und Souveranität: Die päpstliche Unfehlbarkeit im System der ultramontanen Ekklesiologie des 19. Jahrhunderts* (Mainz: Matthias-Grünewald-Verlag, 1975).

[30] Jean-Pierre Torrell, *La théologie de l'épiscopat au premier Concile du Vatican* (Paris: Cerf, 1961); J.M.R. Tillard, *The Bishop of Rome*, 25–34.

[31] *Mansi*, 52, 1215.

[32] Gustave Thils, *Primauté et infaillibilité du pontife Romain à Vatican I*, 190–1. See also Heinrich Fries, *"Ex sese, non ex consensu ecclesiae,"* in *Volke Gottes, Zum Kirchenverständnis der katholischen, evangelischen und anglikanischen Theologie*, ed. R. Bäumer and H. Dolch (Freiburg: Herder, 1967), 480–500; Avery Dulles, "A Moderate Infallibilism: An Ecumenical Approach," chapter in *A Church to Believe In* (New York: Crossroad, 1982), 144–45.

[33] Tillard, *The Bishop of Rome*, 38.

[34] Ibid., 40–41.

[35] Gustave Thils, *"Potestas Ordinaria,"* in *L'Épiscopat et l'Église Universelle*, ed. Yves Congar and B.-D. Dupuy (Paris: Cerf, 1962), 689–708.

[36] Tillard, *The Bishop of Rome*, 157.

[37] Yves Congar, *L'Église de Saint Augustin à l'époque moderne*, 221–28.

[38] Tillard, *The Bishop of Rome*, 158.

Chapter 8

[1] Rahner, *The Episcopate and Primacy*, 98.

[2] For a study which has used the communion of churches as a starting point for a consideration of episcopal conferences see James H. Provost, "Episcopal Conferences as an Expression of the Communion of

Churches," in *Episcopal Conferences: Historical Canonical & Theological Studies,* ed. Thomas J. Reese (Washington: Georgetown University Press, 1989), 267–89.

[3] *Lumen Gentium* #12.

[4] Francis Sullivan contends that "the infallibility which this statement of Vatican II attributes to 'universal agreement in matters of faith and morals,' was verified in the case of the doctrines of Mary's Immaculate Conception and bodily Assumption." Sullivan, *Magisterium,* 19. Sullivan admits that Popes Pius IX and Pius XII only sent questionnaires to the bishops, but contends that these bishops attested to the unanimity of the belief of the faithful. While we cannot pursue here an adequate investigation into the events surrounding the solemn definitions of the two Marian dogmas, it seems questionable to assume that the procedures employed by the two popes ensured an adequate verification of the *sensus fidelium.* Further investigation would seem to demand a consideration of at least the following questions. How free were the bishops to communicate their beliefs on the matter? What kind of unanimity was achieved in the polling of the bishops? What was the relationship which the bishops had with the laity? What procedures were employed by the bishops to ascertain the beliefs of the faithful? How were the bishops able to distinguish between pious custom and authentic faith?

[5] Peter Chirico, *Infallibility: The Crossroads of Doctrine* (Wilmington: Glazier, 1983), 245ff.

[6] Ibid., 247–48. Chirico's innovative approach to infallibility draws heavily upon the philosophy of Lonergan and its recognition of the existence of universal meanings which may be embedded in culturally conditioned forms of expression.

[7] Salaverri, *Sacrae Theologiae Summa,* 671.

[8] Rahner, "Dogmatic Constitution on the Church," in *Commentary on the Documents of Vatican II,* vol. 1, 215.

[9] Schmaus, *The Church: Its Origin and Structure,* 158–59.

[10] Gérard Philips, *L'Église et son mystère au IIe Concile du Vatican* (Paris: Desclée, 1967), 325.

[11] However, Yves Congar has offered an exception to the contention that the exercise of the ordinary universal magisterium must occur outside of an ecumenical council. He proposes that the teaching of Vatican II on the sacramentality of the episcopate may have fulfilled the conditions, as he understands them, for the exercise of the ordinary universal magisterium. This, he admits, would appear to be the only example of an infallible teaching of the ordinary universal magisterium taught *in a council.* Yves Congar, *"En guise de conclusion,"* in *L'Église de Vatican II,* vol. 3, 1367. To make this case, however, one would have to account for why the bishops at the council did not solemnly define the sacramentality of the episcopacy if they wished to propose it as "definitively to be held." Congar fails to do so.

[12] Sullivan, "On the Infallibility of the Episcopal College in the Ordinary Exercise of its Teaching Office," 191–92.

[13] *Modi in Caput III Constitutionis de Ecclesia,* n. 176.

[14] Karl Rahner and Karl Lehmann, *"Kerygma und Dogma,"* in *Mysterium Salutis,* vol. 1, ed. Johannes Feiner and Magnus Löhrer (Einsiedeln: Benziger, 1965), 655.

[15] Raymond E. Brown, *The Virginal Conception and Bodily Resurrection of Jesus,* 35f.

[16] Raymond E. Brown, *Biblical Exegesis and Church Doctrine,* 27n.11.

[17] Sullivan, *Magisterium,* 56–57.

[18] Magnus Löhrer, *"Das besondere Lehramt der Kirche,"* in *Mysterium Salutis,* vol. 1, ed. Johannes Feiner and Magnus Löhrer (Einsiedeln: Benziger, 1965), 573.

[19] Henri Gouhier, *"Infaillibilité et nature,"* in *L'Infaillibilité: Son aspect philosophique et théologique,* ed. Enrico Castelli (Paris: Aubier, 1970), 229. See also Yves Congar, *"Infaillibilité et indéfectibilité,"* in *Ministères et communion ecclésiale* (Paris: Cerf, 1971), 159–60; Sullivan, *Magisterium,* 80–81.

[20] See Sieben, *Die Konzilsidee der Alten Kirche,* 171–91. Sieben claims that the monk Theodor Abu Qurra (d. 820/5) was the first to write on the infallibility of ecumenical councils.

[21] See Brian Tierney, *Origins of Papal Infallibility 1150–1350* (Leiden: Brill, 1972).

[22] "Common Statement," in *Teaching Authority & Infallibility in the Church,* ed. Paul C. Empie, T. Austin Murphy and Joseph A. Burgess (Minneapolis: Augsburg, 1978), 25.

[23] Avery Dulles, "Infallibility: The Terminology," in *Teaching Authority & Infallibility in the Church,* 74.

[24] Sullivan, *Magisterium,* 85–86.

[25] C. Langlois, *"Die Unfehlbarkeit—eine neue Idee des 19. Jahrhunderts,"* in *Fehlbar? Eine Bilanz,* ed. Hans Küng (Zurich: Benziger, 1973), 146–60.

[26] Sullivan, *Magisterium,* 96.

[27] Newman, *On Consulting the Faithful,* 106. See Robert Murray, "Who or What is Infallible?" in *Infallibility in the Church: An Anglican-Catholic Dialogue* (London: Darton, Longman & Todd, 1968), 32.

[28] This account of the four conditions of *Pastor Aeternus* is drawn from Dulles, "Moderate Infallibilism: An Ecumenical Approach," 136–38.

[29] *"Infallibiliter definita nulla intellegitur doctrina nisi id manifeste constiterit." Code of Canon Law,* # 749.3.

[30] Dulles, "Infallibility: The Terminology," 76.

[31] Sullivan, *Magisterium,* 106–07.

[32] See the July 25th, 1986 letter from Cardinal Ratzinger to Charles Curran in Charles E. Curran, *Faithful Dissent,* 268–69.

[33] Richard McCormick has suggested that the assistance of the Spirit is conditioned upon the adequate fulfillment of the human responsibilities for evidence gathering and evidence assessing, at least in its non-infallible magisterium. Should the activity of the teaching church be lacking in either of these areas, the free influence of the Spirit may be subsequently limited. McCormick further contends that the relationship between the infallible and the non-infallible magisterium is one of analogy rather than continuity. Too often, by assuming a relationship of continuity, we have considered the non-infallible magisterium as "just a little less than infallible." Richard A. McCormick, *Notes on Moral Theology: 1965 through 1980* (Lanham, Md.: University Press of America, 1981), 261n.72.

[34] Tillard, *The Bishop of Rome,* 172.

[35] I am employing the term "dissent" reluctantly. Ladislas Örsy's observes that the term "dissent" connotes a negative stance and even an ill will toward the legitimate teaching authority of the church which is often far from the intent of a theologian positively assisting the church in its attempt to commit itself more fully to a particular doctrinal formulation. See Ladislas Örsy, *The Church: Learning and Teaching,* 90ff.

[36] Ibid., 85–86.

Index of Names

Acton, Lord, 65, 71
Alberigo, Giuseppe, 34
Alexander III, Pope, 14
Alzog, J. B., 22
Antonelli, Giacomo, Cardinal, 23
Athanasius, St., 11, 71
Aubert, Roger, 21–22, 195n.3
Augustine, St., 9, 11, 98, 187

Baader, Franz, 20
Barth, Karl, 98
Bartz, Wilhelm, 75
Bautain, Louis, 196n.6
Bellarmine, Robert, St., 38
Betti, Umberto, Cardinal, 223n.45
Billot, Louis, Cardinal, 17, 50, 97, 104, 162
Boff, Leonardo, 2
Bonald, Louis de, 19, 160
Bonaventure, St., 108
Boyle, John, 25–27
Brown, Raymond, 174, 226n.75

Cajetan, Cardinal, 95
Caudron, Marc, 30, 31
Chenu, M.-D., 13, 193n.16
Chirico, Peter, 170–171, 231n.6

Clemens, F. J., 197n.17
Congar, Yves, 9, 10, 34, 72, 81, 92, 93, 98–112, 113, 138, 153–156, 165, 184, 186, 190, 191n.1, 192n.3, 192n.5, 193n.13, 214–215n.15, 215–216n.19, 216n.24, 217n.31, 217–218n.37, 218n.44, 229n.23, 232n.11
Curran, Charles, 2, 5, 183
Cyprian, St., 10

Deufel, Konrad, 33
Deutinger, Martin, 20
Dieckmann, Hermann, 48–49, 59–60, 168, 204n.42
Dionne, J. Robert, 122, 168, 205n.50, 221n.24
Döllinger, Ignaz, 2, 20–24, 33, 182, 196n.9
Drey, J. S., 19
Dulles, Avery, 71, 180, 191n.1, 208n.16
Dummett, Michael, 136

Eriugena, John Scotus, 98

Fenton, Joseph C., 162
Fichte, Johann, 19, 37
Ford, John C., 5, 127–138, 144, 165, 223n.45